CONGRESSMAN
LINCOLN

The Making of America's
Greatest President

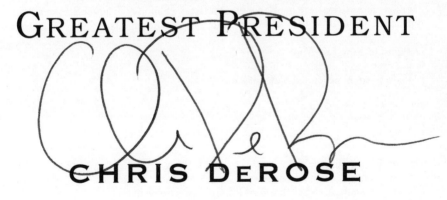

CHRIS DeROSE

THRESHOLD EDITIONS

NEW YORK LONDON TORONTO SYDNEY NEW DELHI

Threshold Editions
A Division of Simon & Schuster, Inc.
1230 Avenue of the Americas
New York, NY 10020

First Threshold Editions hardcover edition January 2013

THRESHOLD EDITIONS and colophon are trademarks
of Simon & Schuster, Inc.

For information about special discounts for bulk purchases,
please contact Simon & Schuster Special Sales at
1-866-506-1949 or business@simonandschuster.com.

The Simon & Schuster Speakers Bureau can bring authors to your live event.
For more information or to book an event, contact the Simon & Schuster Speakers
Bureau at 1-866-248-3049 or visit our website at www.simonspeakers.com.

Designed by Ruth Lee-Mui

Manufactured in the United States of America

10   9   8   7   6   5   4   3   2   1

Library of Congress Cataloging-in-Publication Data

DeRose, Chris (Christopher)
   Congressman Lincoln : the making of America's greatest president /
Christopher DeRose. — 1st Threshold Editions hardcover edition.
      pages cm
   1. Lincoln, Abraham, 1809–1865—Political career before 1861.   2. United States—
Politics and government—1845–1861.   3. United States. Congress. House—Biography.
4. Legislators—United States—Biography.   5. Presidents—United States—Biography.
I. Title.
   E457.4.D46 2013
   328.73092—dc23
   [B]   2012038827

ISBN 978-1-4516-9514-4
ISBN 978-1-4516-9515-1 (ebook)

To Catherine DeRose, my sister,
a scholar of books who now has one dedicated to her,
this work is lovingly inscribed by the author.

CONTENTS

LINCOLN AS LEGISLATOR

When telling a story, we seldom begin with the end or skip over the middle. But for the most part, this is what we've done with the life of Abraham Lincoln. We've heard of his hardscrabble upbringing, his time as an Illinois legislator, his success as a lawyer, and his debates with Stephen Douglas. Lincoln is well known to us as the Civil War president, the author of the Emancipation Proclamation and of the Gettysburg Address, and the victim of a cold-blooded assassination. In just the past few years, more has been written about the latter alone than has ever been published on Lincoln's time in Congress. In our mind's eye we see him with his trademark beard, something he didn't wear until his first inauguration day. But what about his time as a member of the Thirtieth Congress, from 1847 to 1849?

More has been written about Lincoln than any other American. According to Ford's Theatre, home of the final scene in this extraordinary story, its recently built thirty-four-foot tower of Lincoln books represents less than half of the fifteen thousand volumes published on his life. Yet only two previous works, Paul Findley's *A. Lincoln: The Crucible of Congress*, and Donald Riddle's *Congressman Abraham Lincoln*, published in 1979 and 1957, respectively, have focused on this formative time.

This story urgently demands to be told, not only in light of new evidence uncovered in the past thirty-three years, but because of its shocking relevance to our present time. Abraham Lincoln was part of a Congress that was paralyzed by partisan divisions, struggling to make laws for a bitterly divided America. People legitimately wondered whether their leaders were up to the task. Might we not learn from and do better than this?

The lack of attention to Lincoln as a member of Congress is all the more remarkable when one considers that Lincoln held but three elected offices: state legislator, congressman, and president of the United States.

That presidency with which we are so familiar is in many ways informed by, and a continuation of, Lincoln's service in Congress, which had ended twelve years earlier. In 1861, when Lincoln stood on the back of a train in the Springfield, Illinois, depot, bidding farewell to his hometown on his way to Washington, he said, "I now leave, not knowing when or whether ever I may return, with a task before me greater than that which rested upon Washington."

This president who faced the worst crisis in our nation's history was, at least formally, perhaps the least prepared to do so. One term in the House of Representatives was all that Lincoln knew of the federal government he now would lead. James K. Polk was the only one of his predecessors that he witnessed on the job. Zachary Taylor was the only president that Lincoln watched assemble an administration. In both cases, they were examples he largely tried to avoid. But whether prepared or not, Lincoln had to quickly decide how he would govern. How would he award jobs in his administration? How would the most important wartime commander in chief relate to his generals? How would he work with Congress to achieve his goals? How would he as president maintain support among the people? To answer these, Lincoln had but little more to draw on than the memory of his two years in the Thirtieth Congress.

Lincoln's service in the House exposed him to the deeply divided country he now presided over, working closely with members both from North and South, and some of his friendships there would be critical in his rise to power. And it was in the Thirtieth Congress that Lincoln first worked to limit slavery, the evil he one day would end.

Abraham Lincoln's preparation for power and his decisive blow against slavery can all be traced back to this time in the House. For too long we have tried to understand Lincoln while virtually ignoring the events of this story. This book represents my humble attempt to put Congressman Lincoln in his proper context, at the forefront of the Lincoln story, the catalyst for all that followed.

Growing up in Illinois, the self-proclaimed "Land of Lincoln," one can't escape the long shadow of our sixteenth president. His (bearded) visage smiles at us from license plates. Throughout the state, streets, schools, businesses, and a town bear his name. As a boy, there were class field trips to Springfield, where within a few blocks one can see Lincoln's home, law office, and the state capitol where he served and made his "house divided" speech. The Lincoln of my childhood was beyond criticism. Despite such tangible evidence of his existence, such reverence for Lincoln made it hard to think of him as a human being. Lincoln himself believed biographies were "false and misleading," too quick to cover up the subject's faults. Many have erred in equal measure, in their eagerness to criticize Lincoln, attributing to him dishonest motives and tyrannical tendencies. Much of this proceeds from our modern political experience of broken promises and starry-eyed would-be saviors who continually disappoint.

As an adult, my understanding of Lincoln has fallen apart, only to be reassembled on sturdier ground. Lincoln is great *because* of his humanity, not despite it. Not because his life was error-free, but because of how he learned from his mistakes. Not because he was always right, but because of his tremendous capacity to grow and acknowledge when he was wrong. Lincoln's life challenges us to consider that there was once, and could be again, a person with all the failings that the human condition is subject to who could still live up to his billing.

In these pages, we discover how he became the Abraham Lincoln we know today. I hope you will experience some small measure of the joy that I've experienced in getting reacquainted with Lincoln for the "first time."

Chris DeRose
Phoenix, Arizona
October 17, 2012

CONGRESSMAN

LINCOLN

—◦•◦—

AN EPISTLE TO
THE MUSE OF HISTORY

Today it is known as Statuary Hall, a semicircular museum on the way from the Rotunda to the modern House of Representatives. The strange acoustics send the sounds of footsteps bouncing against the walls of the former House chamber. People quietly examine the men commemorated in marble and reverently walk along the floor where plaques mark the seats of the presidents who served in the House. The most popular is that of John Quincy Adams, "the whispering spot." From there, due to the strange reverberations of the chamber, it is said that he could hear everything that was discussed among the opposing party. The room has the feel of a temple, somber and solemn, and this is appropriate, in honor of the great men who walked and worked here. But to know the story of Congressman Abraham Lincoln, we must go back to the Thirtieth Congress, the first illuminated by the power of gas, back to a time when this was the Hall of Representatives, the cockpit of a young republic, replacing the marble with men, and replacing the respectful silence with bedlam.

Clio, the Greek Muse of history, was there and she saw it all, perched above the entrance to the chamber. In Franzoni's *Car of History*, the marble Clio stands atop a winged chariot, a scroll in her hand to faithfully record the deeds of man. Her presence is a reflection of an earlier era's classical fascination, ignited by the 1748 discovery of the ancient ruins of Pompeii.[1] The wheel of Clio's chariot is the face of a clock, the most temporal of all things. It is also a not so subtle reminder to those who look to her; its hands and face may help them navigate their day, to committee hearings and appointments and their sundry other tasks as members of Congress, but Clio's perspective could not be measured in minutes or even hours. There she stood, preserving the history of the House as honestly as the ash of Mount Vesuvius.

On February 21, 1848, John Quincy Adams bounded into the House chamber, walking beneath Clio on the way to his desk. The first and last man to spend his postpresidency in the people's House was full of energy, ready to debate a war he believed unjust and wanted to end.

Proxy fights over the war with Mexico dominated the beginning of the Thirtieth Congress. Even the most anodyne measures served as vehicles to express support or opposition to the war. On this day, a series of resolutions thanking various military officers was one such fight. On procedural motions to bring them to the floor, Adams voted no, joined by a freshman congressman from Illinois, Abraham Lincoln.

They were outvoted, and the clerk read the resolutions a third time. The Speaker rose to put the question before the House.

For the final time, John Quincy Adams, who had once stood atop the world stage, rose under his own power. Intending to be heard on the matter, he lost his balance, grabbing his desk for support even as it slipped slowly from his grasp. He was prevented from falling by his neighbor, Dr. David Fisher of Ohio, who caught him in his arms. William Cocke of Tennessee, standing nearby, described it to a reporter in 1891 as if it were yesterday: "In his feeble effort to rise . . . he caught hold of either side of the narrow desk in front of him, and was tremblingly pulling himself to his feet, when, half way up, his hold gave way; he sank . . . back into his chair, and was dying before he spoke one of the words his lips parted to say."[2] Confusion reigned on the House floor. Members close to the scene yelled for the Speaker to stop. "Mr. Adams! Mr. Adams! . . . The House was in great commotion, every eye being directed to his seat, and every countenance expressing intense anxiety."[3] He appeared in "the agonies of death," according to the *Congressional Globe.*

Adams was placed on one of the sofas that straddled the entryway and removed to the Rotunda. Like actors in a tragic comedy, his handlers brought him out to the balcony and just as quickly decided it would be better to bring him back inside. Finally, Adams was placed in the Speaker's office. "This is the last of earth," he said. "I am content."

There was a "gloomy pause" to the raucousness of the House. "Some members sat in mute suspense; others stood in groups, and made or answered inquiries as to the cause and the probable issue of the attack."[4]

But through it all, Clio was serene. "Her attitude is graceful and beautiful; her light drapery floats around her, and the winged car in which she stands seems to be in motion over the globe."[5]

Adams, who had known an America before the Constitution, who had served Presidents Washington, Madison, and Monroe, who had in turn held that high office, was the last of a generation that had steadily maneuvered the nation through its earliest challenges. His death signaled the passage of stewardship to a new generation, who would soon be asked to weigh in on the greatest and most inflammatory questions ever put before the Republic.

In his desk was found a poem, written in the last hours of his life, to the statue on the wall.

> *Muse! Quit thy car, come down upon the floor,*
> *And bring with thee that volume in thy hand;*
> *Rap with thy marble knuckles at the door,*
> *And take at a reporter's desk thy stand.*
> *Send round thy album, and collect a tome*
> *Of autographs from rulers of the land;*
> *Invite each Solon to inscribe his name,*
> *A self-recorded candidate for fame.*

The Thirtieth Congress of the United States was in its first weeks. The 230[6] members of the House hailed from twenty-nine states. Each had been sufficiently esteemed by his community to serve in this high office. Many, perhaps most, saw themselves as major historical figures who would someday merit a chapter in Clio's records. Of these it has been said, "Few of whom were less known than his which was destined to a fame more wide and enduring than all the rest together."

Abraham Lincoln, the seminal figure in American civilization, was then a rough frontier lawyer and politician, in his first movements on the national stage. Here he worked with many of the greatest figures of the age, and many who would prove significant in his later journeys and in the great coming contest that defined his abbreviated life. It was here that the most significant wartime president tried to end a conflict he believed unjust; here that Lincoln played presidential kingmaker; here that he first tried to limit the reach of an evil he one day would end.

This is the story of Congressman Abraham Lincoln.

CHAPTER 1

THE MOST AMBITIOUS MAN IN THE WORLD

On a cold winter's day in February 1843, attorney Richard Thomas went to his post office in Virginia, Illinois, to retrieve the mail. In his pile was a folded-up parchment bearing a Springfield postmark. The message was from his friend Abraham Lincoln. Thomas paid for his mail (the stamp still being one year off, all mail came postage due) and unfolded it.

"Now if you should hear any one say that Lincoln doesn't want to go to Congress, I wish you as a personal friend of mine, would tell him you have reason to believe he is mistaken. The truth is, I would like to go very much."[1]

With that, Abraham Lincoln, a Springfield attorney and a leader in the Illinois Whig Party, began in earnest his first attempt to win a seat in Congress. Thomas, a Cass County attorney, knew Lincoln from their work together on the Eighth Judicial Circuit. On the frontier of Illinois, no lawyer could earn a living in just one county. Throughout the year, the Eighth Circuit traveled from county seat to county seat, from courthouse to courthouse, handling a variety of causes and controversies.

The Illinois General Assembly, now three years removed from the last census, was far behind on drawing new congressional maps. But when it did, surely there would be an opportunity for Lincoln. Westward migration meant Illinois would grow from three to seven seats in the House of Representatives. John T. Stuart, the incumbent congressman and Lincoln's former law partner, was unlikely to run again, and by this time had probably already signaled this decision to his friends.*

The same day Lincoln penned his letter to Thomas, he also wrote to Alden Hull, a friend from Tazewell County with whom he'd served in the General Assembly. "Your county and ours are almost sure to be placed in the same Congressional district," he wrote. "I would like to be its Representative."[2]

Through his service in the legislature and in Whig Party politics, and his work on the circuit, Lincoln had made a wide network of friends and acquaintances. He would now begin to put the pieces in place, his eyes fixed to the east toward the national seat of power.

Lincoln's early campaign letters caught few by surprise. Those who knew him attested to Lincoln's aspirations, going back to his earliest youth. His cousin remembered that "even in his early days he had a strong conviction that he was born for better things than then seemed likely or even possible."[3] A childhood friend recalled, "Abe was just awful hungry to be somebody."[4] Even the nation's top position did not seem out of reach to Lincoln, who said "he did not recollect the time when he did not believe that he would at some day be President."[5]

For a desperately poor young boy on the frontier, who lost his mother at age nine, such a life should well have been unimaginable. But history remembers few who did not take seriously what others found laughable. That Lincoln maintained this belief through backbreaking labor on the farm, long days on a Mississippi flatboat, a failed general store that left him with crippling debt, or a failed first legislative race may have seemed to others like a missed reality check. But refusal to accept the death of a dream would seem a historical imperative in realizing it. And like others who have risen in politics, Lincoln interacted with men who were reputed to be great, only to find that while they might be exceptional, they were still humans, in

---

*It is not totally clear when Stuart declined to run again; on April 6, after weeks of reporting on the campaign to replace him, the *Sangamo Journal* noted, "We ought to have stated several weeks since that Hon. John T. Stuart is not a candidate for Congress."

no material way different from him.[6] The year before he ran for Congress, Lincoln had his first chance to meet someone with a truly national reputation. Martin Van Buren, who had just left the presidency, stopped for the night in Rochester, Illinois, six miles from Springfield.[7] Despite the fact that he was a prominent Whig, the local Democrats invited Lincoln to dinner. It was a testament to Lincoln's good company and sense of humor, for the Democrats wanted their exalted guest to enjoy himself. Lincoln did not disappoint, filling the evening with "a constant supply" of entertaining stories, "each more irresistible than its predecessor,"[8] while the former president insisted "his sides were sore from laughing."[9] Lincoln listened carefully to Van Buren's stories of old New York politics, of the days of Alexander Hamilton and Aaron Burr, and no doubt believed with increasing confidence that he, too, could make a name for himself. Perhaps he would not have been surprised to know that one day, this tiny town of Rochester would build a memorial to commemorate not just Van Buren's visit, but his presence at the dinner as well. William Herndon, Lincoln's law partner from 1844 until the end of his life, remembered him as "the most ambitious man in the world."[10]

Two days removed from his thirty-fourth birthday when he wrote to Thomas and Hull, Lincoln was already an experienced politician. After losing his first attempt for the legislature in 1832, he had come back to win the next four elections. The time spanning Lincoln's first bid for office and his retirement from the legislature saw a breakdown in the national consensus, division, and the rise and crystallization of new political parties. For his part, Lincoln was a Whig.

Although we remember Lincoln as a Republican, or as someone who was "above" party politics, he was a member of the Whig Party for most of his political life. The Whigs, little understood and largely forgotten, were for a time one of two major American political parties. They elected two presidents, and due to their untimely deaths produced two more, and at times controlled the Senate and House of Representatives.

The Whig coalition came together in response to the policies of President Andrew Jackson. Like all movements born in opposition, they were a disparate bunch. The Whigs included everyone from genteel former Federalists, who traced their most recent lineage to James Madison, to members of the populist Anti-Masonic Party, sworn enemies of secret societies. The latter was formed after William Morgan, a Mason from upstate New York, let it be known that he was publishing a book revealing the secrets of Free-masonry.[11] When Morgan was arrested on a petty charge, four men bailed him out, paid his debt, and took him off in a carriage, never to be seen again.[12]

The essence of Whig Party policy was Henry Clay's "American System." It called for a high protective tariff to shield infant American industries from foreign competition; a system of internal improvements such as ports, canals, roads, bridges, and railroads to create a truly national marketplace; and a national bank for stable currency and a source of financing for com-merce.

In 1832, Jackson vetoed the reauthorization of the national bank. The mercantile class of the United States, who relied on the credit to fund their operations, was driven to the Whig Party. Then Jackson went further, re-moving deposits from the national bank and violating federal law.[13] Two Treasury secretaries were fired, in a nineteenth-century version of Nixon's Saturday Night Massacre. Meanwhile, South Carolina attempted to "nul-lify" the national tariff, which provoked a strong reaction from Jackson and a deep resentment among supporters of states' rights.[14] While northern Whigs were upset about banking policy, southern supporters of state prerogatives were also driven to join the Whig Party, despite its support for the tariff.

Whigs were focused on economic progress. They pushed the nation's first bankruptcy law and the creation of limited liability companies.[15] The Whigs anticipated and advocated for many of the features now associated with the modern economy, while Jackson and the Democrats had a nostalgic view of a nation of yeoman farmers toiling away.

The Jacksonian era, which gave rise to a new party system, also saw the dramatic expansion of voting rights. New tactics would be necessary to win over this broad new electorate. These included new newspapers, and events such as campaign "rallies, parades, barbecues, and pole raisings."[16]

The Panic of 1837 allowed the Whigs to present a unified and national economic message, discussing what they were for and not what they were against.[17]

Lincoln would recall that he "was always a Whig in politics,"[18] and called the Whig platform "the right to rise." [19] While many have celebrated the extreme poverty from which Lincoln emerged, he was never among that group. It was his desire to foster a society with social mobility, in which everyone could rise according to his talents and hard work. Henry Clay was Lincoln's "beau ideal of a statesman, the man for whom I fought all my humble life." [20]

In 1838, John Stuart, Lincoln's law partner, decided to run for Congress. His Democratic opponent was Stephen Douglas, then only twenty-five. Stuart and Douglas traveled the broad district, one of only three in the state of Illinois, and even rode to debates together. One night they arrived late at an inn, and the innkeeper roused his guests from their beds, telling them to make room for two more (it was not uncommon, with the scarcity of sleeping space on the frontier, for innkeepers to ask patrons to share a bed with strangers). Upon learning the partisan affiliations of the two existing guests, Douglas said, "Stuart, you sleep with the Whig, and I'll sleep with the Democrat." [21] But the campaign was not always a model of civility. In a debate at the Market House in Springfield, Stuart lifted Douglas by his head and paraded him around the square. [22] With limited options, the diminutive Douglas closed his jaws around Stuart's thumb, scarring the latter for life. [23]

On May 10, 1838, Abraham Lincoln filled in on the campaign trail for Stuart, who was sick—it was the first Lincoln-Douglas debate. [24]

Stuart won, becoming the first Whig representative from Illinois. On September 29, there was a barbecue for two thousand in celebration at Porter's Grove. Three of the prominent speakers—Abraham Lincoln, John J. Hardin, and Edward D. Baker—were probably even then contemplating how they would win the seat when Stuart gave it up.

By 1843, Lincoln was one of the senior leaders of the Illinois Whig Party, and "the most ambitious man in the world" was itching to move on to the next level. With his behind-the-scenes campaign for Congress revving up, Lincoln participated in a Whig meeting on March 1 to organize for the upcoming elections.

From his home at the Globe Tavern on Adams Street, where he lived with Mary Todd, his wife of four months, Lincoln could see the Illinois State Capitol, his destination. The Globe advertised itself as "well provided with rooms for families and travelers . . . one square southwest of the state house," charging twenty-five cents a meal, fifty cents per day for people, and to stable horses twenty-five cents per night.[25]

Lincoln would have been an instantly recognizable sight on the streets of the town. He weighed 160 pounds, ridiculously thin for his six-foot-four-inch frame.[26] His height was all the more distinctive due to his long legs.[27] Though he stood head and shoulders above nearly everyone he met, when seated he was "no taller than ordinary men."[28]

The capitol stood in stark relief against the scattered structures of the sleepy town of Springfield, the seat of government for an infant state on the western frontier of a young republic.[29] Months earlier, in response to a sermon on the second coming of Christ, Lincoln had said of his town: "If the Lord has been in Springfield once, he will never come the second time."[30] But that view of the capitol must have served as a constant point of pride for Lincoln. Nearly six years earlier, he and the other legislators from Sangamon County had secured Springfield as the site of the new capital for Illinois.* This Classical Revival building was created out of limestone from a local quarry, giving it an unusual brown and yellow color, crowned by a white cupola and a modest red dome, topped by an American flag with twenty-six stars.

Inside the packed Hall of Representatives, enthusiasm ran high as Whigs readied for the next contest. Their optimism was a triumph of hope over experience.

The Whigs of Illinois had "never carried a presidential election, never elected a United States Senator, never elected a Governor or Lieutenant Governor," were in the minority in the General Assembly, and had never held more than one of the state's three congressional seats.[31]

The meeting made a number of resolutions and committed them to a policy paper, "An Address to the People of Illinois."[32] Lincoln was one of three assigned to craft it.† The address offers the clearest possible insight

---

*Remarkably, all were taller than six feet, and they were collectively dubbed "the Long Nine."

† Also on the committee were Stephen Logan, Lincoln's law partner, and Albert Bledsoe, a lawyer who occupied the office next to Lincoln's, who would later serve as assistant secretary of war for the Confederacy.

into Lincoln's philosophy as he first set his sights on national office, covering not only political issues but also best practices for local party organizations. The address advocated for a tariff on imports to fund the operations of the federal government and eliminate the need for direct taxation, which the Whigs opposed. In such a case, Lincoln argued, "The land must be literally covered with assessors and collectors, going forth like swarms of Egyptian locusts, devouring every blade of grass and other green thing." Whigs also favored a tariff to protect American manufacturing from competition with foreign goods.[33]

The address denounced deficit spending and borrowing by the national government, "growing with a rapidity fearful to contemplate." Indebtedness "is a system," Lincoln wrote, "not only ruinous while it lasts, but one that must soon fail and leave us destitute. An individual who undertakes to live by borrowing, soon finds his original means devoured by interest, and next no one left to borrow from—so must it be with a government."

The third point of the circular was the "necessity and propriety of a National Bank," one of the most contentious national issues. As to the advisability of the bank, the circular simply asks its readers to compare the economy now with what it had been under the bank's existence, a predecessor to the perennial question: "Are you better off now than you were four years ago?"

The fourth resolution regarded Henry Clay's bill on public land sales. This would allow states to keep a percentage of federal property sold within their borders, money that could be used to promote economic development in the form of internal improvements. The benefit to Illinois from this bill, Lincoln reasoned, "seems to us the clearest imaginable." Illinois would receive substantial annual revenues, "no part of which we otherwise receive. . . . Shall we accept our share of the proceeds, under Mr. Clay's bill; or shall we rather reject that, and get nothing?"

Resolutions five through nine concerned organizing and preparing the Whig Party for victory. A Whig candidate should be slated for every seat in Congress, Lincoln argued, regardless of how difficult the district.

In addition to fielding a full slate of candidates, the circular prescribed the use of a convention system to narrow the field to a single candidate. "This we believe to be of the very first importance. Whether the system is right in itself, we do not stop to enquire; contenting ourselves with trying to show, that while our opponents use it, it is madness in us not to defend ourselves with it. Experience has shown that we cannot successfully defend ourselves without it." Today it is nearly universally accepted that parties, mostly through primary elections, must narrow down the field for the final ballot, but that was far from the case at the time. Lincoln reported that "go where you would in a large Whig county, you were sure to find the Whigs, not contending shoulder to shoulder against the common enemy, but divided into factions, and fighting furiously with one another." Consequently, the Whig counties sent twenty-seven Democrats to the Illinois House. Conventions were so controversial within the party that Whigs who ran against the convention choice frequently polled ahead of their rivals, only to see themselves lose to the Democrat, "the spoils chucklingly borne off by the common enemy."

"That 'union is strength' is a truth," Lincoln observed, "that has been known, illustrated and declared, in various ways and forms in all ages of the world." In an analogy that Lincoln would later use to unforgettable effect, "He whose wisdom surpasses that of all philosophers, has declared that 'a house divided against itself cannot stand.'"

"If two friends aspire to the same office, it is certain both cannot succeed. Would it not, then, be much less painful to have the question decided by mutual friends some time before, than to snarl and quarrel till the day of election, and then both be beaten by the common enemy?"

The simple formula for victory, to render Whig candidates "always successful," was to get them all to the polls, and to vote unitedly. "This is the great desideratum. Let us make every effort to attain it. At every election, let every Whig act as though he knew the result to depend upon his action."

But hatred of political conventions had contributed to the founding of the Whig Party. In 1832, the Democratic Party held its first national nominating convention. The renomination of Andrew Jackson for president was beyond doubt. At issue was who would serve as his running mate and vice president in his second term, and so at its heart it was a decision on who would succeed him as president and party leader. Richard Mentor Johnson was extremely popular in the West and among the grass roots of the party. Johnson, a colorful but largely forgotten figure, held out one of his slaves,

Julia Chinn, as his wife (though of course they could not legally marry), and, much to the chagrin of Kentucky's debutante set, even tried to have their daughters presented to society. Johnson had won a massive following in the West for his efforts to eliminate indebtedness as a criminal offense.[34] But while Johnson may have held the hearts of the grass roots, it was Martin Van Buren of New York who was selected. Elected officials and party bosses were overrepresented in the convention, and "steam roller methods" were used to rubber-stamp the predetermined vote.[35] Many of the disappointed joined the Whig Party, bringing with them their antipathy for conventions. One of these was Joseph Duncan, a former Democratic governor of Illinois. Duncan replied to the circular Lincoln had drafted by saying, "I look upon the convention system as designed by its authors to change the government from the free will of the people into the hands of designing politicians."[36]

As a legislator, Lincoln was part of a nucleus of influential Whigs who refused to cede the tactical high ground to the Democrats. Referred to by their detractors as "the Springfield Junto," they worked quietly behind the scenes to slate ambitious Whigs for office and deter others to avoid dividing the vote. The Junto's "saving grace," it was reported, "was the lack of reliable information about it."[37]

Many Whigs still prided themselves on being "too independent to wear the collar of party discipline,"[38] but there is nothing like the crush of persistent political reversals to open minds to new approaches. In October 1839, the Whigs had their first state convention, in Springfield. Counties that had honored the result of conventions were successful.[39] Lincoln tried to capitalize on that success by publishing a handbook for party organization. It read as follows:

Lincoln's Plan of Campaign in 1840[40]

1st.   Appoint one person in each county as county captain, and take his pledge to perform promptly all the duties assigned him.

Duties of the County Captain.

1st.   To procure from the poll-books a separate list for each Precinct of all the names of all those persons who voted the Whig ticket in August.

2nd. To appoint one person in each Precinct as Precinct Captain, and,
by a personal interview with him, procure his pledge, to perform
promptly all the duties assigned him.

3rd. To deliver to each Precinct Captain the list of names as above,
belonging to his Precinct; and also a written list of his duties.

Duties of the Precinct Captain.

1st.   To divide the list of names delivered him by the county Captain, into
Sections of ten who reside most convenient to each other.

2nd. To appoint one person of each Section as Section Captain, and by a
personal interview with him, procure his pledge to perform promptly
all the duties assigned him.

3rd. To deliver to each Section Captain the list of names belonging to his
Section and also a written list of his duties.

Duties of the Section Captain.

1st.   To see each man of his Section face to face, and procure his pledge
that he will for no consideration (impossibilities excepted) stay
from the polls on the first Monday in November; and that he will
record his vote as early on the day as possible.

2nd. To add to his Section the name of every person in his vicinity who
did not vote with us in August, but who will vote with us in the fall,
and take the same pledge of him, as from the others.

3rd. To *task* himself to procure at least such additional names to his
Section.

Instead of capitalizing on that success, as Lincoln argued, the Whigs backed
off the convention system, running a disorganized campaign in 1842, and
were routed throughout the state.

When the redistricting maps were completed, the Whig stronghold of
central Illinois found itself in the Seventh District.* Though competition for

---

*The Seventh Congressional District included the counties of Sangamon, Scott, Morgan,
Cass, Menard, Logan, Mason, Tazewell, Woodford, Marshall, and Putnam. Of these,
Sangamon, Menard, Tazewell, and Woodford were in Lincoln's Eighth Judicial Circuit.

the spot would be intense, all sides seemed to agree that a nominating convention was the fairest method of ensuring the seat remained in their hands.

On the morning of March 6, the Whigs of the Seventh District met to decide the date and place of their congressional convention. The next day, Lincoln wrote to his old friend John Bennett, a Whig living in Petersburg, Menard County. "I am sorry to hear that any of the Whigs of your county, or indeed of any county, should longer be against conventions . . . the right way for you to do, is to hold your meeting and appoint delegates any how; and if there be any who will not take part, let it be so. The matter will work so well this time that even they who now oppose will come in next time."[41]

The race would be covered by newspapers, each openly affiliated with one political party or another. In Lincoln's day, this primarily meant the Whig-allied *Sangamo Journal* (later the *Illinois State Journal*) and the *Illinois State Register*, the organ of the Democrats.

Both papers featured advertisements, often illustrated, to meet the various needs of their frontier readership; these included "incorruptible teeth," balm to restore lost eyesight, lozenges (the "Greatest discovery of the age"), glasses, putty, hand pumps, plows, and other farm implements. As time went on, these ads reflected advancements in technology such as spectacles and daguerreotypes. Flashy drawings or headlines helped the ads compete against their neighbors (WAR IN TEXAS! preceded a blurb for a local apothecary). The local papers featured divorce decrees (in one memorable ad, a man warned merchants that he was no longer responsible for paying his ex-wife's creditors), New Hampshire Senate elections, riots in Canada. The papers reprinted the queen's speech at the opening of Parliament and reported Indian slayings on the frontier and alongside revolutions in the Punjab region of India, as well as strange lights witnessed on the Illinois horizon.

Unlike today, when news outlets and reporters make a pretense at impartiality, the newspapers proudly advertised their partisan and ideological identities. Readers were invited to digest the news accordingly. The *Register* featured a recurring column titled "Whig falsehoods." The Whig-affiliated *Journal*, with overstatement characteristic of the partisan press, called the new congressional maps the worst "specimens of gerrymandering, the equal of which was never before exhibited in a representative government."[42]

The Whig nomination would not come easily for Lincoln. For ambitious, experienced Whigs, there was no realistic chance of being elected governor, or to statewide office, or to be elected by the General Assembly to the United States Senate. The Seventh District was the funnel of Whig aspirations. Though many expressed interest, Lincoln's true competitors were John Hardin of Morgan County and Edward Baker, who like Lincoln lived in Sangamon.

Hardin was from one of the elite families of Kentucky. Lincoln had lived the first seven years of his life in Hardin County, Kentucky, named for his adversary's grandfather, a Revolutionary War hero killed by the Indians to whom he'd been sent by George Washington. Hardin's father was a United States senator who had served as Kentucky's Speaker of the House and secretary of state.[43] Hardin's reputation was that of an "honest, upright, and inflexible public servant."[44] Hardin's wife once received a letter from a friend advising her to "put yourself down as favored among women," noting that she'd be hard-pressed to "challenge the annals of matrimony to produce another specimen of husband."[45] Though serious in demeanor, Hardin was sweet with his children, and a doting father. "You are at an age where you are forming habits which will last you through life," he once wrote his daughter. "Be studious, and you will store your mind with useful knowledge, which will be a resource to you whenever you may be left with a lonesome or idle hour on your hands."[46] To his son, during a Christmas when they were separated, he wrote, "It is a great sacrifice for me to be without the society of my two oldest children, and nothing in this world can give me so much pleasure as to hear from them and learn they are good and happy, and improving in knowledge, and learning something of the great responsibilities of life."[47]

Though Lincoln and Hardin were always more professional colleagues than friends, Abe was as close as could be with Edward Baker. It was said that "wherever he spoke he carried his audience captive by the power of his eloquence and the strength of his arguments."[48] Baker was an incredible showman, who liked to deliver speeches with "a pet eagle chained to a ring."[49] When denouncing Democratic failures, the eagle was trained to "lower its head and droop its wings," but when discussing the promise of

Whig policies, the eagle would "spread its wings and scream."[50] Even the *Register* thought Baker "a very handsome man ... an eloquent speaker ... naturally good natured."[51] Such was Baker's drive that he denounced his parents for having him in England, once he found out its impact on his eligibility to be president.[52] The *Register* ribbed Baker, saying that he "has neglected everything else this session in order to get himself a district made here ... we hope our legislature will have mercy on Congress."[53]

It is a maxim of politics that intraparty contests are the most vicious of all. Elections are about offering contrasts to voters and clarifying choices. With Lincoln, Baker, and Hardin in harmony on the issues, with each an experienced legislator and lawyer, that left their supporters limited options to advance their candidate's cause. They could trump up minor or nonexistent policy differences or attack the opposition personally.

The Congressional District Convention would be made up of delegates nominated at smaller county conventions. Lincoln's first hurdle was getting past Baker in their shared home county of Sangamon.

Leave it to the *Register* to cover Whig infighting with feigned shock: "Our ears are stunned here, just now, by the din of the Whigs, concerning Lincoln and Baker as to which shall go to Congress from this district. If we are to believe either of the two factions, it would be difficult to decide which is the bigger rascal."[54] The *Register*, which had contributed mightily to the mythos surrounding the "Springfield Junto," reported that their "secret agents" are "ready to visit the several counties."

Lincoln had a number of challenges to overcome. The first was Baker's popularity and long standing in Sangamon County. The rest were personal to him. First, his association by marriage with the Edwards family led to charges of elitism and aristocracy.

Mary Todd was descended from Kentucky high society and could reportedly trace her lineage back to the sixth century.[55] She came to Springfield at age twenty-one, where in the course of time she would be united to a man with an undistinguished past but a promising future. Mary Todd's sister, Elizabeth, was married to Ninian Edwards, scion of a prominent Illinois family and one of Lincoln's fellow legislators.[56]

Mary Todd's education, intelligence, and pedigree made her popular among the many single men of the frontier. In time, Lincoln joined the others in calling on her. Elizabeth remembered her sister as "the most ambitious woman I ever knew."[57] But it was a man's world, and Mary's ambitions would have to be satiated by her husband's successes. She was reported to have said that, from her many suitors, she would marry "him who has the best prospects of being President."[58]

Their mutual friends thought Abraham and Mary an improbable match.

For his part, Lincoln grew to realize the wisdom of these observations. One evening, he summoned his friend Joshua Speed to his home, handing him a breakup letter to convey to Mary. In an act with wide-ranging and unforeseeable consequences, Speed threw it in the fire, insisting that Lincoln tell her himself.[59] But Lincoln had written the letter for a reason, and what happened next he probably anticipated. Lincoln told Mary that he did not love her, and she burst into tears.[60] Lincoln hugged her and kissed her and backed down. He reported the news that evening to Speed, who told him that he was a fool, and that the die was now cast.[61] Lincoln said, "Well if I am in again, so be it. It's done, and I shall abide by it."[62] Then on January 1, 1841, after food had been prepared and the guests arrived for the event, Lincoln simply didn't show up for his wedding.[63]

When Lincoln was finally located, he was so frantic and upset that his friends undertook a suicide watch, with Speed recalling, "Knives and razors, and every instrument that could be used for self destruction were removed from his reach."[64] In the weeks that followed, Lincoln reported, "I am now the most miserable man living. If what I feel were equally distributed to the whole human family, there would not be one cheerful face on earth. Whether I shall ever be better, I cannot tell."[65] Lincoln, diligent in his attendance at the legislature, now absented himself for weeks.[66] Returning, he barely kept his seat warm during the remainder of session. During this time, Congressman John Stuart, his former law partner, recommended him to Secretary of State Daniel Webster for a diplomatic post in Bogotá, Colombia.[67] Nothing came of it.

After the session, Lincoln repaired to Kentucky, where Speed was now living. Speed was still frightened of his guilt-ridden friend harming himself. Why Lincoln did not may be found in something he said to Speed during the course of this visit. Lincoln despaired that "[h]e had done noth-

ing to make any human being remember that he had lived; and that to connect his name with the events transpiring in his day and generation, and so
impress himself upon them as to link his name with something that would
redound to the interest of his fellow-men, was what he desired to live for."[68]
Even the most miserable man living could survive, it appears, with something to hope for.

Lincoln returned to Springfield, still burdened by "the never-absent idea
that there is one still unhappy whom I have contributed to make so. That
kills my soul. I cannot but reproach myself for even wishing to be happy
while she is otherwise . . . I must gain confidence in my own ability to keep
my resolves when they are made. In that ability I once prided myself as the
only chief gem of my character; that gem I lost, how and where you know
too well. I have not regained it; and until I do I cannot trust myself in any
matter of much importance."[69]

The wife of Simeon Francis, editor of the *Sangamo Journal*, conspired to
bring Lincoln and Mary Todd back together.[70] After a party held for that
sole purpose, to which neither knew the other had been invited, they continued to see each other at the Francis home.[71]

In November 1842, James Matheny was awakened from sleep by a
knocking at his door. He opened it to find his friend Abraham, informing
him that he would be married later that evening, and asking him to serve as
best man.[72]

As Lincoln dressed for the occasion at his friend's house, their little
boy came up to him, and "in boyish innocence asked him where he was
going."[73] "To hell, I suppose,"[74] was Lincoln's response. One can only imagine the look on the boy's face.

This time, Lincoln showed up for his wedding, "as pale and trembling
as if being driven to slaughter," and went through with the ceremony. In
William Herndon's view, Lincoln, caught between "honor and domestic
peace . . . chose the former, and with it years of self-torture, sacrificial pangs,
and the loss forever of a happy home."[75] Now it was hurting Lincoln's
chances of going to Congress. With a growing movement against central-
ized control and the perceived machinations of the Springfield Junto, Ninian Edwards was defeated in his attempt for renomination to the legislature
at the 1840 Sangamon Whig convention. Lincoln grumbled that he himself

would have lost had the Whigs not desired his speaking skills out on the stump.[76] Lincoln's marriage into what passed for Illinois aristocracy, ironically, would hamper the chances of this former farmhand.

Religion was also a factor. Baker was a member of the Campbellite religious movement and received perhaps every vote from that quarter. But Lincoln, who was not a member of any church and whose personal beliefs were considered suspect, faced great resistance from some religiously motivated voters. If that were not enough, there was the Shields affair.

The trouble began with a decision by the leadership of Illinois to stop accepting taxes in notes from the state bank. In criticism, Lincoln penned "A Letter from the Lost Townships," purportedly written by a widow flush with notes from the state bank but unable to pay her taxes.[77] Lincoln's rapier wit was deployed to full effect, with Treasurer James Shields bearing the brunt. Shields demanded of the newspaper editor the name of his anonymous attacker, which Lincoln gave him permission to provide, and Shields challenged Lincoln to a duel. Lincoln received some bad advice from the person he'd chosen as his second and issued a highly technical response that made things worse. Eventually, Lincoln responded that the letter was of a political, not a personal nature, but that if this was unsatisfactory, Lincoln (as the challenged party) would choose to fight with broadswords, across the Mississippi River from Alton on the Missouri side.[78] As Lincoln pointed out, "I did not want to kill Shields, and felt sure I could disarm him . . . and furthermore, I didn't want the damned fellow to kill me, which I rather think he would have done if we had selected pistols."[79] The duelists and their parties (and a substantial crowd) had made it all the way to the dueling site before their seconds and a number of others, including John Hardin, who had come down in an attempt to prevent the duel, found a way to do so. Lincoln would spend the rest of his life embarrassed and reminded of the incident, saying years later, "If all the good things I have ever done are remembered as long and well as my scrape with Shields, it is plain I shall not soon be forgotten."[80]

Baker had campaigned hard. The *Register* described him "running this way to catch a man by the hand, then that way to pat another on the shoulder, then starting off to seize a third by the buttonhole—nodding and bowing to people two or three squares distant—running into a knot of Whigs, and offering his hat full of cigars with astonishing liberality."[81]

March 20 was the day. The Sangamon County Whigs met at the capitol to appoint delegates to the Seventh District Convention. Lincoln must have felt knots in his stomach as he watched so many familiar faces enter the convention, to weigh in on whether he or Baker should be the nominee.

Political conventions take on a life of their own, more than the sum total of their parts. The palpable feeling of who has momentum often exceeds the predictions of the best head counter. It is likely that Lincoln could feel that the tide was not in his favor. The convention was more similar to a primary with one polling location. The Whigs of Sangamon County filed in, hundreds of them, and probably signaled their preference to a teller, who recorded their vote in a poll book. The *Register* reported that Baker's forces came as early as possible, as Lincoln's friends were trickling in. Around noon, Lincoln was convinced to withdraw. After more than eight hundred votes, Lincoln trailed Baker by fifty-one.[82] Lincoln's acquiescence, however, seems to have been a fatal political mistake. According to the *Register*, Lincoln stepped aside before "his real strength was apparent." As the day went on, delegates in favor of Lincoln arrived in greater numbers. In fact, the *Register* reports that "Lincoln would have 'paralyzed' Baker's support by nightfall."[83] Mary "berated him for not exerting himself hard enough to win."[84] Indeed, it seems as though Lincoln failed to heed his own advice. If he had identified his supporters throughout the county, and made note of who had voted and who was outstanding, he may well have realized that the contest was not yet over.

Baker would carry delegate-rich Sangamon County to the district-wide convention in Pekin. Despite his best efforts to decline, the disheartened Lincoln was selected as a delegate to the district convention, committed to supporting Baker. Lincoln compared it to "a fellow who is made grooms-man to the man who has 'cut him out,' and is marrying his own dear gal." He predicted that Hardin would prevail.[85] It surely wasn't easy for Lincoln and Baker, two friends, to stand in each other's way as they had, and it was probably just as difficult for the Whigs of Sangamon to choose between friends. According to the *Journal*, "At the end of the meeting Lincoln was loudly called for and addressed the meeting."[86] No doubt he gamely congratulated Baker and preached the familiar gospel of party unity.

Lincoln's loss in Sangamon very nearly, but not entirely, ruined his chances for 1843. Though Lincoln himself was a pledged Baker delegate, his allies throughout the district could still send pro-Lincoln delegates to the district convention. Menard County, meeting shortly thereafter, instructed its delegates to support Lincoln. Menard included Lincoln's original Illinois home of New Salem, and the town of Petersburg, which Lincoln had plotted as a young land surveyor. Petersburg had attracted many former New Salem residents when that town failed.[87] If other counties followed suit, or if a compromise candidate was needed at Pekin, Lincoln might still have emerged the nominee.

Lincoln wrote to his friend Martin Morris, "It is truly gratifying to me to learn that while the people of Sangamon have cast me off, my old friends of Menard, who have known me longest and best, stick to me."[88] He related to Morris the litany of charges he faced from Baker supporters. "It would astonish, if not amuse, the older citizens to learn that I (a stranger, friendless, uneducated, penniless boy, working on a flatboat at ten dollars per month) have been put down here as the candidate of pride, wealth, and aristocratic family distinction. Yet so, chiefly, it was ... it was everywhere contended that no Christian ought to go for me, because I belonged to no church, was suspected of being a deist, and had talked about fighting a duel ... those influences levied a tax of a considerable per cent upon my strength throughout the religious controversy. But enough of this."[89]

Lincoln took a long walk in the woods with James Matheny, the best man at his wedding, to further vent his frustration. "Why Jim," he protested, "I am now and always shall be the same Abe Lincoln I was when you first saw me."[90]

While Lincoln stewed over the "bitter features of the canvass,"[91] Hardin and Baker campaigned intensely. Both frantically wrote to supporters throughout the district. In Hardin's letters he manifested an intense attention to detail, knowing the particulars of the local convention in Visalia, Woodford County.[92] Hardin had traveled to Versailles, and then to Lacon in Marshall County, visiting the opinion leaders and power brokers at each stop, knowing which delegates were committed and which ones were uninstructed.[93] In five days he traversed an astounding two hundred miles on horseback. Writing from Tazewell, Hardin believed the delegates there would go for "Lincoln, Logan [Lincoln's law partner, who was also interested but not actively campaigning], Baker, or myself," while in Woodford "they are instructed to go for Baker as a 2nd choice," and in Putnam the first choice.[94] Hardin, never prone to problems with self-esteem, wrote that if he believed any man from (his home county) Morgan could defeat the nominee of Sangamon, "I should not have taken the field."[95] He pledged to do "anything which is honorable and fair to get the nomination."[96] Hardin seems to have been looking past the convention, and upon encountering Baker supporters he could not persuade, asked them to commit to supporting him in the general election.[97]

Toward the end of April, Baker traveled from Cass County to Petersburg, in Menard, "in low spirits," recorded one of Hardin's informants.[98] Baker, with some of his comrades from the Black Hawk War, had a muster on the other side of the river "and at Clary's Grove."[99]

That same informant noted, "At present there is more excitement with us than we usually have between Whig and Locos on the eve of an election."[100] Loco Focos, originally a name for a wing of the Democratic Party, had by now become a Whig epithet for the entire group.

On May 1, Lincoln arrived in Pekin for the districtwide Whig convention. If he were best man to the person who was marrying his dear old gal, this was the wedding. That morning featured a long impasse, with Baker and Hardin tied through many ballots. Lincoln watched one round follow the next. Being pledged to support his opponent made the situation difficult enough. But knowing that his support in Menard would have put him over the top had he, and not Baker, been nominated by Sangamon must have been especially painful. Still, Lincoln had been pledged and he did his utmost to bring Menard into Baker's column.

"When the convention assembled," wrote James Ruggles, "Baker was there with his friend and champion delegate, Abraham Lincoln. The ayes and noes had been taken, and there were fifteen votes apiece, and one in doubt that had not arrived. That was myself. I was known to be a warm friend of Baker, representing people who were partial to Hardin. As soon as I arrived Baker hurried to me, saying: 'How is it? It all depends on you.'"[101]

This was not possible, however, as that county's convention had ranked the candidates; if Lincoln could not be chosen, the delegates were instructed to support Hardin over Baker. He relates that he reluctantly broke the tie.[102]

Lincoln as chair of Sangamon withdrew Baker's name and allowed Hardin to be chosen by acclamation.[103]

What Lincoln did next seemed for all the world to be an act of party unity. Though carefully disguised, it was a masterful political power play. As the door swung shut on his congressional ambitions, he managed to stick his boot in its path, just in time.

"Immediately after the nomination," Ruggles remembered, "Mr. Lincoln walked across the room to my table, and asked if I would favor a resolution recommending Baker for the next term. On being answered in the affirmative, he said: 'You prepare the resolution, I will support it, and I think we can pass it.' The resolution created a profound sensation, especially with the friends of Hardin."[104]

It is all the more amazing since he likely thought of it on the spot. There was no way to know for sure that it would come down to one vote. Or that Lincoln would find out that Hardin commanded a majority of the delegates' pledges but not a majority of their preferences. It was the intensity of the fight, and the disappointment from half of the convention, that so easily paved the way for Lincoln to act.

The carefully worded resolution read as follows:

"That this convention, as individuals, recommend E. D. Baker as a suitable person to be voted for by the Whigs of this district, for representative to Congress, at the election in 1844, subject to the decision of a district convention should the Whigs of the district think proper to hold one."[105]

By a vote of 19–14, it was successful.[106]

The measure of the success might be judged against the faux outrage from the *Register*. "Was this fair? Was this not going beyond the line of duty? Although it is only a recommendation, it has the moral force of a nomination. . . . We have never before, in all our political experience, heard of such an instance as this." They likened the Whigs to a "tyrannical despotism, worse than that of Turkey."[107]

Surely Hardin was livid. He would not soon forget what had happened—or at whose hands it had been done. But he was cornered. At a Jacksonville barbecue on October 6, 1843, well before taking office, he publicly announced that he would not run for reelection.[108] But he did not foreclose a political comeback. One upset supporter said, "I am rejoiced to find that you by no means intend to [spend] the balance of your days upon the political laurels you have already won."[109]

While unheard-of today, short tenure in the House of Representatives was the rule, not the exception, in the era of Abraham Lincoln.

The 1840s saw the highest turnover of any other decade, with 60 percent over the course of those ten years.[110] From that number, retirements due to voluntary withdrawal were as high as 75 percent and as low as 55 percent.[111] It was the norm that more than half of any incoming House of Representatives would be freshmen, and not until 1876 did this figure drop below 50 percent.[112] It was not until 1901 that less than 30 percent of the House were freshmen.[113]

One of the reasons for this was that the principle of rotation, introduced to the Seventh District by Lincoln, was common throughout most of the country, more or less for the same reasons. House districts were "artificial political units which generally subsumed several or more separate communities. With few political organizations extending beyond their local towns and counties, district nominating caucuses were pluralistic, frequently fragmented affairs with each local organization sponsoring its own candidate."[114] Like the Seventh, "Districts throughout the country had long found rotation of the nomination to be an acceptable method for resolving conflict."[115] In a few areas the rotation period was a strict "one term and out," whereas in others it was a much more common two-term limit.[116] From 1838 to 1865, 30 percent of freshmen were defeated, compared to 23 percent of more senior members of the House (outside of the South).[117] More than 50 percent of all turnover was due to voluntarily withdrawal.[118] From 1838 to 1853, in nonsouthern states, the figure was 45 percent for freshmen, 61 percent for sophomores, and 42 percent for those with three or more terms.[119]

Why was the South largely exempt from this phenomenon? The reason is as simple as it is sinister. Southern voters believed that slavery was constantly endangered by Congress. Understanding that seniority mattered in obtaining influence and mastering the mechanics of Congress, districts frequently returned the same members. After Reconstruction, southern electorates would employ the same tactic for similar reasons, ensuring that the powerful committee chairs were in place to block civil rights legislation.

So Hardin, loath as he may have been to retire from Congress at age thirty-five, was in the same position as many of his colleagues.

The *Register*, when it had expected Baker to win the convention, had taken a "poor Hardin vs. the Junto" attitude. Now that he'd been nominated, they referred to Hardin as part of the "Springfield Junto Whig Ticket."[120]

Hardin feared that the Sangamon Whigs would be less than enthusiastic in working toward his election. To counter this, Lincoln and his compatriots offered a wager in the *Journal*: Hardin's majority in Sangamon would be double that of his home county of Morgan. "The losing county shall give a free barbeque to the Whigs of the other county. . . . Whigs of Morgan, will you go for it?"[121]

Lincoln wrote to Hardin, assuring him that Sangamon would not only fall in line but deliver big. "You will see by the *Journal* of this week that we propose, upon pain of losing a barbecue, to give you twice as great a majority" as Morgan.

But despite campaigning for the ticket, Lincoln could not bring himself to vote for Hardin, instead casting no vote at all in the congressional race.[122] Nothing could better manifest his hurt at not being chosen.[123]

Hardin won without Lincoln's vote. The *Register* blamed a superior Whig turnout operation, plus the number of Democrats that stayed home.[124]

On the day Hardin left to take his place in Washington, Mary "shed buckets full of tears."[125]

———◦◦◦———

CHAPTER 2

THE RIGHT TO RISE

L incoln had acted brilliantly to keep the path open for himself, but in
the best-case scenario he would not be sworn into Congress until December 1847.

Lincoln had much else to occupy himself; in addition to his travels on
the legal circuit and campaigning for the Whig ticket, he became a father
for the first time.[1]

October 6 was a sweet day for Lincoln. Sangamon had given Hardin
twice as large a majority as Morgan, and as per Lincoln's wager, it was on
this date that the latter held a barbecue. Lincoln, who had failed to vote for
Hardin, would have his barbecue and eat it too.

Hardin and the others in the Twenty-eighth Congress would soon be
faced by momentous questions with enormous consequences.

At the top of the list was what to do about Texas, a former Mexican state
now an independent republic. The cultural, religious, and geographical differences between Texas and Mexico had led to a successful revolution and
independence. What should America's policy be toward this new nation on
its western border, populated as it was by the same people? It was founded
on American ideals, settled largely by Americans, and bordering America. It
seemed natural that Texas should be part of the United States.

But there were other considerations.

While Hardin was receiving the message of the president of the United States, and as a member of Congress would vote on and debate its recommendations, Lincoln was busy scouring the prairie for a copy. The only one he could find, he lamented, belonged to the state library and was not available for reading.[2]

In December 1843, President John Tyler's message to Congress hinted at the annexation of Texas.[3] On December 8, 1843, the *Register* reported, under the headline "Annexation of Texas to the United States," that Great Britain would join with Texas if America did not. In addition to the obvious dangers of a British foothold in North America, the South feared that Britain would abolish slavery there.[4] But if the United States could obtain Texas, the South would have a formidable ally in the case of a sectional war, as well as increased power in Congress.[5]

Abel Upshur, the secretary of state, opened talks with Texas president Sam Houston.[6] It was far from a sure thing. Texas was busy negotiating recognition from Britain and France, which in exchange would insist that they not join the United States.[7]

In moving President Houston, Tyler had one card to play. But it was a powerful one. Andrew Jackson, in retirement at the Hermitage in Tennessee, was sought to press his friend Houston, in a letter that carried great weight with the Texas president.[8]

But it still might not have worked.

On February 28, 1844, the leading lights of Washington gathered about the USS *Princeton* to witness a display of what was billed as the most powerful cannon in the world. At the last minute, President Tyler was detained below deck while the rest of the group gathered above to watch the demonstration. It saved his life, and as he was the first vice president to ascend to the nation's highest office, it also averted a constitutional crisis.*

The test did not go as planned. Congressman John Hardin was "forty or fifty feet" away from the gun as it exploded. With characteristic modesty,

---

*Tyler's own ascendancy after the death of William Henry Harrison had been controversial enough (many believed he was merely acting president, and some felt that a new election should take place), and had he gone above deck that day his death would have further destabilized the young republic.

he remembered, "I do not lose my sense on such occasions, and as many of the officers were injured, I took command of the wounded and dead visitors, and rendered all the assistance possible." The gruesome scene horrified him, and he wondered "what could be done for men who knew not what hurt them." He remembered "the ghastly countenances of the dead, the shattered limbs, the gashes in the wounded and the mournful moaning" that "can neither be described or imagined." His ears were filled by "the wailings and shrieks of agony of the wives of those who were killed."[9] Secretary of State Upshur was dead, along with the secretary of the navy and six others, while many others were seriously wounded by the flying, burning shrapnel.[10]

His entire life, Lincoln had been fascinated by all manner of machines. He loved to inspect them, fiddle with them, and learn about how mechanical things worked. Could he possibly have resisted the chance to board the *Princeton*? Could he have helped but be as near as possible to "the Peacemaker" when it fired? While this question cannot be answered, there are elements of the aftermath of the *Princeton* incident that are concrete.

Abel Upshur would be replaced as secretary of state by John C. Calhoun, an ardently proslavery senator from South Carolina. Calhoun would pursue Texas annexation with a dogged intensity, dramatically accelerating the process. On April 12, the treaty of annexation was signed, and it was sent for ratification ten days later.[11] The treaty would fail, but Calhoun made a critical tactical decision that Texas could be admitted as a state, the same as any other. Instead of two-thirds in the Senate, it would require a simple majority vote in both houses and the signature of the president. Had Upshur lived, it is questionable whether Texas would have then or ever joined the union.

And while Congress grappled with Texas, the campaign for the presidency was beginning in earnest.

Instead of a potentially ill-fated rendezvous on the *Princeton*, Lincoln spoke the next day to farmers in Sugar Creek, in his capacity as an elector for Henry Clay. Electors were designated by the party and would vote in the Electoral College if their candidate won the votes of that state.[12] Part of Lincoln's duties as a Clay elector was to travel the state, campaigning on his behalf, which he did enthusiastically.

Henry Clay was someone Lincoln "almost worshipped."[13] Clay, a senator, former Speaker of the U.S. House, and secretary of state, had run for president unsuccessfully in 1824 and 1832. In 1840, when President Van Buren looked vulnerable, Clay was passed over for General William Henry Harrison. Now, in 1844, Clay's chances burned brighter than ever.

His surprise opponent was James Knox Polk, a serious, pious man, a former Speaker of the U.S. House and governor of Tennessee. The compromise choice of a badly divided convention, Polk was an acolyte of former president Jackson and thus nicknamed "Young Hickory."

Lincoln, Logan, Baker, and Stuart made nightly speeches to packed crowds on behalf of Clay.[14] In the town of Virginia on February 22, Lincoln made two addresses to the Cass County Clay Club. Where Democratic speakers appeared and asked to make their case, the *Journal* reported, Lincoln made "a clean shucking" of his opponent, defending the bank, and was interrupted with "rapturous applause."[15]

Lincoln took advantage of his Eighth Circuit travels to make speeches to local residents.

When the circuit court came to Springfield, Lincoln and a Democratic candidate for Congress debated for a crowded room in the courthouse. While the *Register* reported that the Democrat's arguments were triumphant and "unanswerable," the *Journal* recorded that "we did not discover a single [Democratic] position that he did not entirely demolish."[16] Such was the partisan press—at least they made no bones about it.

On March 9 Lincoln campaigned in Rochester, and on March 16 he had a debate with the Democrats.

It was then on to Tazewell, where attorney David Davis noted: "Politics rage now hereabouts ... the first day of every court is occupied with political speaking, usually by an Elector on each side of politics, each person generally speaking for three or four hours.... Lincoln is the best stump speaker in the state."[17] On April 6, Lincoln rode through the rain to the Peoria courthouse and back to Tremont.

On May 1, the Whig convention unanimously nominated Clay for president. Five days later, Baker was nominated by the Seventh District Whigs at Tremont to succeed Hardin in Congress. In place of his reelection, Hardin was given a resolution of thanks.[18] Hardin was out, Baker was in, and another crucial step in Lincoln's plan to go to Congress was completed.

On May 22, a meeting on the great Texas question was held at the

Illinois Capitol. "After a notice of a few hours, one of the largest meetings ever held by our citizens took place,"[19] the *Journal* reported. Lincoln was the first speaker, disagreeing with Tyler's plan. A year later, Lincoln put in writing his reactions to the Texas issue: "I was never much interested in the Texas question. I never could see much good to come of annexation; inasmuch, as they were already a free republican people on our own model." Lincoln reasoned that slaves would be taken there with or without annexation, without ever increasing the number of people in slavery. "It is possibly true, to some extent, that with annexation, some slaves may be sent to Texas and continued in slavery, that otherwise might have been liberated. To whatever extent this may be true, I think annexation an evil. I hold it to be a paramount duty of us in the free states, due to the union of the states, and perhaps to liberty itself (paradox though it may seem) to let the slavery of other states alone; while, on the other hand, I hold it to be equally clear, that we should never knowingly lend ourselves directly or indirectly, to prevent that slavery from dying a natural death—to find new places for it to live in, when it can no longer exist in the old."

In addition to his tireless efforts on behalf of Clay and the Whigs, Lincoln made a business decision that helped advance his political fortunes. Logan informed Lincoln that he wanted to dissolve their partnership so that he could take on his son as a partner.[20] It was just as well. Logan also had his sights set on the Seventh District.[21] After a long time in Logan's shadow as a lawyer, Lincoln could now be the senior partner of his next venture. He chose William Herndon, who had served as a law clerk to Logan and Lincoln. It was Lincoln's third partnership in the law, and it would last for the rest of his life. Herndon also belonged to the younger set of emerging Springfield Whigs, a group that had supported Baker over Lincoln in 1843.[22] This was a valuable inroad for Lincoln—he had to make sure his Sangamon County base was solid.

As the Lincoln family grew, and his law practice continued to expand, he moved his little family into a five-room house on Eighth and Jackson Streets. It was the first home he'd ever owned, and it was his residence in Springfield for the rest of his life.[23]

Early in the political education of Abraham Lincoln came the most basic lesson: politics is a game of addition, not subtraction.

On June 12, there was a public meeting in Springfield to discuss the Philadelphia nativist riots of the previous months, in which newly arrived Americans had been attacked by angry mobs. Lincoln addressed the meeting and presented a series of resolutions, "supporting them by able and forcible arguments," according to the *Sangamo Journal.* The Democrats had blamed the riots on the Whigs, and their hostility to "foreigners and Catholics." (The Democrats never missed an opportunity to label the Whigs as "bigots.")

Lincoln argued that the Whig position was that citizenship should require "some reasonable test" of one's fidelity to America and its institutions, that one should reside in the country long enough to become familiar with those institutions. Immigration laws "should be framed" to make citizenship "as convenient, cheap, and expeditious as possible."

Further, the Whigs would resist any attempts to make the naturalization process "less convenient, less cheap, or less expeditious than it now is."

The constitutional right of conscience is "most sacred and inviolable" and "belongs no less to the Catholic, than to the Protestant." Any violations of these rights "shall ever have our most effective opposition."

The Whigs would resist any suggestion that they were unwelcoming to foreigners, and even printed campaign literature in German as well as English.[24]

Toward the end of the 1844 election, Lincoln traveled to his boyhood home of Indiana to campaign for Clay. Before the Rockport Courthouse on October 30, Lincoln addressed a large audience. From there it was on to Evansville, Carlin Township, and Gentryville.[25] As Stephen Oates recounts, Lincoln visited his old home at Little Pigeon Creek, walking the "'old field' where he'd toiled and hated to toil for nine long years. . . . He thought of his mother and sister and perhaps even visiting their graves, recalling 'things decayed and loved ones lost.'"[26] Lincoln called on many of his old friends, only to find that "half of all are dead," and another gone completely insane.[27] This visit, sad and sweet, weighed heavily on Lincoln, inspiring him to write a poem, "My Childhood-Home I See Again."

Lincoln would never serve in the Electoral College. James K. Polk would carry Illinois on his way to a surprise national victory. Polk, running on a platform of territorial expansion, ultimately captured the imagination of the ambitious young nation, over Clay, who wanted none at all.

Polk had pledged himself to one term to unify his badly divided party. He was determined to make the absolute most of every second of it.

The vast Oregon Territory had for years been jointly administered by the United States and Great Britain. Each side had varying claims based on expeditions, treaties, and agreements, and this had been a way to avoid untangling these thorny competing arguments. Now Polk was determined to force the issue. For three days in 1845, there was a public meeting in Springfield to discuss this important question. But while testing the British resolve for war, Polk was doing the same to the Mexicans. In August, he ordered General Zachary Taylor to the Nueces River, a westward movement of the army that would inevitably have major consequences for both the United States and Mexico.

John J. Hardin wanted to return to Congress. But if he ever expected a free pass back, he was soon corrected. On September 6, 1845, Hardin learned that Lincoln was building his base for the next congressional election. With Hardin's possible entry into the race, Congressman Baker urged Lincoln to reconsider.[28] Baker was glad, or at least willing, to yield to his friend, but he was concerned that doing so meant Hardin would win, in turn meaning neither of them could have it.[29] There was no love lost between Lincoln and Hardin, or Baker and Hardin.[30] Baker's efforts on Lincoln's behalf did not make matters better.[31]

—◆—

CHAPTER 3

TURNABOUT IS FAIR PLAY

"I would rejoice to be spared the labor of a contest; but 'being in' I shall go it thoroughly, and to the bottom."

—Abraham Lincoln

Population of the counties of the Seventh District:[1]

Sangamon	18,597
Scott	6,553
Morgan	16,541
Cass	5,471
Putnam	3,129
Menard	4,807
Logan	2,907
Mason	3,135
Tazewell	7,615
Woodford	3,288
Marshall	2,883

Abraham Lincoln, who had first faced the voters of the Seventh Congressional District almost three years earlier and lost, would start his next attempt earlier than ever. Baker had understood the spirit of rotation that had given him his window. He seems to have told Lincoln that he would be stepping down before making the knowledge public. The latter, leaving nothing to chance this time, was fast out of the starting gate.

On November 17, 1845, Lincoln wrote to Benjamin F. James, publisher of the *Tazewell Whig*. "Baker is certainly off the track, and I fear Hardin intends to be on it,"[2] he worried. He asked that nothing be printed in James's paper that might hurt his chances for Congress.

The next day he wrote Henry Dummer, a lawyer in Beardstown, Cass County. Lincoln had first met Dummer when the latter was the legal partner of Stuart, and Lincoln would come to their office in Springfield to read books on the law. In his letter, Lincoln referenced a long-standing understanding between him and Baker, and accordingly "the track for the next Congressional race was clear to me, so far as he was concerned; and that he would say so publicly in any manner, and at any time I might desire." Lincoln hoped that Dummer "would set a few stakes for me. I do not know, but I strongly suspect, that General Hardin wishes to run again." Lincoln asked that Dummer help him keep the Beardstown newspaper from promoting Hardin for that office.

Once again, Lincoln and Hardin were on the same side of issues. Personal attacks would only serve to get Hardin's back up against the wall at a time when the goal was to prevent him from running. But worse than in 1843, Hardin now had the experience of serving in Congress that Lincoln lacked. In the preliminary maneuvers for the Whig Party nomination, Lincoln knew that his only real threat was from Hardin, but that it was enough to deny him the dream he had waited so long and worked so hard for. Lincoln would exercise incredible message discipline in advocating the one line of argument that could work. Borrowing from a proverb expressing a sense of fairness instilled in most people since childhood, he told Dummer, as he would tell everyone else: "I know of no argument to give me a preference over him, unless it be 'Turn about is fair play.'"[3]

John Nicolay and John Hay, Lincoln's private secretaries in the White House and later his biographers, reported that "after Baker's election in 1844, it was generally taken as a matter of course in the district that Lincoln was to be the next candidate of the Whig party for Congress. It was charged at the time, and some recent writers have repeated the charge, that there was a bargain made in 1840 between Hardin, Baker, Lincoln, and

Logan to succeed each other in the order named. This sort of fiction is the commonest known to American politics."[4]

They go on to say: "At the same time it is not to be denied that there was a tacit understanding among the Whigs of the district that whoever should, at each election, gain the honor of representing the one Whig constituency of the state, should hold himself satisfied with the privilege, and not be a candidate for reelection. The retiring member was not always convinced of the propriety of this arrangement."[5] If any deal existed, it would have to be that, but it doesn't explain why Hardin's supporters fought the rotation resolution at Pekin.

An agreement among the three could have taken only a limited number of shapes, and each of these seems impossible in light of the evidence.

First, the deal could not have been "Hardin, Baker, Lincoln," since all three ran for the position. Further, none of the three would have been incentivized to make it. All three had a very plausible belief that they could prevail. Hardin did win, Baker came one convention vote away from winning, and Lincoln came dangerously close to being nominated by the Sangamon convention, and if he had gained the votes of Menard and in addition to Baker's other support, he would have beaten Hardin at the convention. In 1843, the candidates were thirty-three, thirty-four, and thirty-five, respectively, with no prospects for higher office in Democratic Illinois. With all three having such a strong chance at winning, it is unlikely that anyone would have taken a voluntary retirement from politics in his thirties. So there was clearly no deal, and no motive to make a deal, before Pekin.

The second possibility for a deal would be that whoever won at convention would be satisfied with one term.

Given the spirited opposition from Lincoln and Baker, it was clear that the deal was not "Hardin, Baker, Lincoln" before Pekin. In assessing Hardin's claims to have not been a party to such a deal, we should start with the following question: What could he possibly have gained? He had bested all comers at the Pekin convention. Baker's forces had fought him right down to the wire, and lost. Why would Hardin fight so hard to win, and having secured the victory, throw away the chance for another term? There was simply no reason to do so. The only motive for so doing would have been to unify the party in a swing district, to ensure that Hardin got at least one term. But this was not the case. A win at Pekin was tantamount to winning the seat. Further, if Baker or Lincoln had sat on his hands, or encouraged others to do so, it would have damaged Hardin tremendously. Further evidence rules out this possibility. Hardin's supporters at Pekin vigorously contested Lincoln's resolution in favor of rotation. If the deal were an open contest for the seat, with the winner serving one term, Hardin's supporters would have been instructed to support the resolution. By withholding his vote from Hardin, Lincoln would have been in violation of any agreement, but Lincoln was consistently and throughout his life a man of his word.

Hardin's announcement shortly after his election that he would serve one term has been held up as proof of his assent to some kind of bargain. But this does not establish any such thing. Rather, it was a grudging nod to the reality that Lincoln had outmaneuvered him in passing the resolution. The Whigs of the Seventh District, reluctant to choose among friends, readily embraced the idea of letting all of them serve. They memorialized that sentiment with the Pekin resolution. If Hardin had sought reelection in light of that, he would have harmed his reputation and likely been defeated by Baker or Lincoln at the next convention. Hardin was perhaps a victim of some kind of deal, but he was certainly not a beneficiary. In the heat of the 1843 campaign, it seems that a good many things were proposed between the parties but nothing ever came of them.

In the preliminary maneuverings for the 1846 nomination, Benjamin Thomas's *Tazewell Whig* promoted Hardin for governor. While Lincoln did not direct this, he learned of it and did not discourage it. Other papers followed suit, and not always with the intent of helping Lincoln. The Whigs were eager to have a strong standard-bearer for the state's top post, a job that always eluded them. Regardless of motivation, Hardin-for-governor chatter made it that much harder for him to chart his congressional comeback.[6]

Much of it, in fact, was coming from Hardin's supporters, and in some cases the idea of having him run for governor originated in his earliest days in the House.[7] Such talk continued throughout his tenure and then after he left office. Martin Morris wrote him on November 19 from Petersburg in Menard County, attesting to "the desire of the Whigs here that you should be the next candidate for governor."[8] Morris noted that "Mr. Lincoln was here at court and I discover from what he says that he wants to run for Congress next August and he doesn't know but you will be his competitor."[9]

Hardin knew he needed to arrest this boomlet, and do it fast. "It is not my desire or intuition to be a candidate for governor," he flatly wrote in the *Tazewell Whig*.[10] He noted that there were many fine aspirants to Congress, and that whether he would be one would be up to the people.

On December 4, Lincoln received the worst possible news in relation to his bid for Congress: confirmation that Hardin intended to run.[11]

Lincoln was well aware of Hardin's sterling reputation, but he may not have known the full scale of the operation he would be up against. As a member of the House, through active correspondence, Hardin had built up a list of reliable Whigs throughout the Seventh District.[12] Hardin bound these together like a book for safekeeping.

Lincoln crunched the numbers for Benjamin James. "To succeed, I must have 17 votes in convention. To secure these, I think I may safely claim— Sangamon 8, Menard 2, Logan 1, making 11, so that, if you and other friends can secure Dr. Boal's entire senatorial district—that is, Tazewell 4, Woodford 1, and Marshall 1, it just covers the case. Besides this, I am not without some chance in Putnam and Mason, the latter of which I verily believe I can secure by close attention. The other counties—that is to say, Morgan, Scott and Cass, he will undoubtedly get." Some of Baker's friends in Cass who were also Lincoln's friends thought he could carry the county, but he was not as optimistic. "Upon the whole," Lincoln thought, "it is my intention to give him the trial, unless clouds should rise, which are not yet discernable." Lincoln believed that Tazewell should be safe. In Woodford and Marshall, "a sharp look-out should be kept, and every Whig met with from those counties, talked to, and initiated. If you and John H. Morrison and Niel Johnson, Dr. Shaw and others will see to this; together with what I have done, and will do, those counties can be saved. In doing this, let nothing be said against Hardin—nothing deserves to be said against him. Let the pith of the whole argument be, 'Turn about is fair play.'" Whenever "you see a 'moccason track' as Indian fighter's say, notify me of it."[13]

Smaller precinct conventions met in advance of the county gatherings. It may well have been at the direction of Lincoln that the Sangamon Athens precinct went first, resolving "our present Representative, E. D. Baker, recognizing the principle of 'rotation in office,' has generously declined a reelection."[14]

In fact, having just been sworn in, not only had Baker taken himself out of the hunt, but events at hand would soon lead to his resignation from Congress.

On New Year's Day, 1846, the *Journal* reported that "a Whig of Menard county speaking on behalf of himself and others, expresses a wish, that the convention for the nomination of a Whig candidate for Congress in this District be held at Petersburg. We know no reason why it should not; and if others are agreed, so are we." The push for a convention in Petersburg may also have been a deliberate move by Lincoln or his supporters. Menard County, with his old New Salem friends, was friendly turf, as good a place as any for Lincoln to have a showdown if one proved necessary (Sangamon and Morgan Counties, as the homes of the two candidates, would obviously not be considered).

Lincoln kept in close contact with his supporters throughout the district. Dr. Robert Boal was a state senator who represented three counties and had always believed the 1846 election to be Lincoln's turn, ever since the Pekin convention. The first week of January, Lincoln wrote him: "If Hardin and I stood precisely equal—that is, if <u>neither</u> of us had been to congress, or if we <u>both</u> had—it would only accord with what I have always done, for the sake of peace, to give way to him. . . . But to yield to Hardin under present circumstances seems to me as nothing else than yielding to one who would gladly sacrifice me altogether."

Lincoln asked him for "the aspect of things in your county, or rather your district," as well as "the names of some of your Whig neighbors, to whom I might, with propriety write . . . my reliance for a fair shake (and I want nothing more) in your county is chiefly on you, because of your position and standing, and because I am acquainted with so few others."[15]

On January 10, the *Illinois Gazette* editorialized in favor of rotation in office, "holding up Lincoln as the next on the list for a turn in Congress."[16] It was a beautiful argument: It gave people an excuse for deciding between two friends in Lincoln's favor, it was simple and made sense, and it allowed for Lincoln's supporters to openly, aggressively promote his candidacy.

Hard-pressed were the Hardin supporters to argue against it. And they

were starting to let Hardin know: "The grounds appear to be that the doctrine of 'taking turns' was established by the Pekin Convention, that it has
so far been acted on, that it is now Lincoln's turn, that Hardin has had his
turn, that it is due to Lincoln on account of his great services to the Whig
party on account of his talent and worth, that he is poor and Hardin is
rich . . . that this is the only crumb that a Whig politician can obtain in
the state, and that no one deserves more than Lincoln."[17] The supporter
wrote, "I think highly of Mr. Lincoln, but it is my opinion that you can do
more for your district and state at Washington now than he can."[18]

On January 12, another Hardin supporter wrote him on the state of affairs. "I find upon enquiring among our friends that Mr. Lincoln during
his journey through the circuit sought and obtained pledges from most of
what we call leading men in this vicinity [Tazewell County]. No one supposed here until your letter was published that you had any desire to again
represent us in Congress. Had such a wish been expressed many would have
hesitated before pledging themselves to Lincoln—I know that you have
many warm and ardent friends here, who are ready at a suitable time to do
all you can reasonably ask of them, as the matter now stands." But these
supporters kept hearing "Hardin is a good fellow and did us and himself
great credit and honor by his course in Congress, Lincoln is also a good
fellow and has worked hard and faithfully for the party, if he desires to go
to Congress let him go this time, turn about is fair play. This latter remark
I hear made in the store daily."[19] There can be no doubt: When a political
message resonates so strongly that people hear it at the store, it is working.
The supporter went on to confess "frankly that Lincoln would at this moment be the choice of probably a . . . majority of the Whigs. Lincoln you
are aware has always been in the habit of attending our courts, and has a
very general acquaintance with our people and from this fact would have an
advantage over you."

A supporter in Hennepin promised Hardin to do all in his power to give
him a "fair chance," noting how popular Hardin had been as a congressman.
He also argued that if Pekin had established "the doctrine of rotation in
office they transcended the power given them." Once again, the writer had
nothing against Lincoln but favored Hardin's superior qualifications.[20]

These supporters were not on board with the "turn about" argument. "It is certainly but poor policy . . . to be continually changing our representation."[21] But they still believed Lincoln would get the vote from Tazewell. And again, his supporters heard that "people think that it is Abraham's turn now. Mr. Lincoln spins a good yarn, is what we call a clever fellow, has mixed much with our citizens, and has done much in sustaining Whig principles in Illinois."[22]

The Illinois prairie was a small place. In the midst of this, Lincoln and Hardin found themselves as opposing counsel in a case before the Illinois Supreme Court. Lincoln's clients had retained Hardin's clients to ship lead from Illinois to Boston, in a deal that went horribly awry. Cocounsel with Hardin was Justin Butterfield, who would show up later at a critical time as an adversary to Lincoln.[23]

Lincoln could hardly wait for the Supreme Court's term to close, bringing with it his full-time return to the campaign trail. On January 14, Lincoln wrote again to Benjamin James: "I would rejoice to be spared the labor of a contest; but 'being in' I shall go it thoroughly, and to the bottom." Lincoln ticked off the names of supporters through the tiny towns of the district. "When this Supreme Court shall adjourn, it is my intention to take a quiet trip through the towns and neighborhoods of Logan County, Delevan, Tremont [in Tazewell], and on to and through the upper counties. Don't speak of this, or let it relax any of your vigilance."[24]

The next day Lincoln wrote to John Bennett, an innkeeper in Petersburg, concerned by intelligence that some of those he believed would support him were now in Hardin's camp.[25] Worse, Hardin could do the same convention math that Lincoln could. If the current system made it a tougher row for Hardin to hoe, he would try to create a new one.

Lincoln wrote to James with concern: "A plan is on foot to change the mode of selecting the candidate for this district. The movement is intended to injure me, and if effected, most likely would injure me to some extent." He asked James to put an article in his paper "taking strong ground for the old system, under which Hardin and Baker were nominated."

Behind the scenes, tense words were exchanged between Lincoln and Hardin.

On the nineteenth he wrote to Hardin.[26] "I do not wish to join in your proposal of a new plan for the selection of a Whig candidate for Congress."

It was the same system that had nominated both Hardin and Baker, Lincoln pointed out. He objected to a proposal for an open primary, suggesting that he preferred to leave the matter to the Whigs. As to the proposal for remaining in one's own county during the campaign, Lincoln pointed out, "on reflection you will see, the fact of your having been in Congress, has in various ways, so spread your name in the district, as to give you a decided advantage in such a stipulation." What Lincoln really wanted to say he crossed out, in the name of making the same point more civilly. As originally written, the letter included this sentence: "It would be nothing other than a stipulation in favor of the horse that has got the start, that the others shall do nothing to catch up." Indeed, it was an outrageous and nakedly self-serving proposal from the man with higher name identification, rendered even worse by the fact that when he needed to, Hardin could campaign as hard as anyone. (Who could forget his two hundred miles traversed in five days during the 1843 race?)

"I appreciate your desire to keep down excitement," Lincoln said, "and I promise you to 'keep cool' under all circumstances." But "I am satisfied with the old system, under which, such good men have triumphed."

But while they were on the subject of changing the rules, Lincoln said that if the old system was wanting in anything, it was the proper apportionment of delegates to the convention. He pointed out that though Sangamon had both a higher population and a greater Whig turnout than Hardin's home of Morgan, each had eight delegates.

Lincoln wrote graciously: "I have always been in the habit of acceding to almost any proposal that a friend would make; and I am truly sorry I can not in this." He closed by mentioning that friends throughout the district were trying to secure the congressional convention, and "I feel they would not feel much complimented, if we were to make a bargain that it shall sit no where."

On January 21, Lincoln wrote a remarkably short but on-message campaign missive, saying Hardin "has had a turn and my argument is 'turn about is fair play.' I shall be pleased if this strikes you as a sufficient argument."[27]

Lincoln wrote to Benjamin James on January 27, asking him to call for a convention in his paper for the first Monday of May. In the letter, Lincoln mentioned that he'd been well received in Petersburg the previous Saturday and Sunday.[28]

Hardin accused Lincoln of stirring up the talk of him for governor in order to keep him from the congressional contest. Lincoln pointed out that the paper at Jacksonville, Hardin's hometown, had twice nominated Lincoln for governor.

Lincoln had assiduously courted the press, but Hardin was still able to push his message through the *Morgan County Journal*, in an article that condemned the Pekin resolution and argued that Lincoln wanted to deny the public the right to choose their preferred candidate. With the Whig antipathy high against conventions and party structure, this was a powerful argument. Lincoln wrote Hardin that, having seen the article, "I am almost discouraged of the hope of doing any good by it."[29]

Incensed, Hardin wrote to Lincoln that "the District is a horse which each candidate may mount and ride a two mile heat without consulting any body but the grooms and jockeys," and he denied he'd ever agreed to any deal at Pekin.[30]

Lincoln pointed out that he never understood his agreement to deny one the right to select the candidate of one's choice; merely that no one ought to "be a candidate out of his turn."

Hardin also pointed out that their contest would have the tendency to weaken the party. Lincoln did not disagree. "It is certain that struggles between candidates do not strengthen a party," he responded, "but who are most responsible for these struggles, those who are willing to live and let live, or those who are resolved, at all hazards, to take care of 'number one'?" At some point in the past, Hardin had told Lincoln not to promote Baker as his successor; that if he, Hardin, could serve and retire on his own terms, it would not take nearly as long as waiting out Baker, who he alleged would stay there forever. With Baker retiring at one term, Lincoln noted, "It seems you then thought a little more favorably of 'turn about' than you seem to now. . . . I believe you do not mean to be unjust or ungenerous; and I therefore am slow to believe that you will not yet think <u>better</u> and think <u>differently</u> of this matter."

Lincoln also sent a letter to James to publish. "I send you this as a weapon with which to demolish, what I can not but regard as a mean insinuation against me." It was a rebuttal to the *Morgan County Journal*, which suggested that Lincoln did not want the voices of the people heard.

On February 3, John H. Morrison of Tazewell reported to Hardin that "Lincoln will probably get all the vote of Tazewell County even if Hardin were to run. The regular succession principle has been accepted. It is Abraham's turn now."[31]

Two weeks later, in a public letter, Hardin declined to be a candidate for Congress. The decision would have far-reaching implications for both men, and ultimately for the country. Lincoln, personally popular and well connected, had gotten the drop on his opponent. Hardin, no doubt, could not stomach the possibility of losing a bid for a job he'd already had.

In leaving the field, Hardin took pains to relate: "I never made any bargain, or had any understanding directly or indirectly with Mr. Baker, or any other person, respecting either the last or any future canvass for Congress."[32]

Leave it to the *Register* to respond by blaming its favorite bogeyman. The "public are left to infer that General [a reference to his rank during the Black Hawk War] Hardin has declined in consequence of the 'corruption' chicanery and 'management' of the candidate of the Springfield Junto."[33]

Hardin said to a friend, "If he is never in Congress again, he will not canvass the district drumming up his friends." This made its way back to Lincoln through a friend, who relayed it with the obvious conclusion that "this is intended, probably, for a thrust at some one."[34] Again, it was too easy for Hardin to forget the past when it suited him.

Lincoln realized that things "had become a little warm," and believed a face-to-face rapprochement could best put the party back together. For his part, Hardin would soon find a very different campaign that was very much to his liking.

Relations between the United States and Mexico were at a breaking point. Texas had joined the Union, and nearly a decade after its independence, Mexico still claimed Texas as part of its territory. Meanwhile, claims of American citizens against the government of Mexico were completely ignored.

To prevent war, Polk dispatched John Slidell, chosen in part for his ability, alone among the members of Congress, to speak Spanish. On December 6, 1845, he arrived in Mexico.[35] Two weeks later, the Mexican government rejected Slidell on technical grounds; his title, they argued, suggested that the two countries enjoyed normal relations, which Mexico contended they did not.[36] Slidell protested strongly, pointing out that nothing of the sort had previously been argued, and warned of the dangers of breaking off diplomatic relations.[37]* On July 27, Secretary of State James Buchanan offered to receive an envoy or send one to resolve the issue of war, to no avail.[38]

Shortly after Polk learned of Slidell's rebuff, he received intelligence that General Mariano Paredes y Arrillaga was heading for the Mexican capital to overthrow President José Joaquín de Herrera. Incredibly, Herrera's government, which had manufactured a fig leaf to slam the door on Slidell, was targeted for being too open to negotiate with the United States.[39]

On January 13, 1846, General Taylor was dispatched to the eastern bank of the Rio Grande, at the head of 3,550 troops.[40] One of Taylor's officers, Ulysses S. Grant, had been preparing for a career in academia and had approached his mathematics instructor at West Point, seeking employment as his assistant.[41] Grant had been plagued by a wet cough since his time at the university, a sickness he believed would prematurely end his life. But a softer life in the academy would have to wait, as affairs continued to escalate with Mexico.

Instead, Grant was sent to Fort Jesup, between the Sabine and the Red Rivers. Most of his fellow army officers were agnostic about whether Texas should be annexed. "For myself," Grant remembered, "I was bitterly opposed to the measure, and to this day regard the war, which resulted, as one of the most unjust ever waged by a stronger against a weaker nation. . . . The occupation, separation, and annexation were, from the inception of the movement to its final consummation, a conspiracy to acquire territory out of which slave states might be formed for the American Union."

---

*Interestingly, this would not be Slidell's last diplomatic mission. During the Civil War, he was appointed by the Confederacy to seek official recognition in Europe. Though Slidell was captured by Union forces, the outcry led President Lincoln to release him. In any case, his mission ultimately failed.

Grant would come to believe that "the Southern rebellion was largely the outgrowth of the Mexican War. Nations, like individuals, are punished for their transgressions. We got our punishment in the most sanguinary and expensive war of modern times."

But Grant was a soldier, and soldiers follow orders. And soldiers are more cognizant than civilians that their lives are not really their own. While waiting at Fort Jesup, Grant exercised outside and rode his horse. Ironically, he would credit this experience with curing his persistent sickness: "I have often thought that my life was saved, and my health restored, by exercise and exposure, enforced by an administrative act, and a war, both of which I disapproved."

In July 1845, Grant was ordered to New Orleans. The army found the Crescent City plagued by yellow fever, "and the streets of the city had the appearance of a continuous well-observed Sunday." This was the last time that the streets of New Orleans were described in this way.

In September, Grant's regiment headed for Corpus Christi, Texas, by small steamboats. Taylor informed Grant's view of an ideal military commander. He noted that "General Taylor never wore uniform, but dressed himself entirely for comfort. He moved about the field in which he was operating to see through his own eyes the situation. . . . Taylor was not a conversationalist, but on paper he could put his meaning so plainly that there could be no mistaking it. He knew how to express what he wanted to say in the fewest well-chosen words, but would not sacrifice meaning to the construction of high-sounding sentences." [42] Taylor's orders were made "without reference to how they would read in history." [43] Taylor had been commissioned an officer by President James Madison in 1808. In the War of 1812 he had been breveted a major (temporarily promoted for the purpose of the conflict), but was bumped down to captain with the onset of peace. In frustration, he quit the army. In 1816, however, Madison restored his rank. His reward was a post in Green Bay, in the Wisconsin Territory, for the next two years. [44] A series of assignments followed: in New Orleans, during the Black Hawk War, at Fort Crawford, and then in Florida. [45] In 1840, Taylor was given command of the First Military Department, covering the southwestern states of Alabama, Arkansas, Mississippi, and Louisiana.[46] In May 1845, opportunity knocked again, when the secretary of war asked Taylor to position his troops to protect Texas from invasion.[47]

Grant also respected the extraordinary measures taken by Taylor toward the people of Mexico. "General Taylor was opposed to anything like plundering by the troops, and in this instance, I doubt not, he looked upon the enemy as the aggrieved party and was not willing to injure them further than his instructions from Washington demanded. His orders to his troops enjoined scrupulous regard for the rights of all peaceable persons and the payment of the highest price for all supplies taken for the use of the army."

The march to the Rio Grande was uneventful, covering broad, undeveloped land. The only sound the soldiers were liable to hear was the gallop of the occasional pack of wild horses. Grant remembered "rolling prairie . . . the vision was obstructed only by the earth's curvature."

Taylor's army arrived in the middle of March at the blue banks of the Rio Grande and camped opposite the Mexican city of Matamoros. Fortifications began at once. Taylor planted the national flag on the Rio Grande, staking America's claim to the disputed territory.[48]

General Pedro de Ampudia entered Matamoros with three thousand soldiers and demanded Taylor retreat to the east bank of the Nueces.[49] Taylor responded by blocking the mouth of the Rio Grande, preventing the Mexican army in Matamoros from being resupplied.[50]

On April 25, General Mariano Arista crossed the Rio Grande with sixteen hundred troops, north of Taylor's position.[51] Seth Thornton and his dragoons were attacked, with eleven killed, six wounded, and the rest of the sixty-three captured.[52] It would forever be known as "the Thornton Affair," the scene of the first blood spilled in the Mexican-American War. It was a spot that would later become of great interest to Congressman Lincoln.

In his tent Grant could hear the artillery, the first of the war. Grant "had never heard a hostile gun before," and "felt sorry that I had enlisted."

Meanwhile, Lincoln's hard work and perseverance had paid off. On May 2, with Hardin out of the running, Lincoln was nominated by acclamation at the Whig convention in Petersburg.

"Resolved, that we present to the Whigs of this district Abraham Lincoln as the Whig candidate for Congress; that in his part firm and undeviating attachments to and his active and able support of Whig principles, his abilities and integrity, entitle him to their cordial and active support in the approaching election."[53]

The *Journal* was excited by the nomination of Lincoln. "The Whigs of this district have been fortunate in the selection of their candidate for Congress. Mr. Lincoln is one of the strongest men of our state—possessing a well-disciplined, clear and comprehensive mind—a mind able to grasp any subject within the range of the statesman."

The Whig leaders put together $200 for Lincoln. After the campaign, he returned $199.25. "I did not need the money. I made the canvass on my own horse, my entertainment being at the houses of friends, cost me nothing; and my only outlay was 75 cents for a barrel of cider, which some farmhands insisted I should treat them to."[54]

While his first son, Robert Todd, had been born in the wake of Lincoln's defeat in 1843, his second child, Edward Baker Lincoln, named for his friend, had been born two months before his coronation at Petersburg. With his growing practice, young wife, two sons, and favorable position for a seat in the next Congress, he must have wondered why he still wasn't satisfied.

The Democrats, for their part, were optimistic about their chances and not about to back down without a fight. Their nominee for the Seventh, a most unusual candidate, had a background that could enable him to win the crossover vote that would be needed for victory.

Enter Peter Cartwright. A fire-and-brimstone Methodist preacher, he was rough as the towns and terrain he'd traveled in support of the Gospel. It was estimated that by the time of his death in 1872, Cartwright had baptized twelve thousand persons and preached fifteen thousand sermons.[55] Cartwright had "preached to almost every Methodist congregation between Springfield and Cairo [Illinois],"[56] and "had family connections all over the district,"[57] a widespread network that would certainly make this a race.

So the matchup was set, Abraham Lincoln versus Peter Cartwright, "respectively circuit riders of man's and God's law,"[58] who would storm the district for the race for Congress.

Cartwright's ministry was tough and bare-knuckled, and his campaign for Congress unlikely to be more genteel. Cartwright would drink with his congregants,[59] and on at least two or three occasions he left the pulpit to beat up people who were disturbing the peace of the church, incidents Nicolay and Hay take pains to point out "do not turn a parson into a pugilist."[60]

Troublemakers were a common problem at church gatherings, something Cartwright was well equipped to handle. Once Cartwright used a club to knock the lead troublemaker off his horse and delivered him to the authorities. The rowdy's friends planned to avenge him by stoning the preacher's tent. Cartwright, in disguise, was among them, and learned of their plans. When they came, he was ready, driving them off with "a sharp volley of pebbles."[61] Cartwright also had problems with whiskey sellers offering their goods in the church campgrounds. Perhaps aware of Cartwright's reputation, one whiskey dealer was armed with a musket. Acting at night, Cartwright seized the seller, fired off his musket, and "threw away his powder."[62]

In one case, "a fat unbelieving woman" was kicking her faithful daughters as they knelt in prayer. Cartwright grabbed her foot, causing her to fall back. Cartwright continued his sermon as though nothing extraordinary had happened.[63]

There is a story, which may be apocryphal, that when lost in a cavernous New York City hotel, he used a hatchet to mark a trail back to his room.[64]

There was a third candidate in the race, Elihu Walcott of the abolitionist Liberty Party, who stood no chance of winning but could play the role of spoiler. Aware of this danger, Lincoln cultivated the Durley brothers of Hennepin, leaders of the local Liberty Party, abolitionists, and operators of a station on the Underground Railroad.[65] Lincoln was heartened to learn of their hopes to combine the forces of the Whigs and Liberty men, as they were united on all questions "save only that of slavery."[66] Lincoln was especially mindful of the role that Liberty Party supporters had played in Clay's 1844 defeat. If the New York abolitionists had been with Clay, Lincoln wrote the Durleys, he'd have been elected president, and Texas would never have been annexed. This result of the division was that "all that either had in the stake in the contest was lost. . . . If by your votes you could have prevented the extension of slavery, would it not have been <u>good</u> and not <u>evil</u> so to have used your votes, even though it involved the casting of them for a slaveholder? By the <u>fruit</u> the tree is to be known. An <u>evil</u> tree can not bring forth <u>good</u> fruit. If the fruit of electing Mr. Clay would have been to prevent the extension of slavery, could the act of electing have been <u>evil</u>?"

Lincoln would carry this pragmatic viewpoint with him to Congress, where it would lead him to take an early and important position in the next presidential campaign.

President of the United States James Polk, far removed from the theater of war (and unaware that there even was one), had a decision to make. The day after the Battle of Palo Alto, and well before the knowledge of the same reached Washington City, Polk sat down with Secretary of State James Buchanan and John Slidell, the recently expelled envoy.[67] Slidell believed that no hope for peace was left. Nothing was left, save "to act with promptness and energy" in the last course of action left open. The president agreed.

The following day, a Saturday, saw a cabinet meeting on Mexico. The advice was unanimous: If Mexican forces at Matamoros had engaged in any act of hostility toward Taylor's men, the president should ask Congress for a declaration of war.[68] Polk believed casus belli existed without such an overt act. By the end of the meeting, only one member of his cabinet did not share his position. At six o'clock that evening, the adjutant general of the army called on the president, giving him correspondence from General Taylor, telling him of the Thornton Affair.[69] Mexican soldiers had ambushed and killed Americans, and Polk, already near a decision, now made up his mind.

The cabinet was summoned back for an evening meeting at seven-thirty, and this time all were in agreement.[70] A message would be drafted and sent to Congress; correspondence between the administration and Slidell and Taylor would be copied and sent along with it. With only a break for church, Polk labored diligently the next day to complete his message. At 5 p.m., he met with Hugh Haralson, chairman of the Committee on Military Affairs, along with Edward Baker, who served as a Whig member of that committee.[71] They reported that the committee had been convened that morning and had unanimously agreed in principle on a bill appropriating $10 million and raising an army of fifty thousand men.[72] Polk asked them to work with his cabinet in fashioning a final bill.

The next day, Polk asked for Senators Lewis Cass of Michigan and Thomas Hart Benton of Missouri to preview his message. Cass was in full agreement, while Benton had problems with it. Benton favored resources for defense but had not yet come around to the idea of an offensive war in the interior of Mexico. Benton had never agreed with the decision to march troops to the Rio Grande.[73]

Polk submitted his message at noon.

But the goodwill promised by these early bipartisan overtures was about to go for naught. Polk was poised for a nearly unanimous declaration in the House, but then Democrats attached a preamble to the bill: "Whereby, by the act of Mexico, a state of war exists between that government and the United States. . . ." Now one could not simply recognize the existence of war, but had to choose. Swallow the bitter pill of the preamble, a statement with which many members did not agree, or vote against supplying our troops on an active battlefield.

Nathan Sargent, a Washington reporter who would later befriend Congressman Lincoln, observed, "The purpose of this was to compel the Whigs to vote what everybody knew to be a brazen untruth, or else to vote against the bill and thus incur the odium of refusing reinforcements and supplies for our army in its conflict with Mexico."[74] Democratic leadership refused the opportunity to vote separately on the preamble, which would have been customary parliamentary practice at the time.

It is an interesting question what Lincoln would have done, especially in contrast to Baker's militarism in meeting with the president beforehand and working closely with the White House in drafting the resolution. Lincoln did not abstain from any tough votes in the Thirtieth Congress, so this course is probably unthinkable. Perhaps he'd have found himself in the category of representatives who decried the preamble even as they voted for the bill that contained it. Perhaps we'd have seen an earlier version of Lincoln's spot resolutions speech, in which he legally deconstructed the preamble's contents.

Many took the opportunity to explain their decision, disassociating themselves from the preamble but pledging to never abandon American forces at war. Ultimately, the vote was 173–14. Depending on your point of view, the holdouts were known as "the Noble 14" or "the Stubborn 14."

The Senate had adjourned without action. Benton returned that evening with questions, leaving Polk convinced that he would oppose the bill. Calhoun, he believed, would oppose it as well. These Democratic defectors, and any who should join them, along with the Whig Party, might well serve to block the House bill.[75] But at 7 p.m. the next day, Polk's private secretary returned with the news: The Senate had joined the House by a vote of 42–2, with some unimportant amendment that probably served as a fig leaf allowing certain senators to reverse course from the previous day.[76] Three senators, including Calhoun, abstained.[77] In anticipation of this, the House began meeting at 7:30 p.m. and an hour later approved the Senate bill, sending it to the president.

That evening, the White House went through with a previously scheduled reception. In attendance were roughly twenty heads of insane asylums throughout the United States, who were gathered in town for a conference, perhaps a fitting punctuation to the day.[78]

So why was America at war? Many, both pro- and antislavery, believed it was to increase slave territory, and they were right. (Ulysses Grant: "The war was one of conquest, in the interest of an institution."[79]) Others believed that it was because of Mexico's long history of ignoring American claims, and they were right. Others believed that America was at war because Mexican troops had crossed the Rio Grande and killed American soldiers. And they were right as well. The truth is that America and Mexico had arrived at this place as a result of many causes.

On May 13, as Polk signed the bill authorizing war, Abraham Lincoln was likely in Charleston, Illinois, attending to legal work.

The war was exceedingly popular in Illinois. Governor Thomas Ford wrote Hardin, excited at the prospect of "conquering New Mexico and California," and noting that such an opportunity might not come again.[80] Hardin would join the war effort as an officer, and soon his mailbox was filled with eager applicants looking to enlist.

On May 30, Lincoln addressed a war rally after a drill by cadets outside the state house. Again, the war was as popular in Illinois as anywhere in the United States. The state was asked to supply four regiments; she produced fourteen.[81]

As Illinois and the nation mobilized for war, Lincoln had a campaign of his own to win.

CHAPTER 4

LINCOLN FOR CONGRESS

Lincoln, who had worked so long and so hard on behalf of others, applied the same tenacious energy in his own campaign. William Herndon remembered, "He was active and alert, speaking everywhere and abandoning his share of business in the law office entirely."[1]

One campaign swing for which there is a record began July 18, in Lacon, seat of Marshall County.[2] Typically, someone would announce Lincoln's visits in advance with publication in the newspaper, but on this occasion they failed. Still, Lincoln found a "respectable gathering" to hear his message. Lincoln spoke about the tariff and addressed the Mexican War, the annexation of Texas, and the Oregon question. It's thought that he took the same hard-line position on Oregon as the *Journal*, since the two generally seemed to be of one mind.[3] But the *Register* accused Lincoln of dodging the question, asking, "Is Lincoln for 54°40' [the latitude at which hard-liners wished to settle Oregon's boundaries], or is he for 'compromising' away our Oregon territory to England, as his brother Whigs in Congress . . . this the people ought to know before they vote next August. No shuffling, Mr. Lincoln. Come out square."[4]

On July 20, joined by his Lacon friends, Lincoln crossed the Illinois River to speak to two precincts of Marshall County in a "grove of fine trees" on Bonham Farm, near the town of Henry. One who was with him remembered, "Lincoln and his party were in high spirits, as nearly every person of voting age came to hear him. He spoke for two hours, happy and felicitous, discussing every question to the satisfaction of his audience."[5]

But just as Lincoln would not take the election for granted, Peter Cartwright pushed ahead with fervor. The time spent in the saddle was no inconvenience to him, preaching as he had these many years in the far-flung churches of the American West. It also seemed to gall the preacher to think that someone whose religious views were suspect, someone who was not even a member of a church, could defeat someone who had made ministry the purpose of his life. Cartwright, it seems, worked hard to cast doubts on Lincoln's religious beliefs.

According to the *Illinois Gazette*, "Mr. Lincoln is right in supposing that Mr. Cartwright circulated the story in this county, and also that he, Mr. L., lost some votes thereby. It appears the Rev. gentleman circulated the same story in other parts of the district. Well, this is novel business for a minister of the Gospel."[6]

Responding effectively to a negative attack is one of the most delicate and critical maneuvers in politics. It's not enough to craft a counter that rebuts the issue; often the question of whether to answer at all must be addressed. So it was with Cartwright's attacks on Lincoln's religious beliefs.

Lincoln believed nine of ten voters had never heard the charge, and that he could only shine a light on it by responding. Eventually, however, he decided he had to do something. On July 31, Lincoln wrote the "Handbill replying to charges of infidelity."

"To the voters of the seventh congressional district. . . ."[7] Responding to the charge that he was "an open scoffer at Christianity. . . . That I am not a member of any Christian Church is true; but I have never denied the truth of the scriptures. . . . It is true that in early life I was inclined to believe . . . the 'Doctrine of Necessity'—that is, that the human mind is impelled to action, or held in rest by some power over which the mind itself has no control." Lincoln argued that he had not made such an argument publicly, or in private for five years. "I do not think I could myself be brought to support a man for office, whom I knew to be an open enemy of, and scoffer at, religion." He wouldn't blame someone for opposing him if the charge were true, "but I do blame those, whoever they may be, who falsely put such a charge in circulation against me."

Shortly before the election, a Democratic voter told Lincoln he intended to switch sides and support him.[8] Lincoln asked the young man to hold off a bit—there was no sense in alienating his party for a foregone conclusion.[9] He promised he'd tell the young man if he really needed his vote. On Election Day, August 3, 1846, Lincoln told the Democrat that the election was won, and that he was free to vote his party.[10] "I am now satisfied that I have got the preacher by the balls," Lincoln said, "and you had better keep out of the ring."[11]

Lincoln was right. When the votes were tallied, Lincoln had 6,340 votes to 4,829 for Cartwright, with only 249 for Wolcott.[12] Out of eleven counties, Lincoln won all but Woodford and Marshall. Lincoln defeated Cartwright by a majority of 1,511, a remarkable result even in light of the Whig history of the district. Clay had carried the Seventh in 1844 by 914, and Taylor's majority in 1848 was still 10 short of Lincoln's.[13] And as Lincoln surely noticed, his majority was in a different league from Hardin's majority of 874 and more than double Baker's 710.[14]

By a clear and convincing vote, Abraham Lincoln would be a member of Congress.

RESULTS [15]

	Lincoln	Cartwright	Walcott
Cass	546	489	
Logan	390	166	
Marshall	252	323	21
Mason	330	294	
Menard	456	336	
Morgan	979	949	18
Putnam	216	213	139
Sangamon	1,535	845	14
Scott	602	478	
Tazewell	819	436	42
Woodford	215	300	15

The Democratic press was predictably disappointed. "We had hoped better results would have followed the nomination of Mr. Cartwright. But 'General Apathy' seems to have controlled the Democratic party—and wherever he is commander in chief defeat ensues as a natural consequence. Better luck next time."[16]

Though the election was over, terminating convincingly in Lincoln's favor, he still thought it necessary to rebut the charges of religious infidelity. He wrote to Allen Ford, publisher of the *Illinois Gazette* in Lacon. Marshall County's results led Lincoln to "incline to the belief that he has succeeded in deceiving some honest men there.... I here aver that he, Cartwright, never heard me utter a word in any way indicating my opinions on religious matters, in his life."[17]

The religious issue would continue to dog Lincoln. In a canvass of voters during his presidential race, only three ministers in Springfield supported him, something that made Lincoln bitter, and "a great many prominent members of the churches."[18] For Lincoln, who learned to read using his family Bible, and who was as familiar with scripture as any man, one passage was particularly apt to this situation: Only in his homeland is a prophet without honor.

The war in Mexico could not have been going better. While Taylor was to advance into the heart of the country, separate detachments were sent to California and New Mexico. (These two Mexican territories included all of the present-day states of California, Nevada, and Utah, as well as parts of Wyoming, Colorado, New Mexico, and Arizona.) The campaign in California and New Mexico encountered weak resistance, while Taylor was cutting through the Mexican defenses.

On August 8, 1846, as the first session of the Twenty-ninth Congress drew to a close, Polk revealed that he wanted money to purchase land from Mexico—finally, a public declaration of a sentiment, long understood privately, that this conflict would result in the territorial expansion of the United States.

The addition of new territory to the United States was a highly charged matter, one that carried with it the power to destroy the Union itself. But it had not always been so. The Northwest Ordinance, passed by Congress under the Articles of Confederation in 1787, organized the territory comprising Ohio, Indiana, Illinois, Wisconsin, and part of Minnesota. The ordinance declared "[t]hat there shall be neither slavery nor involuntary servitude in said territory."[19] This was a time when most southerners regarded slavery as a "necessary evil," and the ordinance passed unanimously.

By the time of the Louisiana Purchase, however, battle lines had begun to harden as the invention of the cotton gin had dramatically increased the profitability of slavery. In 1819, the Union was threatened by the application of Missouri to the Union as a slave state. One member predicted "a fire which all the waters of the ocean cannot put out, which seas of blood can only extinguish."[20]

The result was the Missouri Compromise of 1820, which admitted Maine as a free state, while prohibiting slavery from land acquired in the Louisiana Purchase north of the 36°30' parallel (roughly the southern border of Missouri), with the exception of Missouri, which joined the Union as a slave state.[21] This was the fragile, delicate state of affairs when Polk set his sights on the West.

The announcement produced a frenzy on the House floor. Robert C. Winthrop of Massachusetts spoke out against the measure, and Hugh White of New York challenged the administration to accept a "no slavery" policy in the new territory. With so many clamoring to be heard, the Democratic Speaker called on David Wilmot, perhaps because of his longtime support of the administration.[22] "Within the allotted ten minutes, Wilmot made a place for himself in history."[23]

Wilmot favored expansion, he explained. He favored protecting slavery where it existed, as in Texas. But upon free land, "God forbid that we should be the means of planting this institution upon it."[24] Wilmot's means of accomplishing this would become a defining political issue for a generation and a cause of the Civil War. "As if by magic, it brought to a head the great question which is about to divide the American people."[25]

The Wilmot Proviso was originally offered as an amendment to Polk's $2 million appropriation request. It stated "that as an express and fundamental condition to the acquisition of any territory from the Republic of Mexico . . . neither slavery nor involuntary servitude shall ever exist in any part of said territory, except for crime, whereof the party shall first be duly convicted."[26]

By a margin of 89–54, the Wilmot Proviso was added to Polk's bill. In a panic, three members of the cabinet raced to the scene to keep their members in order.[27] Southerners then turned on the bill and tried to kill it by tabling it, but the amended bill passed 85–80 along sectional lines.

With little time to spare before the end of session, the Senate planned to strike the Wilmot Proviso and send it back to the House, in an attempt to force them to vote up or down on the $2 million. This plan was thwarted by Senator John Davis of Massachusetts. A supporter of the proviso, Davis planned on holding the floor until the final minutes of session, forcing the Senate to vote yes to the bill with the proviso, or no to both. With eight minutes left on the Senate clock, it was announced that the House had adjourned, their clock running a few minutes faster, thus ending the session and killing the proviso and the bill.

It has been said that the House and Senate cannot even agree on what time of day it is. Here, in one consequential historical example, the analogy proved literally true.

While Congress was debating what to do with new territory, the army was busy acquiring more of it.

General Taylor was ascendant. In September, he scored yet another victory with the capture of Monterrey. These triumphs fueled what was already a promising movement promoting Taylor for president.

In June 1846 came an editorial from Thurlow Weed, publisher and Whig boss of New York, pushing Taylor for the top post. And though Taylor was deep in Mexico, the frenzy was not lost on him. That same month, Taylor had written his son-in-law that Polk and Scott "need have no apprehensions of being interfered with by me for that high office, which I would decline if proffered, and [if] I could reach it without opposition."[28] His position had not changed by summer's end, writing in August that he wanted "nothing to do with that high office."[29]

Shortly thereafter, Polk decided to open a new front in the war. General Winfield Scott would land with an army at Veracruz and push westward to conquer Mexico City and deliver a knockout blow. To do this, Scott would take from Taylor a majority of his professional troops. The dramatic reduction in forces meant an end to Taylor's ability to make offensive war.

Why dismantle an undefeated fighting force, or assign it to someone new? The political affiliations of military officers were well known, in sharp contrast to today. In the Mexican-American War, Scott had initially been sidelined. This seems partially due not only to his membership in the Whig Party, but also the perception that he harbored national political ambitions. Taylor, though also a Whig, was thought to be mostly apolitical (in fact he had never voted). Many believed this move was engineered by Polk to arrest Taylor's growing popularity.[30] Some historians have defended Polk from charges of playing politics, while others have considered it beyond dispute, with one saying, "it was well known that politics entered largely into this question. Polk had no desire to aid the Whigs by advancing to prominence successful generals belonging to that party."[31]

What Polk did next seems to comfortably resolve that question. In a special message to Congress, he called for the creation of a new "lieutenant general," who would oversee the entire war effort.[32] His plan was to install Democrat Thomas Hart Benton, esteemed senator of Missouri. Though Benton had feuded with Polk, and even blamed him for initiating the war, Polk was eager to have a Democrat who could run for president with a thread of Mexican War glory. Leading Democrats in Congress resisted Polk's attempt at politicization, finding it incredible that such a successful war effort needed new leadership. The coup de grace to Polk's plan appears to have been delivered by his own secretary of state, James Buchanan. Buchanan, front-runner for the 1848 Democratic nomination, was none too eager to give Benton such a massive advantage.[33]

The Whig press vigorously opposed Polk's move, pointing to "unequivocal signs that an effort will be made by the administration to destroy him [Taylor],"[34] and a "war upon General Taylor by the administration and its hangers on."[35]

Taylor had kept his army intact through several spectacular battles, only to see it amputated by his commander in chief. Instead of arresting the Taylor for President movement, Polk may have facilitated the realization of its fondest hopes. By December, Taylor said while he would still not be seeking the presidency, "at the same time I will not say I would not serve if the good people were to be imprudent enough as to elect me."[36]

Congressman-elect Lincoln was paying attention. Polk's feuding, sometimes publicly, with his generals, and his attempts to politicize the war were bad for morale, cost him support in Congress, and hurt him in the court of public opinion. With the outbreak of the Civil War, President Lincoln aggressively filled the top ranks of the military with members of important constituencies, Democrats at the top of the list.[37] Among his first appointments as generals were Democrats John McClernand, his colleague in the Thirtieth Congress, who strongly opposed the Wilmot Proviso; Benjamin Butler of Massachusetts, who had supported Jefferson Davis for the 1860 Democratic nomination;[38] and John Dix of New York, who had served as secretary of the Treasury under President Buchanan.[39] As president, "Lincoln never accused Democratic generals of sabotaging the war effort. Polk rarely mentioned Taylor and Scott without making such an accusation."[40] Lincoln knew he could not confront the Confederacy if he also faced the opposition of a united Democratic Party. Though his political generals were sometimes a disaster in the field, they prevented him from a defeat that no commander in chief could overcome, and maintained for him the goodwill and support that Polk aggressively forfeited. This lesson is at the top of the list of things that Congressman Lincoln would learn from President Polk.

Since 1843, Lincoln had been waiting with a measure of uncertainty about whether his chance would ever come. As a member-elect of the Thirtieth Congress, that uncertainty was gone, but the waiting game continued. By custom and law, the Twenty-ninth Congress would expire in March, but the first session of the Thirtieth Congress would not begin until December 1847. After his election to Congress, Abraham Lincoln would sit for sixteen months before taking the oath of office or casting his first votes.

On October 22, Lincoln wrote to Speed saying, "Being elected to Congress, though I am grateful to our friends, for having done it, has not pleased me as much as I expected." This significant admission occupied but a single sentence in a much longer letter.[41]

On December 28, Baker returned to the House for one last speech. Baker resigned his seat and returned to his regiment in Mexico.

This meant the Seventh District would be unexpectedly open. On December 30, 1846, Lincoln and the other leading Whigs met in the office of the *Sangamo Journal* to nominate someone to fill Baker's seat. Congressman-elect Lincoln made no attempt to obtain the spot, which surely would have been his had he wanted it. But it made no sense for Lincoln to instantly drop his law practice, leave his family, or hurriedly spirit them on a long, uncomfortable journey across the country, simply to chase the crumbs of Baker's congressional term, set to expire in less than two months. Instead, a man named John Henry was selected to replace Baker. Henry's pitch to the Whigs was a little unorthodox. He pleaded that his financial difficulties would be ameliorated if he could only earn the mileage from traveling to and from Washington. It's debatable which is sadder: that someone once made a case for high office on this basis, that it worked, or that it is not the worst reason for which someone has ever run for Congress. The reimbursement was forty cents per mile to travel, which would have resulted in a nice sum for Henry.[42] Wisely, his address in the newspaper pledged that he would focus on the war, tariffs, and internal improvements, and not on how badly he needed the money. In the end, "Henry got his election and his mileage."[43] He would end up serving only from February 5 to March 3.

Just one victory. Antonio Lopez de Santa Anna had recently seized power in Mexico. He was dismayed at the state of the war, but believed that American public opinion would accomplish what the Mexican army could not. To reduce support for the war, he believed that he had to engage the American forces and defeat them. Any kind would do.[44]

Taylor's army was jumpy. On February 4, John Hardin wrote to Senator Stephen Douglas and described the army hastily coming to order in the face of false information about Mexican troop movements.[45] "I am not satisfied with the part of the war I have seen," Hardin said, noting that his discharge date was approaching and that he had no plans to sign up for another tour. "I am very anxious to meet the Mexicans," he concluded.[46]

But in a matter of days, the false alarms would be at an end, and the listless Hardin would get his wish.

After Scott departed for Veracruz, Taylor was left with 4,073 men, of whom 10 percent were regulars,[47] and "exceedingly vexed,"[48] in Hardin's recollection. His forces divided, Taylor was concerned about intelligence of the movements of Santa Anna, at the head of twenty thousand men. Before long, Santa Anna sent an emissary into Taylor's camp, informing him that he was surrounded by twenty thousand soldiers.[49] Taylor refused to surrender. Both sides prepared for battle.

On the morning of February 23, Santa Anna mustered his men and Mass was said.[50]

The colorful Mexican uniforms and the Catholic Mass lent a surreal quality to the field: "red, green, yellow, crimson, sky-blue, turkey-blue ... silken banners and plumes of many bright hues floated on the breeze."[51]

Along the American lines, Hardin rallied his troops: "Soldiers! You have never met an enemy, but you are now in front. I know the 1st Illinois will never fail. I will ask no man to go where I will not lead; this is Washington's birthday—let us celebrate it as ... true soldiers who love the memory of the father of their country."[52]

As the heavy artillery "came thundering down," Hardin and his men stood firm. Whether guarding their position or charging the enemy, Hardin was also in front, shouting, "Remember Illinois—give them blizzard boys!"[53] After nine hours, Santa Anna hoisted the black flag, signaling that no surrender was possible. "It comes to victory or death," Hardin yelled.[54]

Hardin's regiment, along with one other, bore "the whole brunt of the Mexican charge."[55] It was the height of the battle, the position of the First Illinois boys the center of the action. "Santa Anna had become desperate and led the charge in person—his horse was shot from under him."[56] Suddenly, Hardin was cut off by Mexican lancers, twenty firing at him at once. "Hardin fell wounded, with his holster pistol fired and killed one lancer." As the rest approached, they threw their lances at him. John J. Hardin would be one of the last to die at Buena Vista.

On March 25, under the headline DREADFUL BATTLE, the earliest reports on Buena Vista appeared in the *Journal*. Scanning the frantic initial accounts of such events is fascinating. Such accounts appear before everything can be known, and frequently do not bear the name by which the event is later immortalized. But by April 1, the *Journal* was able to reprint the *New*

Orleans Picayune's story, headlined "Glorious News from the army! Battle of Buena Vista. General Taylor Victorious!" It also brought with it the sad news: "This great victory has been accompanied by the death of the gallant, chivalrous, talented, and popular Illinoisan," John Hardin.

Four days after the news broke, Lincoln addressed a group at the courthouse, saying, "While we sincerely rejoice at the signal triumph of the American arms at Buena Vista, and contemplate with the highest pride, the imperishable honor won by our Illinois brethren, upon that bloody field, it is with the deepest grief we have learned of the fall of the many brave and generous spirits there, and especially that of Colonel J. J. Hardin."[57]

The public went berserk for Buena Vista. Part of the reaction was surely cumulative. From the fields of Palo Alto and Resaca de la Palma, to the streets of Monterrey, Taylor had consistently been isolated and outnumbered, and he had with equal consistency delivered victory for the United States. Now with his forces reduced to almost nothing, he had whipped Santa Anna and a force five times greater than his on their home terrain.

The war was sensationalized in popular culture. In New York, a stage show *The Triumph of Rough and Ready* packed the Bowery Theatre, "crowded to suffocation."[58] Popular new dances were named General Taylor's Encampment Quickstep and Santa Anna's Retreat from Buena Vista.[59] America's first mass-market paperback books were rushed to feed the public demand, with titles such as *The Mexican Spy* and *The Bride of Buena Vista*.[60] Taylor's image appeared on ice cream trucks, fish stands, butcher shops, and cigar boxes.[61] "Rough and Ready" almanacs were sold, and Taylor was toasted and cheered at any public gathering where Mexico was mentioned.[62]

Such popularity inevitably led to widespread talk of a national candidacy. A nonpartisan group in New Jersey assembled to nominate Taylor for president immediately upon hearing the news.[63]

Less than a month after Buena Vista, Winfield Scott and his men executed the largest amphibious landing in American history, and shelled the city of Veracruz into submission in a matter of days.[64]*

*In this he was assisted by officers such as Lee, Grant, George Meade (later commander of Union forces at Gettysburg), James Longstreet, and Thomas "Stonewall" Jackson.

In his report, General Scott commended the work of Captain Robert E. Lee. In this and in other battles, Lee would prove indispensable to Scott's successes, something the general never forgot. On his first day in Washington as president-elect, Lincoln visited Scott's home to seek his counsel on preparing for war.[65] Scott recommended that Lee be made head of the Union army. Lincoln made the offer, and if accepted it would have dramatically altered the course of history. However, Virginia left the Union, taking her most celebrated soldier with her.

In the next phase of the drive to Mexico City, Scott and his men encountered Santa Anna near Cerro Gordo.

Cerro Gordo was too large to attack head-on, and so the Americans searched for a route around it. The alternative was a strip of land so narrow, Santa Anna believed that not even a goat could approach him from that direction.[66] While scouting the location, Lee hid under a tree, which Mexican soldiers passed, even sitting nearby and entering into conversation.

Grant believed there may never have been another battle, ever in the world, "where orders issued before an engagement were nearer being a correct report of what afterwards took place."

"I am compelled to make special mention of Captain R. E. Lee, Engineer," Scott wrote in his report. "This officer was again indefatigable during these operations in reconnaissances as daring as laborious, and of the utmost value. Nor was he less conspicuous in planting batteries and in conducting columns to their stations under the heavy fire of the enemy."[67]

Every day seemed to bring with it some new victory on the road from Veracruz to Mexico City, but nothing captured the public imagination like Rough and Ready and the Battle of Buena Vista. One theory holds that Buena Vista arrived at a period of extreme fear and anxiety over the war, whereas Scott's campaign occurred at a time of clear American advantage.[68]

Whig candidates doubled down on their antiwar position, to the delight of Democrats. Elections for Congress were held on different days, depending on the state. Triumphs in states such as New York and Pennsylvania in 1846 had, in the minds of Democrats, caused the Whigs to misread the hawkish electorate of the South, particularly in light of popular victories at Buena Vista and Veracruz. Southern Whig candidates responded by promoting Zachary Taylor as their nominee for president, a weapon that would, from its first suggestion until actual deployment, allow the Whigs to have it both ways on the war.[69]

Virginia's Democrats had the unfortunate timing to be facing election in April, in the afterglow of Buena Vista, and to be opposed by the Whigs, who liberally used the name and likeness of Rough and Ready. The Democrats were routed, and saw their share of the state's congressional delegation drop from fourteen seats to nine.

Perhaps following their example, several Whig candidates in Louisiana declared their support in the summer of 1847 for Taylor's presidency.[70]

Doubtless Taylor is not the only reason for the Whigs' surprising southern successes. Another, for instance, was that Democrats loyal to Calhoun's antiwar position may have stayed away from the polls.[71] Despite a number of factors working against them, hopes for the Democrats to maintain their majority were strong. All they had to do was not get completely flattened on their most favorable terrain.[72] From here forward, the Democrats held twenty-nine of the forty-seven seats left in play.[73]

On February 28, 1847, in the aftermath of Buena Vista but before the triumph was made known to the world, the Wilmot Proviso was reintroduced in the House.[74]

In the public life of Congressman-elect Abraham Lincoln, the Chicago River and Harbor Convention stands out as the most important. For the first time in his life, Lincoln would interact with the most prominent names in America, elected officials, members of Congress, newspapermen, and opinion leaders.

There were 3,000 delegates, though some thought twice that number. At least 10,000 people showed up in the city of 16,000, though by one account it could have been as many as 20,000.[75]

Publisher of the *New York Tribune* Horace Greeley referred to it as the largest meeting in American history.[76] During the River and Harbor Convention, some stayed on boats. One member was offered a mattress on the floor of a law office on Lake Street.[77]

Edward Bates, who served in Lincoln's cabinet after losing to him in the 1860 convention, was chosen as president.[78]

There were a number of speakers, mostly attacking Polk. Letters were read by those unable to attend, such as Henry Clay and Democrats Silas Wright, Martin Van Buren, and Thomas Benton.[79] The idea of internal improvements—roads, canals, bridges, lighthouses, and harbors—to facilitate commerce and create opportunity, was clearly one that enjoyed bipartisan support.

David Dudley Field of New York was permitted to speak in favor of Polk, defending the constitutionality of his implacable opposition to any internal improvements.[80] As the Whig congressman-elect from the host state, Lincoln was asked to speak on July 6.[81] "His dress and personal appearance could not well be forgotten," said one observer. "It was then for the first time I heard him called 'Old Abe.'" Lincoln seemed "strange enough, as he was then a young man, only thirty-six years of age.... Tall, angular, and awkward, he had on a short waisted thin swallow tail coat, a short vest of the same material, thin pantaloons, scarcely coming down to his ankles, a straw hat and a pair of brogans with woolen socks."[82] One attendee referred to him as "a tall specimen of Illinoian."[83]

"We meet here to promote and advance the cause of internal improvement," he said. Acknowledging the division over this issue, Lincoln asked his hearers to meet "in the spirit of conciliation and good feeling." In responding to Dudley's speech, he made certain to acknowledge his love for country, despite their disagreements. "He loves it in his way; I, in mine."

J. H. Buckingham, a reporter for the *Boston Courier*, shared a coach with Lincoln on his return to Springfield. He reported: "We were now in the district represented by our Whig Congressman, and he knew, or appeared to know, every body we met, the name of the tenant of every farm house, and the owner of every plat of land. Such a shaking of hands—such a how d'ye do—such a greeting of different kinds as we saw, was never seen before; it seemed to me as if he knew everything, and he had a kind word, a smile and a bow for every body on the road, even to the horses, and the cattle, and the swine."[84]

Lincoln could have returned in time, and was likely present for Hardin's funeral, which had been delayed by the time necessary to return his body to Illinois. The procession began in the Jacksonville public square at 10 a.m., with a eulogy and a preacher's sermon. There was a prayer at Hardin's house, after which they proceeded to the burying ground. A number of speakers, including Baker, attested to the high worth of their fallen friend. Lincoln was as good a stump speaker as any, and rarely did he attend a public meeting where he was not asked to make remarks. One wonders whether the organizers, aware of or carrying hard feelings from the previous year's campaign, excluded him from the program.

In the Battle of Buena Vista, the violent, untimely death of Colonel John J. Hardin may well have had the most significant long-term impact. Had Hardin returned from the war, he would have returned as the undisputed leader in the Illinois Whig Party (David Davis argued that "he would have controlled the politics and the affairs of the state") and subsequently of the new Republican Party.[85] It is unlikely that either group would have considered Lincoln, rather than Hardin, the strongest candidate to run for Senate in 1856 or 1858. And Lincoln, author of the Pekin resolution and the man who had elbowed him aside in 1846, could have expected nothing good at the hands of Hardin and his supporters. But that, of course, is not what happened.

As Illinois was mourning a favorite son, it was also busy with a convention to rewrite its constitution. With his move to Congress right around the corner, Lincoln held a reception for twenty of the delegates. "Mrs. L. I am told accompanies her husband to Washington City next winter," wrote one. "She wishes to loom largely." He also didn't think his host looked much like a congressman. "You can't make a gentleman in his outward appearance, out of Lincoln to save your life."[86]

As Lincoln readied for his term in Congress, a number of soldiers on one-year enlistments were returning to Illinois.[87] There were "meetings, bands, speeches, the huzzas of great crowds, the glad welcome of relatives and friends."[88] One morning, Reverend Albert Hale had opened the Illinois Constitutional Convention with a prayer, condemning the war as unjust and bad for morality. He was "grossly insulted and menaced with bodily injury," and the morning prayer was canceled for days.[89] Before heading to Washington, Lincoln would have these powerful examples fresh in his mind.

The summer also provided no clue to whether Lincoln, who had served in the minority all eight years in the Illinois legislature, would for the first time serve in a majority.

As states continued to vote throughout the South, the Whigs picked up three seats in North Carolina, doubling their former number. But this had been expected, as a newly elected Whig legislature had redrawn the districts.[90] The Whigs gained three spots in Indiana, a result that was blamed on Democratic infighting. One of the new members was Elisha Embree, who would live with Lincoln during the Thirtieth Congress.

Embree's example illustrates the importance of candidate recruitment and capitalizing on opportunities in years when one party has momentum. Embree was drafted to run in what appeared to be a safe Democratic district. The Whigs were "exceedingly averse"[91] to giving the incumbent a pass, and felt "like General Taylor [they] should never surrender."[92] They turned "their eyes toward" Embree as the standard-bearer.[93] Embree campaigned against the cost of the war, asking his audiences to imagine better uses, such as "wagons filled and . . . children educated."[94] When the Whig wave hit the Hoosier State, Embree was elected and his opponent "beaten badly—whipped clean of his coat, shirt, pants," in the words of one exuberant Whig. In addition to good candidate recruitment, political parties succeed by convincing incumbents to seek reelection. Indiana Whigs successfully pressed Richard Wiggington Thompson into running for a fourth term in the House. Thompson had "seen enough of public service, not only to gratify to the full my highest ambition, but to convince my mind that the path[s] which politicians generally tread are not the paths of peace."[95] But implored by local leaders, he acknowledged that "there are times when we seem not to be the arbiter of our own destiny."

As the rolling campaign for Congress continued, the Whigs gained but one seat in Alabama, while losing three in Kentucky and making no advancement in Polk's Tennessee.[96] One Whig chosen from Kentucky was army officer John Pollard Gaines, who has the distinction of being the only member of Congress elected while in a Mexican prison (though perhaps not the only member to have seen the inside of one).

Zachary Taylor and Henry Clay were like two on a seesaw. As prospects brightened for the Whigs, there was doubt about whether they needed

Taylor to win, and support increased for a true believer like Clay. When the Democrats showed signs of strength, however, the Whigs clung tighter to the cloak of the winner of Buena Vista.

As Democrats looked increasingly beatable, Clay made a celebrated visit to the East and Winfield Scott was dominating the headlines, both causing Taylor's support to wane.[97] But then a series of victories at the state level for Democrats showed that they were "clearly back on [their] feet in many parts of the nation on both sides of the Mason-Dixon line."[98] With Democratic successes and the prospect of losing the next election, Taylor gained strength, the seesaw moving once again.[99] In the words of one historian, "The indecisiveness of the results of 1847 suited the general's needs admirably."[100]

On July 20, 1847, Taylor was increasingly asserting his place among the presidential field. If he ran, he would refuse to withdraw for anyone, saying, "The people are capable of attending to such matters."[101]

In concert with the Illinois Constitutional Convention, fifty delegates held a meeting resolving to support Taylor. The *Sangamo Journal* was also an early endorser, writing "Taylor for President" on every edition published between then and the election. And Lincoln had resolved, or soon would resolve, the presidential question in his own mind.

As summer gave way to fall, Winfield Scott and his army stood at the gates of Mexico City. The difficulty of capturing the capital was not the issue. Rather, the Americans were fearful that toppling the last vestige of a national government would leave them no one to negotiate with.[102]

Nicholas Trist, a State Department clerk, was with the army and was sent to conclude peace negotiations if possible. He presented Polk's terms to the Mexican government and waited for a response. Mexico must give up all claims to Texas, and New Mexico and California must be sold to the United States for an amount to be agreed to later.[103] The Mexicans were so enchanted by these terms, they began preparing the city for battle without bothering to notify the Americans that the truce was over.

On September 14, the United States Army under the command of Winfield Scott entered Mexico City. One observer called it a "city of the dead," with random sniper fire punctuating the eerie silence.

In the days leading up to Lincoln's departure for Washington, he would take on one final client, Robert Matson of Kentucky. The Thirtieth Congress would be dominated by debates over slavery and that issue would be at the very heart of his final case before he entered Congress.

Four years earlier, as Lincoln first began agitating for the seat, Matson had purchased Black Grove, a farm in Coles County, Illinois.[104] During the harvest season, he would bring his slaves there to work on a seasonal basis, which under the law at the time prevented them from gaining their freedom. Every fall, when the crops were gathered and stored, the slaves were returned to Kentucky. All except for one.

Anthony Bryant was kept as a foreman. In 1847, Bryant's wife, Jane, and six children were brought to Black Grove to live with him. At one point, Matson's housekeeper got angry with Jane and threatened to have her family broken up and sold in the South.[105] Jane and Anthony were understandably quite alarmed.

Late at night, Bryant fled with his family to the inn of abolitionist Gideon Ashmore in nearby Oakland, Illinois.[106] Antislavery men in the area were put on notice to be ready for trouble.[107]

Matson could not persuade Bryant to come back. In what appeared to be a retaliatory prosecution, Matson was arrested for adultery with Mary Corbin, the housekeeper whose intemperate threats had started the whole mess.[108]

In consequence, Matson filed suit against Ashmore for damages, along with Dr. Hiram Rutherford, who had assisted the slaves in their escape. Matson also had Jane and her children arrested.[109] Matson hired Usher Linder to represent him. Linder, a former state attorney general, had once led a mob that had dispersed a meeting of abolitionist Reverend Elijah Lovejoy.[110]

In his defense, Dr. Rutherford hired Orlando Ficklin, a legislative and soon to be congressional colleague of Lincoln's, to represent him.

Lincoln, in town for two other cases, agreed to join Linder in representing Matson.[111]

Rutherford had initially wanted Lincoln, and searching him out, found him "sitting on the veranda, his chair tilted back against one of the wood pillars entertaining the bystanders and loungers gathered about the place with one of his irresistible and highly flavored stories." Rutherford reported his "head was full of the impending lawsuit and I found it a great test of my patience to await the end of the chapter then in process of narration."[112]

But Matson had spoken with him first, and Lincoln was bound to represent him unless released.[113] It was, and still is in some quarters, considered unethical to turn away representation on the basis of ideological disagreement with the client. Lincoln would have been obligated to represent the first person with a credible legal argument to hire him.

Ficklin remembered Lincoln's argument of "trenchant blows and cold logic and subtle knitting together and presenting of facts favorable to his side of the case."[114] Lincoln simply argued that since Jane and her children had been brought there for a temporary time, with the intention to return them to Kentucky, they had not been granted freedom.

Lincoln and Linder lost the case, and Matson fled to Kentucky, never paying his fee, proving that he did not discriminate when it came to depriving people of the fruits of their labor.[115]

For the next two years, the law practice of Abraham Lincoln would be on hold. Herndon would shoulder the burden, as Lincoln had done for Stuart while serving as his junior partner.

On October 23, just days before leaving Springfield, Lincoln leased out his home to Cornelius Ludlum, who agreed to pay him ninety dollars in quarterly rent. The lease terms specified that Ludlum would be "especially careful to avoid destruction by fire," and permit Lincoln to use the north upstairs room to store furniture.

During his time as congressman-elect, Lincoln posed for a daguerreotype, a forerunner of the photograph. It was the earliest-known image of him ever made.[116]

Biographer David Herbert Donald describes his appearance: "In his best suit he sat stiffly for the photographer, obviously proud of his tailor made clothing, his carefully buttoned satin waistcoat, his stiff, starched shirt with gold studs, his intricately knotted black tie."[117]

Then on Monday, October 25, Lincoln, Mary, Robert, and Eddie left for Kentucky, where they would visit her family en route to Washington.

The *Journal* gave him a nice send-off: "Mr. Lincoln the member of

Congress elect from this district, has just set out on his way to the city of Washington. His family is with him; they intend to visit their friends and relatives in Kentucky before they take up the line of march for the seat of government. He will find many men in Congress who possess twice the good looks, and not half the good sense, of our own representative."[118]

The Lincolns' patchwork journey was illustrative of the transportation challenges facing the country. From Springfield, they probably took a stage to Alton or St. Louis, then a river steamer down the Mississippi, up the Ohio, and up the Kentucky River to Frankfort. They then took the railroad to Lexington, where Lincoln stayed with his mother- and father-in-law until Thanksgiving.[119]

"A. Lincoln and family" joined his friend Joshua Speed in staying at Scott's Hotel in St. Louis, October 27,[120] arriving in Kentucky around November 2.[121]

Slavery and war, to the extent they were separate issues, would dominate Lincoln's time in Congress. While in Kentucky, he would come into contact for the first time with his in-laws, the Todds, slaveholders themselves, who lived in a community where the sale and use of slaves was prevalent.

Mary Todd's little sister, then eleven years old, remembered the first sight of her brother-in-law, wearing a "long, full black cloak over his shoulders, and he wore a fur cap with ear straps which allowed but little of his face to be seen." She believed him to be the giant from Jack and the Beanstalk, expecting him to utter "fe, fi, fo, fum" at any moment. But Lincoln was a gentle giant, and his kind voice and smile quickly made her feel at peace.[122]

Lincoln took advantage of the vast library at the Todd house, and several works have his written notes in the margins. These include William Cullen Bryant's poem on death, "Thanatopsis" ("what if thou withdraw in silence from the living and no friend take note of thy departure?"), as well as works by satirist Alexander Pope and, in what would come in handy for his time in Congress, Hugh Blair's "Lectures in Rhetoric."[123]

During his stay in Kentucky, Lincoln had the chance to meet Henry Clay, his "beau ideal" of a statesman.[124] On November 13, Clay gave an address on the state of the war, a discourse seen as the opening of his campaign for president. Lincoln's father-in-law served as vice chairman of the meeting during which the speech took place.[125]

"The day is dark and gloomy, unsettled and uncertain," Clay said, "like the condition of our country in regard to the unnatural war with Mexico." Clay knew that his age would be a serious issue. Modern candidates such as Ronald Reagan (69), Bob Dole (73), and John McCain (72) have all had to confront the age question. One can only imagine the perception in 1847, when Clay, in his seventieth year, had passed average life expectancy by a matter of decades. Clay would try to turn that to his advantage. Instead of a comfortable retirement at Ashland, content with a record of service nearly unequaled in American history, he declared that "while a single pulsation of the human heart remains, it should . . . be dedicated to the services of one's country. . . . In the circle of the year, autumn has come, and the season of flowers has passed away. In the progress of years my spring time has gone by, and I too am in the autumn of life. . . .

"War, pestilence, and famine, by the common consent of mankind, are the three greatest calamities that can befall our species; and war, as the most direful, justly stands foremost and in front." While the others are "inflictions of providence," war is the "voluntary work of our own hands. When it breaks out its duration is indefinite and unknown, its vicissitudes are hidden from our view. In the sacrifice of human life, and in the waste of human treasure, in its losses, and in its burdens, it affects both belligerent nations, and its sad effects of mangled bodies, of death, and of desolation, endure long after its thunders are hushed in peace."

Clay observed that in eighteen months of war, America's loss was already equal to half that of the seven years' war of the Revolution.

He referred to the conflict as the result of "unnecessary and of offensive aggression. It is Mexico that is defending her firesides, her castles, and her altars, not we."

Clay spoke of the Constitutional Convention, and of the historical tendency of kings to rush to war without justification. The framers guarded against it and placed the power in Congress. If the president could make war as he pleased, what separated him from czar, emperor, or king?

It is up to Congress to "to decide the objects and purposes for which it was proclaimed, or for which it ought to be continued. And I think it is the duty of Congress, by some deliberate and authentic act, to declare for what objects the present war shall be longer prosecuted."

Clay declared that the war was caused by the annexation of Texas, and that no new territory should be conquered or added to that for slavery.

Lincoln, watching from the crowd, had much to think about. In a few short weeks, he would be tasked with making very real decisions about whether, when, and under what terms to conclude the Mexican-American War.

Three days after Clay's speech, Nicholas Trist received a disturbing message from Washington. He was "to discontinue all activities previously assigned and return at once to Washington. There would be no further peace offers from the United States."[126]

On November 25, the Lincolns left Kentucky by stage, headed for Winchester, Virginia, and then traveled by railroad to Harpers Ferry, where they transferred to Relay Station, outside Baltimore.

Seven miles away was 62 Exeter Street, where seven-year-old John Wilkes Booth was staying at the winter home of his family.[127] There was nothing to suggest Booth's future notoriety, or his connection to the young congressman-elect who was standing on the train platform. Nothing save one bizarre event. When Booth was a baby, his mother was lying on the bed next to him when she had a vision of his tiny right hand, morphing into a hideous, monstrous paw.[128] Booth's sister would later relay this story, lamenting that our course in life is fixed for us before we're even born.

The train ride to Washington City from Baltimore was $1.60,[129] and the Lincolns probably departed at 5 p.m.[130] At half past seven, Abraham Lincoln first arrived in the nation's capital.[131]

CHAPTER 5

A HOUSE DIVIDED

The capital of the United States has always been a study in contrasts.

The Lincolns' train steamed into a town "surrounded by pretty hills, covered with greenery and cultivated on some of their slopes."[1] As they rolled along the tracks into the city, the natural beauty of the landscape was accented by something created by man, as Abraham Lincoln first cast his eyes on the United States Capitol.

"On a hill which dominates the surrounding panorama rises the American capitol,"[2] wrote one foreign visitor that year, the "tabernacle of the Union."[3]

The splendid Capitol stood in "relative isolation . . . thrown up as if by chance in the center of a town which is in the center of nothing."[4]

Lincoln witnessed the Capitol as few people ever have. Glimpsing part of a yearlong experiment, he saw an "immense lantern, towering over the dome of the rotunda,"[5] six feet in diameter inside an eight-foot mast.[6]

The illuminated Capitol, in the words of one observer writing just days after Lincoln's arrival, was "one of the most splendid and beautiful spectacles we ever beheld. Imagination could scarcely conceive a scene more brilliant and we cannot command language adequate to its proper description."[7]

After this initial view of Washington, the Lincolns' train pulled into the Baltimore and Ohio train depot.

"The station at Washington was a frail and ugly building of wood," according to one description, "scarcely more than a shed, at Pennsylvania Avenue and Second Street [near the modern Reflecting Pool]. Roughs, loafers, and infidel boys gathered there in offensive crowds when the two daily trains came in from Baltimore."[8]

New arrivals at the station were greeted by cabdrivers who "loudly demanded the patronage of travelers."[9] For Lincoln, whose time in Washington would be dominated by issues of race, his entry to Washington through the train depot was an appropriate case of foreshadowing.

In all likelihood, the Lincolns and their fellow passengers were the only white faces in the crowd. The cabdrivers were almost certainly blacks, as it was the only professional license they were legally allowed to hold.[10] Was Lincoln shocked by the sight of so many free blacks? While on a flatboat trip to New Orleans, Lincoln had been attacked by a gang of black robbers.[11] Did the young father worry about protecting his wife and two young sons?

"Until well into his life, [Lincoln] had only sporadic contact with black people, slave or free."[12] But the District of Columbia was different. Here 9,600 free blacks lived among 36,000 whites and 4,725 slaves.[13] The national capital of a country increasingly divided by race was itself an embodiment of that conflict. The District was originally three different cities: Washington City, Georgetown, and Alexandria.[14] The year before, motivated in part by rumors of emancipation in the District, Alexandria had returned to Virginia.

From the decrepit depot the Lincolns headed to some of the finest quarters in the city. The grand hotels of Washington, such as Jesse Brown's Indian Queen, which was the Lincolns' destination (so named for the "lurid" portrait of Pocahontas that hung outside[15]), provided shuttle service to and from the depot in a giant carrier referred to as an "omnibus."* Lincoln would have taken the omnibus provided for by the hotel, or paid twelve and a half cents for the short trip.[16]

While the Indian Queen and the depot were worlds apart in other ways,

---

*Denizens of Washington are now very familiar with that word as a legislative term for a bill encompassing many subjects, but it was initially a reference to a bus large enough for everybody to ride.

the trip was a short one down Pennsylvania Avenue toward the White House (601 NW). "The Great National Broadway of the Metropolis"[17] was then four miles long and 160 feet wide, "planted on each side with the elm, maple and tree of heaven."[18] Between the Capitol and the White House, Pennsylvania was paved with brick,[19] one of two paved roads in the city, "poorly and in part."[20] It was also the only stretch of road with lights, "smoky oil lamps" that burned only while Congress was in session.[21]

The wide streets and avenues of the District gave off a "straggling appearance,"[22] the streets filled with more "carriages than you ever saw."[23] Apart from the grand government buildings and hotels, it was "an ill contrived, ill arranged, rambling, scrambling village. Its poorly built houses were far apart, with privies, pigsties, cowsheds, and geese pens in the back yards."[24] There were piles of garbage in the alleys and streets, and geese, pigs, and cows wandering about. If there were sidewalks, they were made of gravel and ashes.[25]

It was hard to reconcile one Washington with the other.

After the long journey, the Lincolns were surely grateful to arrive at the "principal hotel in the capital."[26]

It had been the scene of James Madison's second inaugural, and both of James Monroe's. It was there that John Tyler took the oath of office after the death of President Harrison. John Marshall and the entire Supreme Court had lived there for years.[27]

Jesse Brown, the self-styled "Prince of Landlords," delighted in entertaining his powerful guests, and each night laid out a complimentary spread of whiskey and brandy.[28] That evening, his most famous guest signed in as "A. Lincoln & Lady, 2 children, Illinois."[29] This was probably the first time Lincoln signed his name with the aid of gaslight, a technology that was years from making its way to Springfield.[30]

The Lincolns did not stay long at the Indian Queen. Their next stop was the boardinghouse of Ann G. Sprigg. Stuart and Baker had lived there while serving in Congress, and Lincoln likely arrived in Washington with a recommendation to board there. Rather than move during session, which would begin on Monday, or incur the additional expense of staying in a luxury hotel, the Lincolns probably moved to Sprigg's within a day or two of arriving in town. One source reported Brown's cost thirty-five dollars a week,[31] whereas costs at Sprigg's were probably closer to those paid at nearby Mrs. Carter's—fourteen dollars for a married couple,[32] though some members reported boarding for five or six dollars a week by themselves.[33]

Sprigg's boardinghouse was on Carroll Row, "a five-house block of buildings" that "occupied a site from 1st Street to the center of the west front of the Library of Congress, where A Street SE formerly was cut through."[34] It was made up of "five Federal-style townhouses," three stories tall, with five staircases.[35] The Carroll Row buildings had been used as headquarters by the invading British during the War of 1812, and would be used as a prison during the Civil War.[36]

Boardinghouses, lived in by nearly every member of the House and Senate, were the center of a member's life in Washington. Due to the expense and the temporary nature of their stay, only five senators and four representatives in the Thirtieth Congress had homes of their own. So it was at boardinghouses that most members took their meals, and socialized with fellow housemates. They were often self-selecting, with members from similar regions and ideologies choosing to live together. For this reason, they often earned nicknames. Sprigg's was known was "Abolition House." As early as 1842, when the subject was barely mentionable in public or private, the idea of ending slavery was freely discussed at the dinner table.[37]

Eight other members of Congress lived at Sprigg's. John Blanchard, Abraham McIlvaine, John Dickey, James Pollock, and John Strohm were from Pennsylvania.[38] Elisha Embree hailed from Indiana, and Patrick Tompkins, an upset winner riding the Taylor bandwagon, from Mississippi. But it was his housemate from Ohio, Joshua Giddings, who would be significant to Lincoln in ways he couldn't then imagine.

Living at Abolition House put Lincoln in daily contact with some of the most radical members of the House of Representatives. Of the Noble or Stubborn 14 who voted against the declaration of war with Mexico, eight returned to the Thirtieth Congress, and two of them, Giddings and John Strohm, lived with Lincoln. Another, Abraham McIlvaine, had refused to vote.

Five of the eight were from Pennsylvania. The Keystone State's politics were tough, and so was its congressional delegation. One southern member thought "Pennsylvania is one of the meanest states in the union."[39]

Though most Whigs opposed the Mexican War, Giddings and McIlvaine were among a handful who refused to vote supplies to the troops. Giddings believed that every death in Mexico was a murder, and every vote in favor meant complicity with the crime.[40]

While Lincoln was close to the average age of the House, he was by far the youngest of the congressmen who lived at Sprigg's. He was 38, Tompkins and McIlvaine both 43, Embree 46, Giddings 52, Dickey 53, Strohm and Pollock both 54, and Blanchard 60.

Many were lawyers like Lincoln, but their pedigrees ranged from the Ivy League to what Lincoln, referring to himself, described as "defective" education.

John Blanchard was a Dartmouth-educated attorney, serving his second term. He was elected to the Twenty-ninth and Thirtieth Congresses.

John Dickey had been a postmaster, like Lincoln, as well as a sheriff and legislator, and was returning to the House after serving in the Twenty-eighth Congress.

Elisha Embree and Patrick Tompkins, like Lincoln, were freshmen with limited education, but they had served as lawyers and judges before their victories.

John Strohm was a farmer, a former Speaker of the Pennsylvania House, and was serving his second term.

James Pollock had graduated from Princeton, was a lawyer and a judge, and had won a special election to the Twenty-eighth and served in the Twenty-ninth and Thirtieth Congresses. Director of the U.S. Mint in Philadelphia under President Lincoln, he was behind the inscribing of "In God We Trust" on currency.

The other Abraham at Mrs. Sprigg's, McIlvaine, was a farmer and former state legislator serving his third term.

But of all the housemates, only Joshua Giddings was a "name familiar to the public ear." In the combustible House of Representatives, it was observed, "we have seen him lash its inflammable elements into fury, he alone remaining calm amid the storm."[41]

In what his detractors saw as an insult, one remarked that Giddings's "mind seems capable of containing but one idea, slavery."[42] Undeservedly forgotten by history, Giddings was a giant in his time, the leader of the antislavery movement in Congress. He'd been described as "fearless, self possessed and not to be put down by threats or bluster."[43] According to one critic, Giddings recognized "no expediency, and sparing no object which he regards as legitimately open to his attacks, there is an intense bitterness in his expression."[44]

He was described as a "tall man, of stout proportions, with a stoop in his shoulders, the face marked, and the hair gray." He and Lincoln seem to have found common cause in their utterly impoverished upbringings. Giddings was from the Western Reserve of Ohio, "unbroken wilderness" devoid of schools, and he "was accustomed to almost every hardship incident to a new and rugged country."[45] After a term in the legislature, Giddings had won a special election to Congress in 1838,[46] and made a name for himself by fighting "the gag rule," a controversial order of the House prohibiting discussion of slavery or consideration of petitions covering the subject.[47] Giddings was known as an abolitionist, but what did that mean? In many ways, it was a question of style over policy. Giddings had voted for a resolution acknowledging that Congress had no jurisdiction over slavery in the states where it then existed, which was true.[48] What Giddings was for, he argued, was the freedom to debate, and while Congress could not ban slavery in the states where it existed, he insisted that no northern states be taxed to subsidize the evil institution. He didn't want the army or navy or any federal agents to be used to retrieve fugitive slaves, and he opposed an Indian treaty requiring repayment for stolen slaves. Though fiercely antiwar, when Texas was annexed he became hawkish over the Oregon question in order to counterbalance southern influence in Congress.[49]

Giddings was often a target of southern violence in the House. "Did he think the people he represented would send a coward here?" Giddings challenged one would-be attacker. "He had never seen an infernal coward that did not talk loud."[50]

Giddings had risen to national popularity after an incident aboard the ship *Creole*, on which 135 slaves bound from Virginia to New Orleans revolted in November 1841. The ship landed in Nassau, New Providence. As this was a British colony, the government decided that the mutineers were free. Giddings argued that slavery did not exist without a positive law to the contrary, and that slaves ceased to be slaves upon the high seas.[51] While many wanted the federal government to protest the decision of the British, Giddings argued that using taxpayer money to do this, or to try to recapture the slaves, was "incompatible with our national honor."[52]

The others at Sprigg's came from a variety of backgrounds and became Whigs for varying reasons.

John Blanchard was seventy years old and looked every minute of it, if contemporary descriptions are to be believed. One writer said that, in light of his sickly effect, one could probably buy the rest of his life for a quarter.[53] This was not just from age; he had been sick his entire life, including five years of complete bedridden debilitation.[54] Blanchard became a Whig after Jackson's veto of the bank charter in 1832, and nine years later as a congressman gave a famous speech defending the tariff of 1842.[55]

Abraham Robinson McIlvaine was "among the earliest and most constant opponents" of Texas annexation. When debating the measure to send troops to Texas, he asked, "Where are the strict constructionists, who can not find power in the Constitution to improve your harbors, clear out your rivers, and protect the labor of the country?"[56] McIlvaine had refused to vote for the declaration of war with Mexico, after the Democratic preamble was attached.[57] In June 1846, he said he "washed his hands of this war . . . unnecessarily and unjustly forced upon the country by the president, without authority of law, and in violation of the Constitution." He would gladly resupply the troops, but he would not appropriate money for an offensive war. "No one is mad enough," he argued, "to suppose that this country is, or could be, in any danger from Mexico." McIlvaine firmly believed that the purpose of the war was conquest. He did not believe that one could be against the war while voting to supply the troops, arguing, "The war will continue as long as the majority desire it, and no longer."[58]

The Lincolns were very happy at Mrs. Sprigg's, as were the others. At times when competition for boarders was fierce, and when other houses were lowering their prices, Sprigg's was the only house at capacity.[59] Years later, when Sprigg fell on hard times, President Lincoln arranged for her appointment as a clerk in the Treasury Department.[60]

Her boarders ate in a common dining room, with a view of the Capitol and the park that surrounded it.[61] On the menu were staples such as bread, "mush" (thickened cornmeal), milk, and potatoes, "spinach, eggs, almonds, raisins, figs." For dessert the boarders ate "puddings, pies," and "cakes."[62]

A team of black servants, perhaps eight or so, served the boarders of Abolition House at mealtime. While Mrs. Sprigg did not own slaves, she hired them from their masters. It was likely that all of them were in the process of earning their freedom, a condition her guests probably would have insisted on.[63]

One boarder described his room favorably: "a good bed with plenty of covering, a bureau, table, chairs, closets and clothes press, a good fire place, and plenty of dry wood to burn in it."[64] The Lincoln family, Abraham, Mary, Robert, and Eddie, would have shared one of these rooms.

Safely settled in at Sprigg's and getting to know his new housemates, Lincoln prepared for one of the most important votes of his time in Congress, one that would occur even before his swearing in—choosing a Whig nominee for Speaker of the House. The contest would prove to be a convergence of the violently different beliefs running through the country, and an important one in Lincoln's education on the tumultuous nature of politics in the era of war and slavery.

Robert Winthrop of Massachusetts wanted the job. Of all the members of Congress, none had a more distinguished pedigree. In 1630, his ancestor John Winthrop had been elected governor of the Massachusetts Bay Colony (coining the phrase "shining city on a hill"). Winthrop had gone to Harvard, graduating at the top of his class, and studied law under the legendary Daniel Webster.*

Winthrop had bitterly opposed the gag rule, saying the constitutional right to petition was "as poor a pretense, as miserable a mockery, as empty and unmeaning and worthless an abstraction as was ever dignified by a swelling name or a high sounding title."[65] With equal fervor he fought annexation, which he argued would lead to war and disunion. "I spurn the notion that patriotism can only be manifested by plunging the nation into war, or that the love of one's own country can only be measured by one's hatred to any other country."[66] But he had clashed with the Conscience

*Winthrop is also the great-great-grandfather of Senator John Kerry.

Whigs of Massachusetts, allies of Joshua Giddings who wanted a more aggressive approach against slavery. At that summer's state party convention, Congressman John Palfrey had tried to pass a resolution threatening to withhold support for a nominee for national office who did not clearly oppose the extension of slavery. Winthrop was opposed, and promised to support the nominee.[67] Winthrop had also voted for the war, while seven of his Massachusetts colleagues made up half of the Stubborn 14 who had voted against it. Because of his vote in favor, there was a serious effort to defeat him, though his district had given him a higher margin of victory than ever before.[68] Charles Francis Adams, son of John Quincy Adams, was a leading Conscience Whig and believed the Democrats had shown up for the purpose of sustaining him in his reelection.[69] But if the Conscience Whigs didn't trust him, the proslavery Cotton Whigs worried about his opposition to Texas annexation and support for the Wilmot Proviso. Winthrop would have to carefully thread the needle to win.

Winthrop left Boston for Washington City the day after Thanksgiving, arriving at Coleman's Hotel on December 1. There he "found a few members . . . very busy about the organization of the House."[70] As the Lincoln family's train headed for Washington, Winthrop observed "everything uncertain . . . the south are afraid of me as a Wilmot proviso man, and the north a few only as not sufficiently antislavery."[71] The next day he called on Samuel Vinton of Ohio, who was talked about as the next Speaker, and John Quincy Adams, recording, "The contest thickens. . . . My chances begin brighter."[72]

While Winthrop was careful to avoid the appearance of campaigning for the job, his supporters were active on his behalf. His home state colleague Joseph Grinnell wrote fellow Bay Stater Artemas Hale that the contest would be between Vinton and Winthrop, and was certain "the latter will exercise the duties of the chair more in conformity with the opinions of N. England than the former. I beg of you to be present [at the Whig caucus]."[73]

On the day Lincoln arrived in Washington, Winthrop wrote, "The idea of spending the greater part of a year in a House so closely divided as this will be, battling to no purpose till past midsummer, is full of horror to me."[74] Caleb Smith of Indiana was also angling for the spot, "electioneering in a way," and if Winthrop was to be believed it might be just as well that he get it instead.[75]

On Saturday, two days after reaching Washington, Lincoln joined the Whig congressional caucus at the Capitol. Out of the 117 Whigs, it seems only 84 attended.[76] Some were still on their way to Washington, while others, such as David Outlaw, a Whig from North Carolina, had little interest in "the little dirty intrigues and maneuvers which precede the organization of the two houses."[77] Giddings and other abolitionists stayed away, in order to have no ownership in the result.

While many presumed that Vinton would win, "[i]n a very handsome speech"[78] he bowed out and endorsed Winthrop, who defeated Caleb Smith 57–25.[79] Whom did Lincoln support? With so little to guide him, it is quite possible that regional affinity would have inclined him toward Smith. Where did Smith's twenty-five votes come from? Indiana had but three other Whigs. As for the rest of the Midwest, Ohio had eleven Whigs, but Giddings did not attend and Samuel Vinton had just made a speech on Winthrop's behalf, and no doubt brought some of his Ohio colleagues along. Likely both Smith and Winthrop benefited from the support of some friends from previous Congresses, but with such high turnover, this number cannot have been very high for either. Lincoln may have attended the caucus with his housemate from Indiana, Elisha Embree. A recommendation from Embree would have gone a long way in the absence of other information. To get to twenty-five, it is very likely that Smith counted on the lone Whig from Illinois, who spent much of his boyhood in Indiana. It would have been the first, but not the last time, that Lincoln selected Caleb Blood Smith for an important post.

In addition to nominating a Speaker, the Whigs also ran a slate for sergeant at arms, doorkeeper, and postmaster. "The Whig majority in the House is so small," Lincoln wrote Herndon, "that, together with some little dissatisfaction, [it] leaves it doubtful whether we will elect them all."[80] The "little dissatisfaction" he referenced was coming in major part from Sprigg's boardinghouse.

Starting with this contest for Speaker and continuing through the presidential election, the Whigs would time and again be forced to answer questions that have plagued political parties from the beginning of the republic to the present day. When, and to what degree, is it ever permissible to moderate their views to obtain a practical political result? And exactly where is the line when it would be better to suffer defeat rather than compromise? And in light of these compromises, is there such a thing as a victory not worth winning?

The day after he was nominated for Speaker, Winthrop received a letter from John Palfrey, who had tangled with him at the summer Whig convention in Massachusetts.[81] He asked whether Winthrop would appoint members of the Ways and Means Committee who would end the war in Mexico, and whether he would choose members of the Committee on Territories who would prevent the expansion of slavery. Palfrey also asked whether his selections for the Judiciary Committee would repeal a law banning jury trials for those accused of being slaves, and who would consider the abolition of slavery in the District of Columbia.

Winthrop replied that he would take office with no promises, encouraging Palfrey to look at his character and record in office.[82] For Palfrey, Giddings, and their allies, this was what worried them in the first place.

Lincoln would face a steep learning curve in Congress, but some things would be familiar. One of these was the partisan press. Replacing the *Register* and *Journal* were the *Washington Daily Union*, the organ of the Democratic Party, and the *National Intelligencer*, allied with the Whigs. The day before Lincoln arrived in Washington, the front page of the *Union* referred to him and his colleagues as the party of "national humiliation and disgrace."[83]

Monday, December 6, was the appointed day for the gathering of the Thirtieth United States Congress. That day's *National Intelligencer*, a newspaper read by Lincoln, carried an ominous warning: "Congress has never, at any time, assembled under a more grave responsibility to the people than on this day."[84]

One of Lincoln's new colleagues wrote in his diary that the "present session of Congress is one of vast interest to the country for good or ill. If its doings and measure shall result in an early and honorable termination of the president's war, it will richly merit the lasting honor and gratitude of the country and of all future generations. . . ." If not, "then will sadness and mourning fill the land and cover with sackcloth all the friends of liberty in the world."[85]

With this great task before him, Lincoln, perhaps joined by his house-mates, crossed the street and walked fifty yards to the cast-iron gate that then ringed the Capitol grounds.

Entering the gates was like leaving one Washington and entering an-other. The well-manicured lawn and shady trees boasted priceless artwork and "several beautiful fountains of water."[86]

In the garden was the colossus of Washington depicted as Zeus, which had scandalized the nation. Originally in the Rotunda, it had been banished outside.[87] One guidebook at the time thought "posterity may be better pleased with it than the present generation."[88] In this they were correct, for today it is one of the most popular items at the Smithsonian's National Mu-seum of American History. Lincoln walked past this statue every day on his way to work, and at night from his window could see it illuminated by four lamps.[89] Lincoln probably entered from the ground floor next to the East Portico. It was from that platform that he would later take the oath of office as president in 1861 and 1865, and from there that he delivered both of his inaugural addresses.

Joining a throng of people filing into the building, Lincoln would have a chance to take in what still today is an awe-inspiring sight. No public buildings in Illinois or anywhere else in the country could compete with its splendor. Congress had commissioned two statues flanking the steps of the portico, but only one had been finished. *The Discovery of America* by Persico was "the most miserable conceit I ever saw," in the words of one of Lincoln's colleagues, which "ought to be removed . . . as an eyesore."[90] "In [Christo-pher Columbus's] right hand he holds a globe aloft," and America kneels before him personified "in the figure of a beautiful female Indian" covered in very little clothing.[91] After years of criticism, *Discovery* was quietly removed and is currently in deep storage.

Climbing the stairs with his fellow House members, along with clerks, reporters, lobbyists, and spectators, Lincoln entered the Rotunda, the cir-cular room beneath the dome that connected the House and Senate wings, ninety-six feet across and ninety-six feet high to the ceiling.[92]

The massive portraits on the walls told the story of American history. The *Landing of Columbus*, the most recent addition, had been placed there earlier that year, joining the *Embarkation of the Pilgrims* and the *Baptism of Pocahontas*.[93] Then there were the paintings by John Trumbull: the Declaration of Independence presented to the Second Continental Congress; the surrender of General Burgoyne after the Battle of Saratoga; the surrender of Lord Cornwallis at Yorktown; and General George Washington resigning his commission. An empty square held the place now occupied by De Soto's *Discovery of the Mississippi*. Lincoln couldn't help but consider that as a member of Congress, he was now a part of this amazing story depicted on the white walls of the Rotunda, and would have a hand in fashioning its future chapters. What he might not have predicted was the statue of himself that now stands in that room alongside those of Washington and Jefferson.

Above each entrance to the Rotunda was a panel featuring a scene from American history. Over the door to the House was Daniel Boone fighting a tomahawk-wielding Indian,[94] symbolizing the untamed West from which Lincoln had come. Through that doorway Lincoln passed into the Hall of Representatives to begin his new job.

The hall is designed like an ancient Greek theater, shaped like a crescent ninety-five feet long and sixty feet high, ringed by twenty-four[95] Italian columns made with marble from the Potomac River.[96]

When Lincoln entered, he would have passed beneath Clio and looked directly at "the Speaker's chair . . . elevated on a platform richly draped," above which is Causici's *Liberty and the Eagle* statue. The question of who would fill this empty chair would dominate Lincoln's first day as a congressman.

Looking above, Lincoln could see the domed ceiling with painted caissons, "to represent the pantheon at Rome."[97] It was a "beautifully painted roof," observed one guidebook, which also took note of "the vast pillars, the red drapery about the Speaker's chair and between the columns."[98]

On either side of the Speaker's chair, facing inward, were portraits of Washington and Lafayette that still hang in the current House of Representatives.

The scene on the House floor was chaotic: old friends getting reacquainted after nine months apart, new friends being made, people huddling in corners discussing the presidential election or the upcoming vote for Speaker. It was no doubt intimidating to Lincoln, facing a floor full of new people, all of whom were members of Congress, just like him. Aside from the three who had served with him in the Illinois legislature, the group from Sprigg's, and whomever he'd managed to meet at Saturday's caucus, Lincoln saw nothing but unfamiliar faces.

But while their faces were unfamiliar to Lincoln, their path to this place would not be. Abraham Lincoln was very much a typical member of the House. Like 75 percent of his colleagues, he was an attorney.[99] And like Lincoln, roughly two in three had served in their respective state legislatures. Fewer than one hundred had ever attended college. Nearly 20 percent had served as a prosecuting attorney; most of these were elected district attorneys, representing either a county or group of counties, in addition to a handful of U.S. attorneys. Nearly one in ten representatives had served as judges before their election. There were a smattering of former statewide officeholders and local elected officials. Nine members were medical doctors.

The demographic breakdown in Congress helps explain why Lincoln had arrived there. Why did lawyers dominate the chamber? First, because of the mid-nineteenth-century division of labor. Today there are a number of professions whose prestige and income can produce members of Congress; only 40 percent have a law degree, nearly half the number it was in the Thirtieth Congress.[100] Modern Congresses are made up of professions that in many cases did not exist (or barely existed), such as accountants, psychologists, physicists, engineers, radio and television personalities, professional athletes, and musicians. The organized labor movement, then a generation away, had not yet opened the doors to the carpenters and auto, iron, and factory workers who now serve.[101] MBAs and business professionals were nearly nonexistent; in 1847, the largest corporations in America (and there were few) might have two or three executive employees, and circumstances rarely permitted absenteeism.

Lincoln's profession afforded him the time to attend meetings, speak to groups, and serve in the legislature. To run for Congress and to serve, one needed a flexible schedule and income sufficient to spend substantial time away from the office. During presidential years, Lincoln always missed the fall term of the court and the business that came with it in order to campaign for the national ticket.[102] Though agricultural pursuits were the primary work of Americans, farmers were dramatically underrepresented in the Congress. The first session of the Thirtieth Congress would run from December straight until the middle of August. Staple crops such as wheat, corn, and cotton are planted in April or May and harvested in September, October, and sometimes November.[103] The second session began in December and ended in March. Most farmers simply could not be away from home at such critical periods in the planting and, when significant travel time is taken into account, the harvest season.

In 1847, one of the most common pathways to serving in today's Congress did not yet exist; nearly one in four members of the House today have served as a congressional staffer.[104] Lincoln and his colleagues did not have personal staff, while the Speaker and committee chairmen maintained a modest number of clerical workers.

Most important, however, in explaining a Congress dominated by lawyers and former legislators is that these were among the few people who had networks that extended beyond their home communities, into the surrounding counties within the congressional district. Of the eleven counties of the Seventh Congressional District, four were in Lincoln's Eighth Judicial Circuit. Attorneys developed relationships not only with their counterparts in other counties, but also with clients, members of juries, and the many spectators who attended court proceedings for entertainment. Similarly, service in the state legislature guaranteed a network of the most prominent citizens in other counties. Stuart, Hardin, and Baker had all been lawyers and legislators. Witness how Lincoln began his congressional campaign in 1843 by writing to a friend from the legislature in Tazewell and a friend from the Eighth Circuit in Cass, or how he used his trip on the circuit in 1845 to baffle Hardin's plans for a comeback.

It should also be noted that the critical political skills of this time were highly correlated to those of the legal profession. A politician's public-speaking skills, capability in debate, and writing ability were crucial. This is still the case, but in the modern era such deficiencies are easily overcome. Voters are far more likely to see a brief advertisement for a candidate or read a mail piece carefully crafted by others than they are to personally examine a candidate. At the time of the Thirtieth Congress and for many years thereafter, even presidential candidates would personally put pen to paper and respond to questions from voters. Rhetorical prowess, verbal agility, and fluency with the written word were everything.

The members of the Thirtieth Congress were the sons and grandsons of the Revolution, and two standing committees were charged with handling the claims and pensions from that war. Weeks away from his thirty-ninth birthday, Lincoln was slightly younger than 43, the average age in the House. The three youngest members were all 27. The oldest member was John Quincy Adams, born in 1767, 15 years older than his next-oldest colleague. Twelve members were born in the 1780s, 50 in the 1790s. Like Lincoln, 105 of the members were born in the first decade of the nineteenth century; 68 were born in the second. Only two members were over 62.[105]

There were some standouts among the crowd. At the top of the list, and in a category of his own, was former president John Quincy Adams. Also on the list were diplomats to Portugal and Chile, former governors of Virginia and Alabama, and a number of former state house Speakers and senate presidents (a list that would have included Lincoln had the Whigs ever won the majority in Illinois).

If the Thirtieth House followed a similar route to Washington City, they followed many different paths upon leaving. In addition to one previous president, there were also two future presidents. As Nathan Sargent said: "A future president was a member of that House, yet no one surmised the fact, and perhaps the last one to suspect such a thing was the individual himself."[106] Sargent, sergeant at arms for the Thirtieth House and who dined at Mrs. Sprigg's, noted that Lincoln was not the only future president in the room. "Who could then have imagined the occurrence of such a marvelous concatenation of circumstances as would place Andrew Johnson, a most radical Democrat, on the ticket, as Vice-President, with Abraham Lincoln, a staunch Whig, as President! Truly the whirligig of politics makes strange bedfellows. Johnson was the antipodes of Lincoln, not only in politics, but in everything else. He was taciturn, ungenial, utterly devoid of humor, had no relish for a story, and no capacity to tell one; was as grave as a tombstone, and as guiltless of a loud, hearty laugh as an undertaker at a funeral. And yet those two opposites were brought together, for a short period, by the terrible events which could not then have been dreamed of, as President and Vice President of the United States!"[107]

In the Thirtieth Congress there were future delegates to the Republican Convention of 1860, which nominated Lincoln for president, and delegates to the state conventions who voted for secession. There were Union generals and Confederate generals, and officers on both sides. When Lincoln spoke at the dedication of the cemetery in Gettysburg, pledging that the dead shall not have died in vain, their number included one of his House colleagues, a colonel who was killed in the battle. Of the doctors, one served as a surgeon for the North, another for the South. The Thirtieth Congress included the four most powerful members of the Confederacy. Its president, Jefferson Davis, served in the U.S. Senate, while its vice president, secretary of state, and Speaker of the House served alongside Lincoln.

But those were courses none in the hall imagined for their life, that day in December 1847. Lincoln would have presented the clerk of the House with his certificate of election, issued by Governor Ford. A challenge facing government in the mid-eighteenth century was producing official-looking documents, or at least ones that appear as such to modern eyes. Lincoln's certificate was probably handwritten on folded-up paper, accompanied by the wax seal of Illinois.

Looking to the "thronged" spectator seats in the balcony above the floor, Lincoln, as if he needed it, had additional reminders of the important work he was about to undertake.[108] Initial seating was first come, first served, and Lincoln would sit in an armed chair and fold his long legs beneath a tiny mahogany desk like an overgrown schoolboy. Without an office, this desk served as the only place provided by the House for Lincoln to perform his duties.

Visible from this temple of democracy, here in the city of contrasts, was a most unsettling and surprising sight. Lincoln recalled: "In view from the windows of the Capitol, a sort of Negro-livery stable, where droves of Negroes were collected, temporarily kept, and finally taken to Southern markets, precisely like droves of horses."[109]

Congressman John Wentworth of Illinois, who later became mayor of Chicago, remembered, "Within sight of the capitol, not far from the lower gate, and near, if not upon, the land where the public garden now is, was a building with a large yard around it, enclosed with a high fence. Thither slaves were brought from all the slave holding regions, like cattle to the Chicago stockyards, and locked up until sold. There were regular auction days for those not disposed of at private sale."[110]

Washington City was home to some of the busiest slave pens in the nation. A typical one was two stories high, surrounded by a tall fence.[111]

There was "the Yellow House," and "Robey's Pen," a "wretched hovel," half a mile from the Capitol.[112] But on the walls of the hall were two copies of the Declaration of Independence, announcing that it was "self-evident, that all men are created equal." Only one version of reality was right—whose was it?

Lincoln had a lot to process on his first day. Finally at noon, House Clerk Benjamin French called the roll of states. The strange shape of the chamber caused persistent audio difficulties. One member thought it was "built as if to illustrate the successful ingenuity of an architect, who had staked his reputation on the erection of a building wherein the sound of the human voice might be lost in its own ascending echoes. The loudest voices, not caught precisely in the proper angle, are frequently the least heard."[113] Members "in close proximity" to whoever is speaking "are often at a loss to know what is said, and receive the first intimation of some serious or important matter in the papers the next morning."[114]

Together this group would now decide who would lead them. John Quincy Adams moved that the House have elections for Speaker.

At its commencement, the Thirtieth Congress had 117 Whigs, 110 Democrats, and 1 Native American,* but not all had shown up in time for the vote. And not all would vote for their party. Two of Sprigg's boarders, one from the North, one from the South, would oppose Winthrop. Lincoln, the consummate party man, would certainly have had some interesting conversations with these two in the run-up to the vote.

In the first round of balloting, Winthrop received 108 votes, Democrat Linn Boyd of Kentucky 61, and Robert McClelland, Democrat of Michigan and supporter of the Wilmot Proviso, 23, nearly all of them from northern Democrats, while John McClernand, an Illinois Democrat who

---

*A minor party that opposed immigration and Catholicism.

strongly opposed the Wilmot Proviso, received 11, mostly from the South, with 7 other candidates in single digits.

Five Whigs defected from the caucus choice: Giddings, Palfrey, William Cocke of Tennessee, John W. Jones of Georgia, and Patrick W. Tompkins of Mississippi. Tompkins voted for Alabama's John Gayle, and Jones for Kentucky's John Pollard Gaines. Palfrey voted for Charles Hudson, his Massachusetts colleague. Amos Tuck, an abolitionist Independent Democrat of New Hampshire, and Giddings voted for James Wilson of New Hampshire. Tuck considered Winthrop timid, saying, "When he had bid a friend goodnight he would call him aside and ask him not to say anything about it."[115]

In each round of balloting, the number of voters dropped by one. In each, Winthrop gained by one. On the second ballot, Jones of Georgia supported Winthrop, while Tompkins agreed to abstain.

Finally, John Quincy Adams stepped in. He sent George Ashmun, a Massachusetts congressman, to Palfrey with a message: "If I can vote for Mr. Winthrop with a clear conscience, I should suppose Dr. Palfrey could."[116] Palfrey refused to commit. Isaac Holmes of South Carolina, who was thought to be motivated by his friendship with Winthrop as well as his hatred for Giddings, got up and walked out of the chamber, despite the pleas of his neighbors to stay. On the third ballot, then, Winthrop's 110 was the exact number sufficient for election out of the 218 who had voted.

Winthrop would be the Speaker, but the deep divisions created by and manifested in his ascendency would remain.

Charles Francis Adams wrote Giddings that his decision was "perfectly correct. The Whigs ought to be made to understand that there are some men, however few, who look at principle steadily, to the exclusion of every thing else. I am so sick and tired of compromises, that I should be glad to have it understood that we make none."[117] Giddings would come to believe this revolt had been successful in cementing his position in the national antislavery movement. "Though it alarmed my friends," he wrote, his vote against Winthrop "has increased my moral power both in the House and throughout the country."[118] Giddings would only become more satisfied with himself over time, and six months later had come to believe that his opposition "has done much for the cause of humanity."[119]

The abolitionist press praised Giddings in poetry: "Now in our halls of legislation stands old Joshua in his place / the pride and glory of our nation / Yet hated by the loco race."[120] The *Liberator*, the abolitionist newspaper of record, said, "No one," not even Adams, "has so openly, boldly, or so efficiently assailed the slaveholding oligarchy, under whose tyrannical reign the country is groaning."[121]

But the mainstream Whig press assailed Giddings and the other dissenters. They were condemned for "party treachery. . . . Their minds are so utterly obfuscated by the madness of abolitionism, that they can neither see nor feel what is due to themselves or the party to which they profess to belong."[122] Recriminations over this vote would ultimately lead to the breakup of the Whig Party itself, and ultimately, the founding of the Republican Party. Some southern Whigs also felt the heat for backing Winthrop: Edward Cabell of Florida received "the most illiberal and abusive" attacks in newspapers for supporting "the abolitionist Winthrop."[123]

CHAPTER 6

LINCOLN'S WASHINGTON

"It has been said that a residence in Washington leaves no man precisely as it found him."

—John Nicolay and John Hay

L incoln's first hours in Congress were off to quite an exciting start.

Passing through the fire successfully, Winthrop stepped up to the platform and addressed the House.

"Severe labors, perplexing cares, trying responsibilities, await any one who is called to it," he said, "even under the most auspicious and favorable circumstances. How, then, can I help trembling at the task which you have imposed on me, in the existing condition of this House and of the country? In a time of war, in a time of high political excitement, in a time of momentous national controversy, I see before me the representatives of the people almost equally divided, not merely, as the votes this morning have already indicated, in their preference for persons, but in opinion and in principle, on many of the most important questions on which they have assembled to deliberate.... And I hazard nothing in saying that there have been few periods in our national history when the eyes of the whole people have been turned more intently and more anxiously toward the Capitol than they are at this moment."[1]

John Quincy Adams, as the most senior member, administered the oath of office to Speaker Winthrop. In turn, the clerk called the roll of states and each took the same simple oath, written by James Madison and taken by every member of Congress since, "that I will support the Constitution of the United States."

With those words, Abraham Lincoln of Illinois became a member of Congress.

Congressman Outlaw probably spoke for his colleague from Illinois in saying, "One day of my Congressional life has passed and I like the business quite as little as I expected."[2] As for politics, he sighed, "How hollow are its triumphs, and how uncertain too."[3]

The next day, the President's Annual Message was read before the House of Representatives.[4] This was equivalent to the modern State of the Union address, and was typically presented in written form, before Woodrow Wilson established the modern tradition of personally delivering a speech.

"The annual meeting of Congress is always an interesting event," Polk began, with nary a clue as to how "interesting" things were going to get.[5]

Polk announced that no change in the relations with Mexico had taken place since the last meeting of Congress, and "the war in which the United States was forced to engage with the government of that country still continues." He then devoted time to blaming Mexico for the war, and for the breakdown of diplomatic relations that preceded it, pronouncing it a war of self-defense.

Polk argued strongly for territorial acquisition and made the incredible charge that the failure to gain adequate territory would be an admission that America was in the wrong.

Polk was far apart from the House majority that wanted to conclude the war. The president urged a more aggressive prosecution than ever, saying, "The enemy must be made to feel its pressure more than they have heretofore done." When Polk talked of raising additional forces, he could not have been more at odds with the mood in the House of Representatives.

Polk reported expenditures from the last fiscal year of $55 million and a national debt of $45 million. Like the modern State of the Union address, the President's Annual Message had powerful agenda-setting power and included specific requests for legislation. At the top of Polk's wish list was a loan of $18 million to continue the war while fully funding the government.

One of Lincoln's Whig colleagues felt that the messages from previous presidents were "devoted to an enlarged and comprehensive review of the affairs of the republic: now it is a mere party paper intended to defend partisan measures. Formerly the production of the best intellects of the country, how far James K. Polk and his advisors fall short of that I need not explain you."[6]

For his part, Lincoln compared the president's recent message to "the half insane mumbling of a fever dream.... He is a bewildered, confounded and miserably perplexed man. God grant he may be able to show, there is not something about his conscience, more painful than all his mental perplexity!"

President Lincoln's first address to Congress was received by an emergency session that had been called to deal with the secession crisis. Lincoln had taken great pains to explain and justify his actions in the four months since his inauguration, which included mobilizing for war and suspending habeas corpus.[7] Lincoln's address was an impassioned plea for help for an administration desiring peace but reluctantly forced into war. Polk's message of 1847, by contrast, read more like the dictates of a leader hungry for endless war. Granted, Lincoln faced a crisis more exigent than what was happening in Mexico, as well as a strongly Republican Congress. But could his carefully calibrated address, mindful of Polk's tin ear, have been part of the reason that his request for $400 million to build an army of 400,000 men was increased by Congress to $500 million for 500,000 men?[8] Polk, by contrast, acted as though the 1846 elections had never happened, and would see his war objectives frustrated and ultimately blocked by the House of Representatives.

Along with the president's message, the representatives had a number of housekeeping measures to consider. At the top of the list were the appointment of House officers and a lottery for seats on the floor. Lincoln ended up with seat 191,[9] as far back as he could go (sixth row), to the left of the Speaker where the semicircle curved.[10] If the House chamber can be pictured like the top half of a clock, with nine o'clock directly to the Speaker's left, Lincoln's chair was between ten and eleven. To his left sat Jasper Brady, a Pennsylvania hatter by training who became a lawyer, county treasurer, and state representative, now also serving his first term in Congress. President Lincoln would appoint him paymaster in the War Department during the Civil War. To his right was John Van Dyke of New Jersey, also a freshman member, a former district attorney, mayor, and bank president. According to Van Dyke's son, "They became friends immediately. [Van Dyke] was quick enough to see great possibilities in Lincoln. He admired his broad humanity, his unerring sense of right and wrong, his shrewdness of resource, his persuasive speech." [11]

The earliest days of the Thirtieth Congress saw debate over the issues that would dominate throughout to its final highly charged minutes: the war in Mexico, the upcoming presidential contest, internal improvements, and at the heart of all of these, the question of slavery.

By December 9, the House had formed its committees* and the Speaker made his appointments. [12] If the members of the House felt peculiar at investing the power of Speaker in someone they barely knew, it was Winthrop's turn, as he made committee assignments for hundreds of members. He lamented the task of placing 230 people on committees with "due regard to parties, localities, and personal pretensions." [13]

Winthrop, standing at the rostrum and overlooking the House, felt the pressure to learn the complexity of the rules, motions, and protocols, and which had priority over others. [14] This pressure was shared by his colleagues, and especially among new members such as Lincoln. Eager to gain an understanding of his new surroundings, he ordered a copy of previous editions of the *Congressional Globe*, the newspaper of record containing verbatim accounts of the debates and votes of the House and Senate. [15]

Congressmen had to learn by swimming in the deep end. In addition to a brand-new city, the Congress had unfamiliar rules of its own.

One member told his wife that the older members of the House let the junior ones "fend for themselves." [16] He was grateful for a long letter on

---

*These were: Elections, Ways and Means, Claims, Commerce, Public Lands, Post Offices and Post Roads, District of Columbia, Judiciary, Revolutionary Claims, Public Expenditures, Private Land Claims, Manufactures, Agriculture, Indian Affairs, Military Affairs, Militia, Naval Affairs, Foreign Affairs, Territories, Revolutionary Pensions, Invalid Pensions, Roads and Canals, Patents, Public Buildings and Grounds, Revisal of Unfinished Business, Accounts, Mileage, Engraving, Library of Congress, Enrolled Bills, and Rules. In addition there were Committees on Expenditures in the departments of State, Treasury, War, Navy, and Post Office.

etiquette from a former member, "for every body here seems to act upon the motto, 'the devil take the hindmost.'"[17]

Lincoln, like Hardin before him,[18] was appointed to the Committee on Post Offices and Post Roads, and as has been observed elsewhere, his status as a former postmaster probably had something to do with it. This was a major committee, charged with making policy for what was, and still is for many, the function of the federal government most relevant to their everyday lives. At the time, regular mail delivery was not guaranteed, which affected where people could choose to live and do business. The post office was also one of the largest components of the national government. The committee's mandate was "to consider all petitions, resolutions, and matters relating to post offices and post roads."[19] This included 153,000 miles of postal routes; their employees and contractors traveled 39 million miles in the course of a year, 4 million by rail and 3.2 million by steamboat, 15 million by coaches and yet another 15 million by "modes of inferior grade."[20] The committee met in room 42, on the second story in the west side of the Capitol.[21]

Lincoln's other appointment was to the Committee on Expenditures in the War Department. Similar committees existed to oversee the finances of the other major executive divisions.* This committee was charged to "examine into the accounts and expenditures submitted to them," searching for abuses, waste, and whether disbursements were lawfully made.[22] The committee received mountains of reports from the military, and no doubt some members studied them closely, but the evidence suggests that this committee did little and met no more than a handful of times. During debate in the Thirtieth Congress, one member protested having one of his bills sent to one of the expenditures committees, saying that he could not recall their meeting for four years, or at least producing a report in that time.[23] With Lincoln on such a powerful committee as Post Offices, it also stands to reason that his second committee would not be very significant. When they did convene, it was in room 45, in the basement.[24]

One observer felt nothing "in the way of business will be done during

---

*Eventually, all of these would be wrapped into the House Oversight and Government Reform Committee.

this month—indeed there will be a great deal of talk and not much acting during the session."[25] The next day, the same observer said, "There has as yet been no debate in our House of any consequences."[26]

Lincoln and his fellow members had worked hard to get here, and they were eager to make their mark. They were increasingly reminded of how little time they had to do so, as well as the difficulty of doing so.

The members of the Thirtieth Congress were constantly reminded of their mortality. Deaths among members were incredibly common. There would be a eulogy in the House, an adjournment out of respect, a burial at the Congressional Cemetery (if the death occurred in D.C.), and then House members would wear black armbands in a sign of mourning for thirty days. If this were faithfully observed, and there is no reason to believe that it was not, members of the House would have worn armbands consistently from the first days of the session until the summer came. Just north of Mrs. Sprigg's was a stonecutter's yard, filled with tombstones in various stages of production for the Congressional Cemetery.[27]

For his part, Lincoln was quick to play an active role in the legislation working its way through the House.

There were a number of competing resolutions on the war: whether Mexico should be dismembered, whether it should be conquered completely, whether the war was justified, and when or whether peace should be obtained.

Alexander Stephens of Georgia, one of the most powerful members of the House, introduced a resolution for terminating the war "as soon as an honorable peace can be obtained," and condemned wars for conquest.

John Botts of Virginia, chairman of Post Offices and Post Roads, offered one expressing that war for conflict is unconstitutional, "in conflict with the genius and spirit of our institutions.... The war with Mexico was brought on by the unauthorized act of the President of the United States, in ordering the army under the command of General Taylor into territory then in possession of the Mexican Republic ... no new territory can be annexed to the United States by virtue of the war, without involving the agitation of domestic difficulties, begetting sectional animosities, and weakening the ties that connect us together." Some members supported immediate withdrawal to the Rio Grande and the initiation of peace talks.[28]

With such a narrow Whig majority and rampant absenteeism on the House floor, Democrats watched the ebbs and flows of the floor like hungry predators, waiting to pounce with resolutions praising the war. December 20 was racked by "uproar and confusion," and Speaker Winthrop ordered a suspension of all business until everyone took their seats.[29] Members who expected to be absent for any length of time were expected to "pair off" with a member of the party opposite, to guarantee that neither side would gain an advantage.

The members were frustrated by the partisanship and lack of progress. Alexander Stephens wrote, "I fear that we are a doomed people anyhow—I fear that our people are governed too much by passion and prejudice. Reasoned judgment and intelligence have but little to do now in the choice of rulers and lawmakers. The most artful demagogues and the most heartless panderers to popular errors are now generally the most successful candidates for office."[30]

Outlaw felt that things would be fine if we could only bring back the Founding Fathers to run things. The "virtue which distinguished our revolutionary ancestors is gone. Congress is filled not with patriots but with mere politicians eager in the race of power and popularity."[31] A week later, he said: "The more I see of Washington of politics and politicians the more am I disgusted with a political life."[32] A month later, nothing had changed. "The time when great men, I mean intellectually great, can be elected to the highest offices of this government has passed. It is the age of mediocrity of schemes and intrigues."[33]

Armistead Burt of South Carolina thought the House "the only body he had ever known, where vulgarity, ignorance, and impudence were in the ascendancy."[34]

The scene on the House floor was chaotic. Forget the strange acoustics: "There is so much noise and confusion in the House I cannot hear anything,"[35] said one member.

Another of Lincoln's colleagues thought that "there is no such thing as a parliamentary debate in either house of Congress," simply "harangues addressed not to the bodies themselves, but to the passions and prejudices of the people."[36] And a month later: "If the Parliament that Cromwell dispersed was such a mob as the representatives of the great American Republic, they hardly deserve a better fate."[37]

Artemas Hale's daily diary entries read simply "But little done,"[38] "No business of importance done in the House,"[39] and "Nothing was done in the House."[40] Before long, Hale stopped keeping a diary.

Another member observed, "I never saw a district school dismissed at noon so rude and noisy . . . more like a hundred swarms of bees."[41]

It is not surprising that many members stayed away from the House floor whenever possible.

"A man acquires no information as a general rule by listening to the shrill speeches made in the House of Representatives,"[42] said one. "Many of these men run into the House to vote and are out again as soon as their names are called,"[43] said another member.

The average voting record for a member in the House was 74 percent; missing more than one in four votes was the norm in the Thirtieth Congress.[44] Lincoln maintained a 97 percent record, missing seven votes the first session, and six the second; but they were procedural motions that were not important, such as motions to adjourn.[45]

Even the process of voting was chaotic. Roll call votes in the House took twenty or thirty minutes to complete.[46] Clerks would record the yeas and nays on a printed sheet of paper listing the names of the members. To the left of a member's name was the yea column, to the right the nay column. For example, if Lincoln was the sixty-third nay vote on a measure, the clerk would write "63" to the right of his name. This made for a speedy tally and announcement at the end of a vote.[47]

William Wick of Indiana had made a "sliding scale of the means of acquiring notoriety as a member of this House":[48] to be gloriously persecuted, to get into a fight, to have many heated altercations, and always get in the way of hard sayings, to move a suspension of the rules often, for the purpose of introducing popular provisions, to make frequent personal explanations.

But away from the madness of the Hall of Representatives were a nearly unlimited number of social and cultural opportunities, far from what the Lincolns had ever experienced.

Shortly after arriving in Washington, Lincoln likely made his first visit to the White House, to call upon President James K. Polk. It was a tradition that one of the first stops in Washington City for a new member of Congress, regardless of party, was the White House to pay his respects to the chief executive.[49] Polk's diary for December reflects a flood of unnamed members.[50] The stream continued to the point where it would have been shocking were Lincoln not in one of these groups.

The Marine Corps band played on the Capitol grounds during the summer and autumn, twice a week, occasions on which "large crowds" gathered.[51]

Dr. Samuel Busey, who dined at Sprigg's, socialized with Lincoln. He remembered, "Congressman Lincoln was very fond of bowling, and would frequently join others of the mess, or meet other members in a match game, at the alley of James Casparis, which was near the boarding-house."

It was Lincoln's first introduction to the sport; no bowling alley had opened in Springfield until at least the 1860s, with the earliest confirmed date in the 1870s.* Busey wrote: "He was a very awkward bowler, but played the game with great zest and spirit, solely for exercise and amusement, and greatly to the enjoyment and entertainment of the other players and bystanders by his criticisms and funny illustrations. He accepted success and defeat with like good nature and humor, and left the alley at the conclusion of the game without a sorrow or disappointment. When it was known that he was in the alley there would assemble numbers of people to witness the fun which was anticipated by those who knew of his fund of anecdotes and jokes. When in the alley, surrounded by a crowd of eager listeners, he indulged with great freedom in the sport of narrative, some of which were very broad. His witticisms seemed for the most part to be impromptu, but he always told the anecdotes and jokes as if he wished to convey the impression that he had heard them from someone; but they appeared very many times as if they had been made for the immediate occasion."

Busey recalled Lincoln "was always neatly but very plainly dressed, very simple and approachable in manner, and unpretentious. He attended to

---

*The Greater Springfield Bowling Association has helpfully compiled a list of the earliest alleys in the town and the dates of their establishment (retrieved online at http://www .gsbabowl.com/bc_history.php).

his business, going promptly to the House and remaining until session adjourned, and appeared to be familiar with the progress of legislation."

Busey saw little of Mary Todd, "so retiring she was rarely seen except at the meals." He remembered, "Robert was a bright boy, about four years old, and seemed to have his own way."

In the basement of the Capitol were "two eating and drinking saloons, frequented alike by Congressmen and by the public, and not infrequently the scene of disgusting inebriety."[52] One of Winthrop's first moves had been to close the saloon on the House side, which was probably the best day in the history of the bar on the Senate side.[53] One member noted that no matter how splendid the building, "The great attractions [are] in the lower part of the Capitol."[54]

For those less inclined to the bar scene, there were nearly forty churches in Lincoln's Washington: a handful each of Episcopalian, Presbyterian, Catholic, Methodist, and Baptist churches, four African churches, one Unitarian, and one Quaker.[55] Weekly Sabbath services were held in the Capitol, but there is no evidence of Lincoln ever being in attendance, or joining any of the others.

Lincoln, who didn't drink and wasn't a member of a church, still found great enjoyment in the social and intellectual opportunities of serving in Congress.

"During the Christmas holidays," it was remembered, "Mr. Lincoln found his way into the small room used as the post-office of the House," which was located adjacent to the House chamber on the second story, where the House lobby formed "an angle of the building."[56] Here "a few jovial raconteurs used to meet almost every morning, after the mail had been distributed into the members' boxes, to exchange such new stories as any of them might have acquired since they had last met. After modestly standing at the door for several days, Mr. Lincoln was 'reminded' of a story, and by New Year he was recognized as the champion story-teller of the Capitol. His favorite seat was at the left of the open fire-place, tilted back in his chair, with his long legs reaching over to the chimney jamb. He never told a story twice, but appeared to have an endless repertoire of them, always ready, like the successive charges in a magazine gun, and always pertinently adapted to some passing event."[57]

Benjamin Perley Poore, a national correspondent who hung out in the post office, said, "It was refreshing to us correspondents, compelled as we were to listen to so much that was prosy and tedious, to hear this bright specimen of western genius tell his inimitable stories, especially his reminiscences of the Black Hawk War in which he had commanded a company, which was mustered into the US service by Jefferson Davis, then Second Lt. of Dragoons." Lincoln was "marching with a front of over 20 men across a field, when he desired to pass through a gateway into the next enclosure. . . . I could not for the life of me, said he, remember the proper word of command for getting my company endwise so that it could get through the gate, so as we came near the gate I shouted: this company is dismissed for two minutes, when it will fall in again on the other side of the gate." Here Lincoln was temporarily interrupted by laughter. "And I sometimes think here, that gentlemen in yonder who get into a tight place in debate, would like to dismiss the house until the next day and then take a fair start."[58]

In addition to social outlets like the House post office, Lincoln had nearly endless opportunities to learn more about subjects that interested him. A bibliophile, Lincoln from his earliest days on the frontier had read everything he could get his hands on. Nothing could possibly have prepared him for the Library of Congress, which was then housed in the Capitol.* The ceilings were thirty-six feet high and ninety-two feet long. Marble busts of Washington, Jefferson, Lafayette, Marshall, John Quincy Adams, Van Buren, and Jackson stood on pedestals throughout the room. It was open from 9 a.m. to 3 p.m. and from 5 p.m. to 7 p.m. while Congress was in session, except for Sundays. Depending on the size of the volume, one could take it out for one to three weeks.[59] Thomas Jefferson's seven thousand books had been the foundation of what was then a thirty-thousand-book library.[60] It is something to imagine Congressman Lincoln, lying with his legs stretched out, reading a book from the personal collection of the third president.

In addition to the Library of Congress, the Capitol also housed a law

---

*When the Library of Congress moved to its permanent home across the street from the Capitol, Mrs. Sprigg's boardinghouse was torn down to make way. While in Congress, Lincoln lived roughly where the Madison Building of the Library stands today.

library for the benefit of the Supreme Court. "In each of the alcoves are tables with pens, ink, and paper for copying, which are at the service of any person introduced by a member of Congress." It was open from 9 a.m. to 3 p.m.,[61] and Lincoln probably didn't wait long before finding his way there. The librarian of the Supreme Court remembered his coming in looking for law books. When Lincoln found what he'd needed, "taking a large bandana handkerchief, adjusting the package of books to a stick which he had brought with him through a knot he had made in the handkerchief, adjusting the package of books to his stick, he shouldered it, and marched off from the library to his room."[62]

As a member of Congress, Lincoln was entitled to free magazine and newspaper subscriptions. These reflected Lincoln's broad interests, not only in politics, but in literature, science, and poetry. They included the *National Intelligencer*, the national Whig newspaper, *American Review*, which covered "Politics, Literature, Art, and Science" and featured the first publication of Edgar Allan Poe's "The Raven," *Godey's Lady's Book*, *Graham's Magazine*, the *Boston Atlas*, and the *St. Louis Republican*.[63]

Lincoln loved poetry and Poe; he gave a first edition copy of *The Raven* to the wife of John Van Dyke, his neighbor on the House floor. Published in 1845, on the cover, in ink, it read: "Mrs. Van Dyke with the regards of A. Lincoln, Washington, 1847."[64]

In Washington the Lincolns had their first opportunity to see an art museum. King's Gallery, at Twelfth Street west near F, had two floors. It was reported the "lower room contains about 100 fine paintings," with another 160 in "the gallery or upper room."[65]

There were avant-garde performances such as the "model artists—men and women, who dressed so as to appear nude, represent[ing famous] paintings and statuary."[66] Washington offered a great deal of live theater, and more conventional choices such as *Romeo and Juliet*.[67]

There was a Chinese Museum Exhibition at Odd Fellows Hall: "Chinese figures of life size, several hundred Chinese paintings, splendid male and female costumes." It was very popular and extended its expected run by a week.[68] For perhaps the only time, the *Intelligencer* agreed with the *Union*, stating that it was a "superb display."[69]

But perhaps the most popular form of entertainment for congressmen was visiting with one another. Members would drop by at each other's boardinghouses.[70] People sat and gossiped on doorsteps and porches. They hung out at the stores in their neighborhood. On Lincoln's block there were "two or three groceries, several drug stores, a shop where needles and ribbons were sold, two dram shops, and a taffy dealer 'who spat on his hands' to make his candy brittle."

Being in Congress gave members a chance to connect with others outside their state and region, often for the first time. For many, Lincoln included, this triggered an interest in genealogy. After Lincoln made a speech on the war, he was contacted by a Solomon Lincoln of Massachusetts, inquiring about his background. This seems to have gotten Lincoln thinking seriously not just about where he was going but where he had come from.

Abraham Lincoln was interested in information on his family history, but "owing to my father being left an orphan at the age of six years, in poverty, and in a new country, he became a wholly uneducated man." His grandfather's name was "<u>Abraham</u>, the same as my own." His grandfather moved from Rockingham County, Virginia, to Kentucky in 1782, and two years later was killed by Indians.

Lincoln also reached out to James McDowell, who represented Rockingham County in Congress, to see if any others by his name still resided there. This conversation resulted in a letter to one David Lincoln. "I have concluded to ascertain whether we are not of the same family," Lincoln wrote.[71] After further correspondence, Lincoln believed "[t]here is no longer any doubt that your uncle Abraham, and my grandfather was the same man."

But many members felt out of place in Washington.

David Outlaw's wife was routinely subjected to her husband's voicing of disdain for the city. He felt that people made speeches at him instead of conversing in social settings.[72] He believed Washington was completely phony: "It is all form, there is nothing real, nothing true about it."[73] As for his colleagues, he observed "very short memories and marvelous little gratitude."[74]

In addition to all the other pressures, new members had to acquaint themselves with an unfamiliar city, with few if any friends. Many liked to take walks on Pennsylvania Avenue. Outlaw thought "there is no solitude like that of a crowded city."[75] Once he accidentally passed his hotel and walked all the way to the Capitol before turning around, then passing it again before finding it.[76]

Daniel Barringer of North Carolina felt a "dark shadow of pain and anxiety over the whole city."[77]

Against this awful and wonderful backdrop, the members of the Thirtieth Congress would soon be asked to consider the momentous issues of the day.

CHAPTER 7

THE SECRET QUESTION

"The question of slavery, even where its presence was not avowed, had its secret influence upon every trial of strength in Congress."[1]

—John Nicolay and John Hay

At Ann Sprigg's boardinghouse, Dr. Busey remembered, "The Wilmot Proviso was the topic of frequent conversation and the occasion of very many angry controversies."[2] He remembered John Dickey as "a very offensive man in manner and conversation," who "seemed to take special pleasure in ventilating his opinions and provoking unpleasant discussions with the Democrats and some of the Whigs, especially Tompkins, who held adverse opinions on the Wilmot Proviso."[3] As a housemate of Giddings, who was not famous for getting along with those with whom he disagreed, this is saying something. One can only imagine the daily torments of Tompkins, a Mississippi lawyer and judge whom only pure accident could have placed in Abolition House. Interestingly, Busey thought that Lincoln "may have been as radical as either of these gentlemen, but was so discreet in giving expression to his convictions on the slavery question as to avoid giving offence to anybody, and was so conciliatory as to create the impression, even among the proslavery advocates, that he did not wish to introduce or discuss subjects that would provoke a controversy. When such conversation would threaten angry or even unpleasant contention he would interrupt it by interposing some anecdote, thus diverting it into a hearty and general laugh, and so completely disarrange the tenor of the discussion that the parties engaged would either separate in good humor or continue conversation free from discord. This amicable disposition made him very popular with the household."[4]

Lincoln understood that the Union was a diverse place, even then, held together by a series of compromises. When Tompkins received a constituent letter inquiring about abolishing the Electoral College, Lincoln realized that he'd known the writer, and took the opportunity to reply. "Don't you remember a long black fellow who rode on horseback with you from Tremont to Springfield nearly ten years ago, swimming your horses over the Mackinaw on the trip? Well I am that same fellow yet." Lincoln pointed out that the House was based on population, the Senate on equal representation, and that the Electoral College was a compromise between the two, since each state received two electors for its senators. Don't undo the compromise, Lincoln urged.

But Lincoln, who could get along with everyone and who played peacemaker around the America in miniature that was Ann Sprigg's dinner table, would soon have to take sides on the floor of the House.

Action in the Thirtieth Congress was driven in part by petitions sent from citizens, calling upon the House to act on a particular issue. They were typically referred to the appropriate committee for action.

On December 21, Giddings introduced a petition from eighteen residents of Washington asking for the repeal of all laws sanctioning or authorizing slavery in the District. But there was a motion made to table (kill) the petition, rather than send it to the Judiciary Committee. For the first time as a member of Congress, Abraham Lincoln considered a measure on this issue, and voted to advance the petition. But by a vote of 98–97 the petition was tabled.[5]

On December 28, 1847, came another vote on slavery. Caleb Smith of Indiana presented a petition from his constituents calling for the abolition of slavery in the District of Columbia, and asked that it be referred to committee. Once again the petition was tabled, 76–70, with Lincoln voting against tabling.[6]

On December 30, Amos Tuck introduced a resolution committing the proceeds of public lands to be used to purchase slaves. Again Lincoln voted against tabling, and again he was in the minority, 87–70.[7] It is sometimes argued today that the government should simply have purchased and freed the slaves, to avoid the cost and calamity of the Civil War, by those who believe they've somehow figured out a problem that vexed the greatest minds of the nineteenth century with something that never occurred to them. The truth is, "The economic value of these men, women, and children when considered as property exceeded the combined worth of all the banks, railroads, and factories in the United States."[8] Even if the money could be found, when offered the proceeds of millions of acres of public land sales to fully recompense them for their slaves, the South went ballistic. Even if the nation could afford it, the South was totally uninterested.

The same day, Tuck introduced a petition praying for the abolition of slavery throughout the Union. Not only was it laid on the table, but no recorded vote was necessary.[9]

The slavery issue, which already appeared quite personal to many in Abolition House, was about to come home to the boarders of Mrs. Sprigg in ways they could never imagine.

Late in the evening on Friday, January 14, in the shadow of the United States Capitol, the very symbol of democracy and lawful authority, three armed men embarked on a sinister mission.

After arriving at the door of their intended target, they appear to have forced their way in. They were looking for a black waiter employed at Mrs. Sprigg's, a married man on track to earn his freedom, having paid $240 of the $300 required. In front of his wife, the assailants held him at gunpoint, forced a gag into his mouth so he couldn't scream, and shackled irons onto his body. With that, they stole him away. From what the boarders could learn, he was brought to a slave pen in the city and removed from there to New Orleans over the weekend.[10] As the District had no police force to speak of, it is likely the wife went to Mrs. Sprigg's to ask the boarders for help. By Monday morning in the House, Giddings had a detailed resolution ready for offer, making clear he had learned of the incident over the weekend.

It is an event that is little noticed for the impact it must have had on Lincoln, but he learned, probably within minutes, that a man who had served meals to him and his family for the past forty days had been kidnapped at gunpoint and taken like an animal to be sold into bondage. A married man, so close to buying his freedom. Lincoln was a naturally empathetic person, and his heart would have bled for the man.

After detailing the facts for the House, Giddings's resolution read:

> And whereas said colored man had been employed in said boarding-house for several years, had become well and favorably known to members of this House,
>
> And whereas outrages like the foregoing have been of common occurrence in this district, and are sanctioned by the laws of Congress, and are extremely painful to many of the members of this House, as well as in themselves inhuman: Therefore,
>
> Resolved, That a select committee of five members be appointed to inquire into and report upon the facts aforesaid; also, as to the propriety of repealing such acts of Congress as sustain or authorize the slave trade in this district, or to remove the seat of government to some free State.[11]

By 94–88, the House refused to even investigate. Patrick Tompkins, the accidental southern boarder at Abolition House, voted no. In so doing, one wonders how he felt, having known the waiter personally. Maybe Giddings, in his classic style, had overreached when a clean request for an inquiry would have succeeded. A public investigation might well have yielded the waiter's whereabouts and secured his freedom.

What became of the waiter, whose name we do not even know? We can surmise a great deal from the account of Solomon Northup, a free black man from New York who had been abducted in Washington several years earlier. Northup later secured his freedom after twelve years, and told his incredible story.

Northup had been drugged and woke up weighed down by both chains and disbelief. "It could not be . . . [I] had wronged no man, nor violated any law, should be dealt with thus inhumanly." In the only option available to him, Northup "[c]ommended myself to the God of the oppressed, bowed my head upon my fettered hands, and wept most bitterly."[12] He smelled "damp, moldy odors" and heard the cock crow, but he saw no daylight.[13]

Northup was a prisoner of James Burch, a slave trader in Washington with a partner in New Orleans (the New Orleans connection suggests strongly that Burch was also the slave trader who had arranged the kidnapping and sale of the waiter). Northup remembered being closed in by "walls of solid masonry . . . [the] floor was of heavy plank," secured by an "iron bound door . . . , up a flight of steps into a yard, surrounded by a brick wall ten or twelve feet high. . . . The doom of the colored man, upon whom the door leading out of that narrow passage closed, was sealed."[14]

"Its outside presented only the appearance of a quiet private residence."[15] "Strange as it may seem, within plain sight of this same house, looking down from its commanding height upon it, was the Capitol. The voices of patriotic representatives boasting of freedom and equality, and the rattling of the poor slave's chains, almost commingled. A slave pen within the very shadow of the Capitol!"[16] Northup had protested that he was a free man, with a wife and children who were also free. For this he was beaten with "a piece of hard wood board, eighteen or twenty inches long,"[17] whipped with a cat-o'-nine-tails, stripped naked, and beaten again.[18]

Surely the waiter, too, would have insisted that he belonged to another, was married, and was on track to be free. Northup was beaten until the paddle broke, insisting he was a free man,[19] beaten so badly that he could not stay in the same position for more than a few minutes.[20] In captivity, he met other slaves, including a little boy who cried and called for his mother.[21]

Northrup was awakened in the dead of night, chained, and marched through the city down Pennsylvania Avenue, "through a capital of a nation, whose theory of government, we are told, rests on the foundation of man's inalienable right to life, liberty, and the pursuit of happiness! Hail! Columbia, happy land, indeed!"[22]

Northup was then placed in the cargo hold of a steamboat. "The bell tolled as we passed the tomb of Washington! Burch, no doubt, with uncovered head, bowed reverently before the sacred ashes of the man who devoted his illustrious life to the liberty of his country."[23] He was taken by steamer with thirty others to a pen in Virginia.[24] Chained to a man who was born free in Cincinnati, with a wife and children, who had been lured south with the promise of temporary employment,[25] Northup eventually made it to New Orleans, sold to a cruel slave master. Did the waiter die a slave, never seeing his wife again? Perhaps he lived for sixteen years, to be freed at the hand of the coarse young congressman on whom he used to wait.

—◆—

CHAPTER 8

A GREAT
PRESIDENT-MAKING MACHINE

"This whole session will be devoted to president making, and to this end, the public good will be subordinate."

—David Outlaw

S oon it was 1848. Artemas Hale noted that "among all the anniversaries of the year, there are none so well calculated for solemn reflections as the close of a year."[1] It was a custom on New Year's Day in Washington City to join with friends and pay calls upon its prominent denizens.[2] Members recorded going to the White House at noon to shake hands with President Polk. From there the groups continued to Dolley Madison's, to John Quincy Adams's, to Mayor William Seaton's, and to Speaker Winthrop's.[3] In all probability Lincoln and his friends did the same.

But as 1847 yielded to the new year, James K. Polk was not much for celebrating. Though the fact was known but to few, the senior command of the American army was in meltdown, with accusations flying back and forth like volleys of cannon fire. General Winfield Scott had disciplined his subordinate, General Gideon Pillow, for his publication of a letter taking full credit for the success of the campaign. Pillow, a political ally of Polk, made allegations of his own, setting the stage for a series of courts-martial and investigations.

Senators Lewis Cass and Jefferson Davis met with Polk to recommend the immediate recall of Scott. Polk blamed Scott's "bad temper, dictatorial spirit, and extreme jealously" for the controversy.[4] A trial in Mexico would be a nightmare, but if it were held in the United States, who would have to return to be a witness?[5] Nearly everyone.

Instead they would recall Scott, and have the trials of the others in Mexico. To make matters worse, Polk learned that Nicholas Trist had continued his negotiations with the current Mexican government.[6] The true story of what had happened in Mexico was far more random and far less sinister than Polk suspected. After being recalled by Polk, Trist was expecting a replacement that never arrived.[7] And Winfield Scott could not spare the manpower to safely escort Trist back to Veracruz.[8] So there he stayed. The *moderados* in the Mexican government were devastated by the news of his recall, and eventually started pretending nothing had ever changed.[9] British diplomats urged Trist to disobey the president, to stay and finish what he'd started.[10] The die was cast when he confided in a newspaper correspondent that he was considering staying after all.[11] "Mr. Trist, make the Treaty. Make the Treaty, Sir! It is now in your power to do your country a greater service than any living man can render her."[12] This final push was all he needed. "I will make the treaty," he declared, telling his friend to stay there in order to bring it home.[13]

Trist would stay. But it was not enough to simply ignore his orders. He would tell the administration exactly what he was doing. Trist wrote to Polk refusing to be recalled, insisting that he would stay and complete the negotiations, in what was essentially a sixty-five-page piece of his mind directed at the president. Polk called it "the most extraordinary document I have ever heard from a diplomatic representative."[14] It might have been safe to say that it was the most extraordinary document that *any* president had received from a diplomat. Trist scolded the administration for what one historian described as "blind pride, ignorance, and unwillingness to be informed."[15]

Polk ordered the secretary of war to write General William Butler, a Democrat and Scott's second-in-command, and order Trist to stop, and to tell the Mexicans he was dealing with that he had no authority. "If there was any legal provision for his punishment he ought to be severely handled.

He has acted worse than any man in the public employ whom I have ever known," Polk said.[16] But the administration soon realized that this rogue diplomat had them hostage. Such a letter could not be drafted, unless Polk had already decided to reject whatever Trist brought back. As Polk could not foreclose that option, they had nothing to do but wait.[17] And wait. There was nearly a month's lag time in the fastest dispatch from Mexico, and Polk desperately awaited word.[18]

Polk's position had changed, and Trist's negotiations were not consistent with it. Polk now wanted far harsher terms, wanted to blame Mexico for "the blood which has been shed and the money which had been expended since the date of Trist's instructions in April last, that, if it was an open question, I would not now approve the terms of the treaty which I then authorized."[19]

Meanwhile, Polk consulted his cabinet on the future of the war. He was certain that Congress would not appropriate money for new troops, or would at least wait until the last possible minute of session.[20] The House continued to keep the heat on Polk in a number of ways, by insisting on the production of various documents related to the war. Polk denied many of these on the basis of executive privilege, citing George Washington's 1796 precedent regarding the instructions to the minister of England for treaty making.[21]

Polk had to accomplish this against the backdrop of a presidential election, which would not just intensify partisanship but draw fault lines within the respective parties. Polk's top cabinet appointee, Secretary of State James Buchanan, was a favorite for the nomination to replace him. Polk grew increasingly distrustful of Buchanan, a man he believed was serving two masters. Lewis Cass, another serious contender, accused the State Department of leaking unfavorable information to the press about his conduct as Military Affairs chairman in the Senate.[22]

Congress focused a great deal of attention on the presidential question; meanwhile, the president seemed relieved to be nearly at the end of his term. The Thirtieth Congress was obsessed with the presidential election, the behind-the-scenes intrigues, machinations, and gossip. Much of it was driven by the fact that it was the first time these members had been together for nearly a year, their first meeting since the race began to take shape.

Lincoln wrote: "There is a good deal of diversity among the Whigs here, as to who shall be their candidate for the Presidency; but I think it will result in favor of General Taylor."[23]

It is very likely that Lincoln made up his mind before arriving in Congress. His heart would always be with Henry Clay. But his head was firmly fixed in favor of Taylor. It was simple for Lincoln. Neither Clay nor any other Whig could beat the Democrats. Taylor might be a good president on Whig issues. But the Democrat surely wouldn't be. The *Sangamo Journal* had come out early for Taylor, and in light of the war's popularity in the state and its southern sensibilities, the general was absolutely the perfect candidate for Illinois.

In the first weeks of Congress, Lincoln responded to a letter from the Taylor Committee, which wanted him to attend a convention on the twenty-second in Philadelphia, the two-year anniversary of Buena Vista. "It will not be convenient for me to attend," Lincoln said, "yet I take the occasion to say, I am decidedly in favor of General Taylor as the Whig candidate for the next Presidency." He wrote of the Illinois Constitutional Convention from the previous summer, where the seventy Whig members agreed on Taylor with perhaps six dissents. If Lincoln had lingering doubts, he never expressed them. David Outlaw, who also received an invitation to the Philadelphia meeting, felt "melancholy and indignant" at the readiness of his colleagues to "throw Mr. Clay overboard, a man who in sunshine and in storm, in prosperity and adversity, has always borne aloft the Whig banner."[24]

A week after the Philadelphia meeting, Clay was greeted by thousands in Philadelphia.[25] The *Intelligencer* reported that all stripes of Whig had gathered to see him. Though this was reported as a positive omen, was it not reflective of Clay's core problem? The affection for Clay across the Whig Party could not be matched by another, any more than it could be doubted. The question was his viability, in light of his previous losses, advanced age, and the presence of stronger nominees. At the same time, Edward Baker was addressing a "great mass meeting" in New York City on behalf of his former general, a place where Clay would theoretically be much stronger than Taylor.[26]

Abraham Lincoln was one of the first seven supporters in the House of Taylor's candidacy. At the beginning of the session, Alexander Stephens of

Georgia had put together a group calling themselves "the Young Indians," dedicated to promoting Taylor's candidacy. "For months there were but seven of us," Stephens recalled. "Truman Smith of Connecticut, Abraham Lincoln of Illinois, William Ballard Preston, Thomas S. Flournoy, and John S. Pendleton of Virginia, Toombs and myself of Georgia. We opened an extensive correspondence and put the ball in motion," Stephens said, arguing that the Young Indians (and as their founder, he personally) were responsible for Taylor's presidency.[27]

But if Lincoln were of but a small number of congressmen behind Taylor, the general had widespread support among the public.

On the day the House assembled, Taylor was greeted by thousands in the city of New Orleans.[28] A "great and glorious pageant . . . the streets, housetops, and the decks and yard of every vessel within sight were darkened with human forms, and high above the mass of heads rose the triumphal arch in the place d'armes . . . the cheers which pealed from the assembled thousands were electrifying."[29] From Lincoln's perspective, they simply had to get Taylor the Whig nomination.

Congress was "a great president making machine,"[30] David Outlaw thought. "This whole session will be devoted to president making, and to this end, the public good will be subordinate."[31]

Lincoln's housemate John Strohm observed, "The presidential question begins to be agitated a good deal here."[32]

Outlaw noted wryly that "since the elevation of Polk, almost every body thinks he may reasonably aspire to the presidency."[33] Outlaw was the perfect example of a Whig, especially one from the South, who was wary of the whole Taylor movement. "It is pretty apparent by the times I think that there are large numbers of the Whig party opposed to the nomination of Mr. Clay. They think he cannot be elected, and are willing to go for General Taylor, relying upon their . . . information that he is a Whig. . . . I do not like this idea of voting to build up a man who may turn round and oppose all the principles which I hold dear."[34]

Perhaps no member's correspondents were more engaged in the race than those of Indiana's Caleb Smith. "The Zack Taylor feeling is getting up here pretty strong," wrote a friend from New York. "Taylor could give the

Whigs the state."[35] Meanwhile, Horace Greeley wrote Smith, "The Whigs of this city are Clay all over."[36]

Armistead Burt received a letter from a constituent stating, "Next to Mr. Calhoun, General Taylor is the strongest man in South Carolina and General Cass the weakest . . . Mr. Clay is out of the question. His day is long gone by."[37]

A writer to Democrat George Houston of Alabama said, "I fear it will be Taylor. We can beat any other man . . . I sincerely hope Clay will be the nominee."[38]

Another of his correspondents said, "General Taylor is popular but all parties seem to be somewhat uncertain as to his real sentiments touching the great questions lately at issue between the Whigs and Democrats."[39]

Speaker Winthrop felt that "the hurrah for Taylor is likely to carry every thing before it. You will agree with me that we might do a great deal worse."[40] "I have had but one opinion about the Presidency from the first. If Taylor and the Whigs can make a joint in any way, on fair terms, we can carry the country."[41]

By January, former governor William Seward of New York, a prominent Whig leader, believed the race had been reduced to Clay and Taylor.[42]

At the end of the month, the Whigs had a caucus and voted "by a very large majority" to have a national convention.[43] Some of Taylor's most fervent supporters wanted to dispense with it and have him nominated, while many of his supporters understood that this would never work. Lincoln was surely in the latter category. As a party man, an advocate of conventions as a means to win elections, and a pragmatist, Lincoln knew that Taylor could not win without the Whigs who were now cool to him, and those could never be brought to support him lest he fairly beat their preferred candidates. While Lincoln could have been counted on to support the convention's pick, there were a number in the room who pledged to support Taylor no matter what, even if he ran without party affiliation.[44]

Outlaw believed Taylor would need to prevail in a national convention. "If he would avow himself a Whig, I [believe] that in all human probability he will receive the nomination. This not because he is the first choice of a large body of the Whig party, or a majority of it, but because it is thought he would be the most available man to turn out the present corrupt party."[45] He would later joke that if those who aspired to be his vice president were excluded, he'd have no supporters at all.[46]

But Taylor had his detractors, and none was stronger than Joshua Giddings. Just as Lincoln had probably arrived in Washington a Taylor supporter, and served as part of the nucleus of his presidential effort, Giddings had long since been trying to stop the Taylor boomlet, preparing to resist him in equal measure.

Giddings kept in regular correspondence with the leading antislavery men around the country. Charles Francis Adams reported, "The cotton men are all for Taylor."[47] Caleb Smith, campaigning on an antiwar platform in Indiana, feared "the Taylor fever which is now sweeping over the country will derange all our calculations. If he is a candidate he will be irresistible in this state. A large number of the Whigs will not vote for him, but he will get more than sufficient [others] to make up for the loss."[48] Columbus Delano of Ohio, one of the fourteen who had voted no on the declaration of war, preferred Winfield Scott. "Perhaps when he comes home he will be sufficiently bloody to satisfy the patriotic portion of all parties," he noted sardonically.[49] "To kill women and children and hurry men unprepared to eternity because they refuse to give us their land, now free, in order that we may cover it with slaves, are certainly high qualifications for the highest office in the gift of a free nation of professing Christians."[50] Delano fumed that Taylor's silence on the issues allowed "lying politicians and newspapers" to "represent him in different [ways] to different coalitions."[51]

Senator Thomas Corwin of Ohio predicted "a final and fatal division of the Whig party. We must prevent this." Corwin believed that if the party under Taylor "puts itself on the right ground as to slavery and the other controlling questions I think it wrong to divide it merely because General Taylor is a slaveholder."[52]

Horace Greeley wrote to James Wilson of New Hampshire: "I can't go for Taylor, for reasons you will appreciate; nor for Scott, who is a vain, headstrong blockhead."[53]

The problem was agreeing on an alternative. Purists such as Giddings and his allies are often better at finding what they're against than what they are for. But the antislavery men, while representing beliefs outside the mainstream, were not totally without practical instincts. Charles Francis Adams noted that Supreme Court justice John McLean, another candidate for president, couldn't win a single slave state, and if nominated would need a strongly proslavery running mate, which would cost them the high ground in the North.[54] But on second thought, though Giddings had assured them Scott was antislavery, he still didn't think he could support "the man who bombarded Vera Cruz and otherwise acted as the instrument of this atrocious war."[55]

But as members of Congress obsessed over promoting a candidate for president, or perhaps stopping one, there was one person in particular who anticipated the upcoming election more than the rest put together. Twenty-one days into the session, Polk took note that in fourteen months, he would be able to retire to Nashville.[56]

When Congress returned in the new year, Whig John Houston of Delaware offered a resolution of thanks to Taylor and his soldiers for "indomitable skill, valor, and good conduct."[57] Thomas Henley, an Indiana Democrat, proposed to add the language, "Engaged as they were in defending the rights and honor of the nation."

But it was George Ashmun's amendment that would strike the House like a lightning bolt. He proposed adding a coda to the resolution: "In a war unnecessarily and unconstitutionally begun by the President of the United States." It passed, 82–81, with Lincoln voting in favor.[58] Where the House had been holding Polk's feet to the fire, they were now on the record officially condemning the war. Weeks later, this position was reaffirmed. When the Democrats tried to reverse the Ashmun amendment, they were rebuffed, 105–95.[59] Now the Whigs were on the record. But what were they going to do about it?

Outlaw said, "They all believe the war to be unjust, to have been unconstitutionally commenced, and now to be . . . for conquest, yet they are afraid to take any decision or efficient measures to advert it, before it is too late, least their popularity may be affected, and they may not be able to obtain seats in the next Congress."[60]

Lincoln made his first remarks in the House early for a freshman.

A rule had been enacted in 1841 limiting a member to one hour of speaking time during debate.[61] As the House generally began at noon and ended at three, this offered very little chance to be heard among the 220-plus members serving at any given time. Lincoln gave four substantial speeches in Congress, and more frequently spoke for shorter periods of time. In light of this, and despite criticism from other histories for not speaking more, Lincoln was actually one of the more active participants on the House floor. Many of the other freshmen were unnerved at the prospect. Artemas Hale felt he "could do little except giving a silent vote upon the important questions that were presented—it afforded me, however, an opportunity for becoming acquainted with members from the various parts of the country and witnessing the manner in which the business of Congress is transacted—which I am sorry to say, is far less creditable to the country, than I had imagined."[62]

Others didn't see the value in participating. Outlaw thought that "there is such a rush to get the floor that a tolerably modest man shrinks from the scramble . . . there is so much noise I am almost afraid to speak."[63] He also felt that the best members of Congress would never come to the attention of the American people, as they did not deliver speeches filled with the puffery that generated news coverage.[64]

On January 5, Lincoln weighed in for the first time as a member of the House. The bill at issue involved a dispute between the postmaster general and a railroad carrier.[65] Years earlier, the Post Office Department had refused to pay what it saw as exorbitant rates to have the mail carried by rail through Virginia to Washington. Not happy to be denied, the railroad owner simply went to President John Tyler, who overruled his postmaster general and signed a contract. Now the contract had expired, and the Post Office returned to using the previous, less expensive route. John Botts of Virginia, chairman of the Committee on Post Offices and Post Roads, now sponsored a bill to force the postmaster general to renew the old, more expensive contract, due to concerns about the speed of mail arriving in the capital.

In his speech, Lincoln demonstrated an intimate command of facts, details, the history of the situation, and operative laws. At first, however, he failed to demonstrate familiarity with a rule that was new to him. He began by explaining that all the Whigs and all but one Democrat on the committee supported the postmaster general in reverting to the previous route. Chatter from the floor of the House intimated that Lincoln was out of order to reference committee proceedings. Rather than lose his composure, Lincoln quickly recovered, joking that if he had been out of order, he "took it all back, so far as he could." He assured the House that he had no desire to be out of order, but laughed that he never could stay in order for long. Lincoln knew nothing of the personal animosity between railroad owner and postmaster. And he didn't want to know anything, "because it had nothing whatever to do with a just conclusion from the premises." The postmaster said he could not give to this company more than $237.50 per railroad mile, and 12.5 percent less for transportation by steamboats. "Further, he would not give more if he could, because in his apprehension, it would not be fair and just."

There were three operative laws, Lincoln argued:

1. The Postmaster General is allowed to pay 25% more to transport over rail than for similar transportation in mail coaches.
2. The Postmaster General shall not pay more than $300 per mile for daily transportation.
3. The Postmaster General has to classify the services rendered.

What did the postmaster do? "He took the most expensive mail coach route in the nation. He took the prices allowed for coach transportation on different portions of that route and averaged them, and then built his construction of the law upon that average. It came to $190 per mile. He added 25% to that rate and offered the result to this railroad company. The gentleman from Virginia says that this was wrong: I say it was right." The amount in controversy was not monumental. "I admit it is very small; and if nothing else were involved, it would not be worth the dispute. But there is a principle involved, and if we once yield to a wrong principle, that concession will be the prolific source of endless mischief. It is for this reason, and not for the sake of saving $2,700, that I am unwilling to yield what is demanded. If I had no apprehensions that the ghost of this yielding would rise and appear in various distant places, I would say, pay the money and let us have no more fuss about it." But "What is just compensation?" Lincoln asked. He noted that the daily steamboat between Troy, New York, and New York City could deliver mail for less than $100 per mile. The Virginia rail company turned down $212–$213 per mile. Lincoln noted the route from Cincinnati to Louisville cost less than $28 per mile. Perhaps there's a reason why it should be more, Lincoln conceded, but a reason why it should be that much more?[66]

Botts's bill went nowhere, and Lincoln's first foray on the floor was a success for taxpayers against an overreaching special interest.

On January 8, Lincoln wrote about it to Herndon. "As to speech-making, by way of getting the hang of the House, I made a little speech two or three days ago, on a post office question of no general interest. I find speaking here, and speaking elsewhere, about the same thing. I was about as badly scared, and no worse, as I am when I speak in court. I expect to make one within a week or two, in which I hope to succeed well enough, to wish you to see it."[67]

Herndon had informed Lincoln that there were those in the district who favored his reelection. Lincoln was open to the idea, having said that he would not run again "to deal fairly with others, to keep peace among our friends, and to keep the district from going over to the enemy," rather than for his own personal inclination. If "no body else wishes to be elected, I could not refuse the people the right of sending me again."[68]

Meanwhile, Mary was not finding Washington to her liking. Lincoln was often busy with official duties, and very few members had brought their wives. At Sprigg's, it is certain that Tompkins had brought his wife, a large woman with whom Mary did not get along. Of Mrs. Tompkins, one member joked: "It is said a man had well have too much of anything as too much wife. She was tremendously large . . . one of the tallest women I ever saw."[69] The Lincolns were back where they started: in a boardinghouse. Mary had hated life at the Globe Hotel in Springfield, and at least among the other residents there, the feeling was mutual.

One thing desperately missing, at least from the perspective of the male party circuit, was eligible women. One of Lincoln's colleagues from Ohio was "requested to invite a few ladies of my acquaintance" to parties.[70]

There were many reasons that members left their wives back home. It was said that Washington was a "scandalous place," where "a married lady ought not remain . . . more than a week without contamination."[71] In their boredom, some wives took "young coxcombs who have about as little brains in their heads as in their heels."[72] When one congressman suggested ladies from the House gallery be allowed on the floor, another objected that the House was bad company, and no place for ladies.[73] Lincoln's colleague Richard Donnell never married, because he desired a career in Congress. And Congress met in Washington, which was no place for a wife.[74]

Instead of the lavish nightly parties she envisioned, most of Mary's life was spent shut away in her room or attending to domestic needs. Anything Mary required could be found at one of the four public markets in Washington, held on Saturdays and every other day except Sunday. The Lincolns would have patronized the market on Capitol Hill. The "abundance of commodities brought there for sale," it was said, "is not excelled by any market in the United States."[75]

The night after Lincoln's first speech, he took Mary to see the Ethiopian Serenaders at Carusi's Saloon, at C Street between Tenth and Eleventh Streets west.[76] The Serenaders were not Ethiopian, but white performers in blackface who had just returned from performing for Queen Victoria and Prince Albert, and it cost twenty-five cents to attend.[77]

If there was little for a spouse to do, there was even less for children. Lincoln did take Robert to the U.S. Patent Office.[78] "The model room [of the patent office] occupied the entire third floor of the building, consisted of four grand halls opening into each other, and contained about two hundred thousand models of American inventions as well as priceless items of historic interest and curiosity."[79]

As a congressman, the mechanically minded Lincoln had voted to increase the number of examiners in the patent office, and voted against attempts to limit that number.[80]

But Lincoln was immersed in his new role as congressman, and believed his family's presence held him back to some degree. There was his work in committee, his business on the floor, the need to build personal relationships, and his participation in the presidential race. And the Young Indians were about to encounter rough terrain on the presidential trail.

Taylor wrote a widely publicized letter, reprinted in many newspapers, saying that if he were nominated, "I must insist on the condition—and my position on this point is immutable—that I shall not be brought forward by them as the candidate of their party, or considered as the exponent of their party doctrines." He closed by saying, "If I were nominated for the presidency, by any body of my fellow citizens, designated by any name they might choose to adopt, I should esteem it an honor, and would accept such nomination provided it had been made entirely independent of party considerations."[81]

Alexander Stephens, Robert Toombs, and Senator John Crittenden of Kentucky sent Taylor a letter addressing this and preparing him for questions that might arise. It was given to Major William Bliss, Taylor's son-in-law, who was then in Washington.[82] This produced another letter from Taylor, promising to be independent of party, but making clear that "I am a Whig, but not an ultra Whig."[83] It turns out Taylor's position was at least a little bit mutable after all.

But as the damage control began in earnest, a second letter surfaced, wherein Taylor denied that he would get out of the race if the Whigs nominated Henry Clay or someone else.[84] This contradicted Taylor's letter to Clay several months earlier pledging to do just that.[85] To get the nominee they believed the party needed, the Young Indians would have to keep working hard—and to keep their candidate quiet.

CHAPTER 9

THE QUESTIONS OF WAR

"What an epitaph: 'Died of the Spotted Fever.' Poor Lincoln!"
—Illinois State Register

O n January 3, the Whigs had declared, 82–81, that "war had been unnecessarily and unconstitutionally begun by the president of the United States." But the Whigs would continue to keep the pressure on Polk to find a way to end the war.

Shortly after arriving in Congress, Lincoln wrote Herndon, "As you are all so anxious for me to distinguish myself, I have concluded to do so before long."

This seeming jest would soon prove serious, and Lincoln and his supporters would find that there was more than one way to be distinguished.

Lincoln the lawyer traveled the Eighth Judicial Circuit of Illinois, across many miles, and appeared in many a crude courthouse, sometimes a one-room wooden structure in a new county on the rapidly growing frontier. As he was a small-town attorney, his practice consisted mainly of divorce, petty crimes, and business disputes, trying cases to pioneer juries. Now his court-room was in the United States Capitol, in the Greek Revival–style Hall of Representatives; his jury was the membership of Congress; the defendant was the president of the United States; the charge, leading America into a war under false pretenses, and in violation of the Constitution.

As each case begins with a complaint, so on December 22 did Lincoln introduce eight resolutions questioning the path by which President Polk took America to war.[1]

These resolutions posed pointed questions to the president concerning the spot where blood was first shed in this conflict. Was it American territory, as Polk had always asserted as the cornerstone of his actions, or Mexican, or disputed? Were the people who lived in this place Americans by consent or conquest? Was General Taylor sent into that settlement after telling the president repeatedly that such a move was unnecessary for the defense of the United States?

The resolutions were read aloud and set aside for future debate.

Before he even spoke on the measure, the fallout was enormous. The Democratic newspapers made a sport of pounding on Lincoln, questioning his patriotism and motivation in the most personal way possible. The *Illinois State Register* on January 7 accused Lincoln of deceiving the voters, who it claimed were caught by surprise at his opposition. A week later the *Register* published an editorial titled "The War—Mr. Lincoln's Resolutions." They pointed out that Illinoisans had volunteered en masse for the war, with six thousand men enlisting. "They cannot accept politically motivated questions of the justness of the war . . . thank heaven Illinois has eight representatives who will stand by the honor of the nation. Would that we could find Mr. Lincoln in their ranks, doing battle on the side of his country as valiantly. . . . He will have a fearful account to settle with them, should he lend his aid in an effort to neutralize their achievements and blast their fame."

In Coles County, the *Charleston Globe*, the hometown newspaper of Lincoln's father and stepmother, reported these resolutions "show conclusively that the littleness of the pettifogging lawyer has not merged into the greatness of the statesman. We regret, as a citizen of Illinois, that a representative from our noble state should thus disgrace her, by offering such trash for the consideration of the grave and dignified legislature of this wide spread republic. Well may the patriotic people of the 7th district lament that they have not a Hardin or Baker to represent them at this important crisis. Alas poor Spotty."[2]

"Spotty" would forever be a sobriquet of choice for Lincoln's enemies, on account of his fixation on "the spot" where the war began.

These editorials were not the worst of it. That distinction belongs to the *Belleville Times*, which argued that his opposition to the war flowed from his "undying hatred to his former and successful rival who fell so gloriously in this very war."[3]

The Whig newspapers came to his defense. The *Quincy Whig* argued that these resolutions were "based upon facts which cannot be successfully controverted, as to which nation was the aggressor and upon whose soil the first blood was shed."[4]

The resolutions even attracted some national attention. The *Baltimore Patriot* observed that "the resolutions of Mr. Lincoln, of Illinois, submitted to the House today, will attract attention from the fact that they stick to the spot in Mexico where the first blood was shed, with all the tightness that characterized the shirt of the fabled Nessus! Evidently there is music in that very tall Mr. Lincoln."[5]

But the truth is that public opinion, even among Lincoln's friends and fellow Whigs in Illinois, was that he had made a terrible mistake. This tempest had been stirred by simply introducing these resolutions to the House for its consideration. This was before Lincoln finally obtained the floor to justify them.

On January 11, Lincoln attempted to get recognition from the Speaker to explain his position. The House adjourned, giving him the floor the following morning.[6] He had much to consider on his walk home to the Sprigg house. Though Lincoln rarely engaged his colleagues politically at dinner, choosing instead to share from his vast collection of anecdotes, maybe that night he discussed what he had meditated for the morning. That evening he likely attended the Whig caucus meeting, which one attendee described as "a miserable affair, and after several speeches it adjourned, just as wise as when it met, without coming to any conclusions on any subject."[7]

Lincoln's written speech is riddled with changes, none of any substance. "Spoken" is struck and replaced with "addressed," "upon" became "on," and sentences were struck for redundancy rather than because of a change in strategy.[8]

When the morning came, Abraham Lincoln as prosecutor finally had the attention of the floor. By the time he sat down, he had in the minds of many completed his act of political suicide.

Lincoln felt he could do no other. At the outset of war, he, along with other "good citizens and patriots, remain[ed] silent on that point, at least 'til the war should be ended," and would have preferred to avoid criticism until that day. But President Polk, Lincoln charged, had argued that every silent vote for supplying the troops constituted "an endorsement of the wisdom and justice of his conduct." This Lincoln could not accept. He had voted to supply the troops in the field at every turn. But he could not accept that those soldiers had been justifiably put in danger.

Methodical in his approach, Lincoln went back to May 1846, and Polk's first wartime message to Congress. The president had declared "the soil was ours on which hostilities were commenced by Mexico," a charge repeated in every subsequent communication, "thus showing that he [Polk] esteems that point a highly essential one." This was a point of agreement between the two men. "To my judgment," Lincoln said, "it is the very point upon which he should be justified or condemned." In December 1846, Polk put forward evidence of the truthfulness of his claims. Lincoln took each of the president's positions in turn.

Polk began his argument by stating that the Rio Grande, purchased from France in 1803, was the western boundary of Louisiana. Lincoln mocked this assertion, not because it was false but because it was so obviously true, and just as much irrelevant to the issues at hand. In 1819, Lincoln pointed out, America sold the land under the auspices of the Adams-Onis Treaty. "What under heaven," Lincoln asked, "had that to do with the present boundary between us and Mexico?" How "the line that once divided your land from mine can still be the boundary between us after I have sold my land to you, is to me beyond all comprehension. And how any man, with an honest purpose only of proving the truth, could ever have thought of introducing such a fact to prove such an issue is equally incomprehensible."

The second plank of Polk's defense alleged that the Republic of Texas had always claimed the Rio Grande as her western boundary. It was true, Lincoln said, that Texas claimed the Rio Grande as her western border, but she did not always make that claim. The state constitution, "the last will and testament" of the Republic of Texas, is silent. "But suppose she had always claimed it?" Lincoln asked. As a good lawyer, Lincoln would argue no more than he had to in order to win his case. "Had not Mexico always claimed the contrary? . . . If I should claim your land by word of mouth, that certainly would not make it mine; and if I were to claim it by a deed which I had made myself, and with which you had nothing to do, the claim would be quite the same in substance, or rather in utter nothingness."

Polk argued that the Mexican general Santa Anna had entered into a treaty with Texas that recognized the Rio Grande as her western boundary. Official recognition by the Mexican government, if it had been offered, would be a powerful, perhaps dispositive factor in favor of the president. Lincoln pointed out that at the time, Santa Anna was held as a prisoner of war and could not bind Mexico by treaty. Lincoln further took issue with the use of the word *treaty*, laughing at "that little thing which the president calls by that big name. . . . I believe I should not err if I were to declare that, during the first ten years of the existence of that document, it was never, by any body, called a treaty; that it was never so called till the President, in his extremity attempted, by so calling it, to wring something from it in jurisdiction of himself in connection with the Mexican War. It has nothing of the distinguishing features of a treaty. It does not call itself a treaty. Santa Anna does not therein assume to bind Mexico; he assumes only to act as the leader of the Mexican army and navy. He didn't recognize the independence of Texas, he did not say one word about boundary, and most probably never thought of it."

Lincoln pointed out that the so-called treaty stipulated that Mexican forces should evacuate the territory of Texas, passing to the other side of the Rio Grande, and that the Texas army should not approach nearer than within five leagues. Now Polk asserted that the treaty setting the contours of Texas said that Texas should not go within five leagues of her own boundary? On its face, the president could find no justification there, Lincoln argued.

Lincoln then turned to whether the Republic of Texas and the United States had exercised jurisdiction beyond the Nueces River, which sits to the east of the Rio Grande and which the Mexicans contended was the true western boundary. Lincoln believed that this, too, was a diversion. He pointed out that while it was true Texas had claimed such jurisdiction, even Polk did not assert that it stretched to the Rio Grande. With self-effacing humor, Lincoln argued that "some simple minded people think it possible to cross one river and go beyond it, without going all the way to the next." And "that jurisdiction between two rivers can be exercised without including all of the area between it." Lincoln knew "a man who exercises jurisdiction over a piece of land between the Wabash and the Mississippi; and yet so far is this from being all there is between those rivers."

Finally, Polk had argued that Congress understood the boundary of Texas as going beyond the Nueces River. "But how far beyond?" Lincoln asked. "The Congress did not understand it to extend clear to the Rio Grande," citing joint resolutions "expressly leaving all questions of boundary to future adjustment" at the time of Texas's annexation.

Having picked apart Polk's case piece by piece, Lincoln deployed his powerful closing argument. "I am now through the whole of the President's evidence; and it is a singular fact, that if any one should declare that the President sent the army into the midst of a settlement of Mexican people, who had never submitted, by consent or force, to the authority of Texas or the United States, and that there, and thereby, the first blood of the war was shed, there is not one word in all the President has said that would either admit or deny the declaration."

Lincoln observed that his own "way of living leads me to be about the courts of justice; and there I have sometimes seen a good lawyer, struggling for his client's neck, in a desperate case, employing every artifice to work round, befog, and cover up with many words, some position pressed upon him by the prosecution, which he dared not admit, and yet could not deny."

Lincoln believed it probably true that Mexico's jurisdiction extended east of the Rio Grande, and Texas's west of the Nueces. Neither river could then be said to be the boundary. This was the key, Lincoln believed, in determining where one land ended and another began—the crucial fact in determining the spot where blood was first spilled in the Mexican-American War.

Lincoln's next comments would be resurrected and repurposed at a future time and place. "Any people any where," Lincoln said, "being inclined and having the power, have the right to rise up and shake off the existing government, and form a new one that suits them better. This is a most valuable, a most sacred right—a right which, we hope and believe, is to liberate the world. Nor is this right confined to cases in which the whole people of an existing government may choose to exercise it. Any portion of such people that can may revolutionize, and make their own of so much of the territory as they inhabit. More than this, a majority of any portion of such people may revolutionize, putting down a minority, intermingled with, or near about them, who may oppose their movements. Such a minority was precisely the case of the Tories of our own revolution."

The land in question was part of the Louisiana Purchase in 1803, sold to Spain in 1819, after which Mexico revolted against Spain. "In my view," Lincoln reasoned, "just so far as she carried her revolution, by obtaining the actual, willing or unwilling submission of the people, so far the country was hers, and no farther."

Lincoln asked for Polk's answer, "fully, fairly, and candidly. Let him answer with facts, and not with arguments. Let him remember he sits where Washington sat; and so remembering, let him answer as Washington would answer. As a nation should not, and the Almighty will not, be evaded, so let him attempt no evasion, no equivocation. And if, so answering, he can show that the soil was ours where the first blood of the war was shed—that it was not within an inhabited country, or if within such, that the inhabitants had submitted themselves to the civil authority of Texas, or of the United States, and that the same is true of the site of Fort Brown." (Fort Brown was built by the U.S. Army on the north bank of the Rio Grande in the run-up to the war.)

Why won't the president answer? Lincoln asked. Because "he feels the blood of this war, like the blood of Abel, is crying to Heaven against him; that he ordered General Taylor into the midst of a peaceful Mexican settlement purposely to bring on a war, that, originally having some strong motive—what, I will not stop now to give my opinion concerning—to involve the two countries in war, and trusting to escape scrutiny by fixing the public gaze upon the exceeding brightness of military glory—that attractive rainbow, that rises in the showers of blood—that serpent's eye, that charms to destroy—he plunged into it, and has swept on and on till disappointed in this calculation of the ease with which Mexico might be subdued, he now finds himself he knows not where."

Now Polk and his supporters asked Mexico to pay for the cost of the war with her territory. Where would the balance come from, Lincoln asked, when America had taken everything that Mexico owned?

The speech took roughly forty-five minutes, so as not to run over the "one hour rule" then in place in the House. It would follow Lincoln all the way to Ford's Theatre.

That night at Sprigg's, Dr. Busey recalled "with vivid pleasure the scene of merriment," as Lincoln and his colleagues delivered postmortems on his first speech, "occasioned by the description, by himself and others of the Congressional mess, of the uproar in the House during its delivery."[9]*

But if Lincoln's Washington friends approved, those in Illinois were appalled in equal measure. Not the least of Lincoln's detractors was William Herndon. Herndon wrote Lincoln on January 19, after learning of the resolutions but before the speech. Herndon argued that Polk had a right to invade Mexican territory if necessary to prevent an attack.

Lincoln responded that "if you misunderstand" what happened, "I fear other good friends will also." Lincoln reaffirmed his previous resolution that the war was "unnecessarily and unconstitutionally commenced by the President; and I will stake my life, that if you had been in my place, you would have voted just as I did. Would you have voted what you felt you know to be a lie? I know you would not."[10]

The Democrats had attempted to "make the direct question of the justice of the war; so that no man can be silent if he would. You are compelled to speak; and your only alternative is to tell the truth or tell a lie. I can not doubt which you would do."

Lincoln had always voted for supplies for the troops, he pointed out. Whig war veterans who had heard his speech "do not hesitate to denounce, as unjust, the President's conduct in the beginning of the war," and do not believe him motivated by "undying hatred to them, as the *Register* would have it believed." Two of those veterans had served with Edward Baker, Lincoln's predecessor.

By the time Herndon read this letter, Lincoln wrote, "you will have seen

---

*Busey says that this happened on the night of Lincoln's maiden speech, but it seems clear that it was actually the night of the "Spot Resolutions" speech, his second. The bland postal issue Lincoln first addressed was not capable of producing much of an uproar. Second, the first speech was probably not even referenced at dinner; therefore this was the first time Dr. Busey, who did not serve in the House, heard about Lincoln speaking. Third, Busey's recollections were recorded many years after the events took place.

and read my ... speech, and perhaps, scared anew by it. After you get over your scare, read it over again, sentence by sentence, and tell me honestly what you think of it."

Herndon wrote again to Lincoln before receiving this letter. Herndon argued that the president had the power to invade a foreign nation if necessary to repel a threat, and that the president was the sole judge of his own conduct in such a case. Lincoln pointed out that this position "neither the President himself, nor any friend of his, so far as I know, has ever taken." The president argued that American blood was shed on American soil, "false in fact, as you can prove that your house is not mine. That soil was not ours; and Congress did not annex or attempt to annex it." And if the president could indeed invade whenever he felt it necessary, "You allow him to make war at pleasure." The framers of the Constitution were motivated to give war-making power to Congress by kings' "involving and impoverishing their people in wars, pretending generally, if not always, that the good of the people was the object." This was something the Founders believed to be "the most oppressive of all kingly oppressions," and they thus built our Constitution so "that no one man should hold the power of bringing this oppression upon us." If this were Herndon's argument, he "places our President where kings have always stood."[11]

The people and papers of Illinois were not content to hear Lincoln's arguments with the open mind of Herndon. As Herndon's letters portended, the fire would not come exclusively from his partisan opponents.

Reverend John M. Peck, an ally and friend of Lincoln's, was recorded in the *Belleville Advocate* as defending the war and opposing the resolutions. "It is the first effort of the kind I have known, made by one appearing to me to be, intelligent, right minded, and <u>impartial</u>," Lincoln fretted. According to Peck, Mexican general Paredes had come to power in the last of December 1845, and from that moment, all hopes of avoiding war by negotiation vanished. All this happened three months before Taylor crossed the Nueces. "You evidently intend to have it inferred that General Taylor was sent across the desert, in <u>consequence</u> of the destruction of all hope of peace, in the overthrow of Herara by Paredes." What is missing is that Taylor was ordered to cross on January 13—the three months was the total time it took for the order to reach Taylor, for preparations for the march, and for the march itself. "Not in the president's waiting to hear the knell of peace . . . The U.S. Army marched into the Rio Grande and a peaceful Mexican settlement. Fort Brown was built in a Mexican cotton field. Then I ask, is the precept 'whatsoever ye would that men should do to you, do ye even so to them' absolute?—of no force?—of no application?"

Much of the reaction was to Lincoln's style, not his substance. Two of his allies in Illinois told him that his position was wrong, and that of Senator Crittenden correct. "Please wherein is my position different from his?" Lincoln asked. "Has he ever approved the President's conduct in the beginning of the war, or his mode or objects in prosecuting it? Never. He condemns both. True, he votes supplies, and so do I. What, then, is the difference, except that he is a great man and I am a small one?" [12]

Lincoln defended his outspokenness; neutrality was not an option. "Their [Democratic war hawks'] very first act in Congress was to present a preamble declaring that war existed by the act of Mexico, and the Whigs were obliged to vote on it, and this policy is followed up by them," their only option to "tell the truth." In the House, Taylor had some forty supporters, all of whom had voted for the Ashmun amendment. Two of them, Colonel Haskell and Major Gaines, were veterans of the war. Only one Whig veteran in Mexico (Captain Bishop) preferred a different candidate.

The most common fallacy about the Spot Resolutions speech is that it was largely ignored, both in and out of the House chamber. It is true that the resolutions never came to a vote, but as will be seen, Lincoln's speech received plenty of attention and fomented plenty of excitement—on the House floor and elsewhere.

It is sometimes alleged that the speech was never debated. This by itself would not be remarkable; for the House to formally consider and vote on the proposals, Lincoln or someone else would have had to obtain the floor and try to move them forward. He did not do this, perhaps because his point was made, and especially in light of the Ashmun amendment, in which the House had formally expressed itself. Had Lincoln spoken just a few days earlier, perhaps his bill would have been the vehicle the House used to condemn Polk and the war. The House usually met for three or four hours a day, members were entitled to one-hour speeches, much of the time on the floor was occupied with housekeeping items such as approval of the journals, or presentation of citizens' petitions, and a simple roll call would average twenty minutes of the House's time. Simply put, obtaining the floor was incredibly difficult, and generally the House would move past the subject one wished to discuss by the time one had the opportunity. In spite of this, the speech had no fewer than three responses in the House, and perhaps one in the Senate.

As was first noted by Donald Riddle, three members of the House sought to refute Lincoln's speech directly. Riddle also argued that Stephen Douglas in the Senate responded to the speech without referencing it or its maker. A reading of Douglas's speech, which does address some of the same issues as Lincoln's, is not conclusive. Douglas addressed his remarks generally to the Senate, and to one senator in particular, and they frankly could have been a response to a number of other speeches.

But six days after this supposed dud of a speech, John Jameson of Missouri responded directly to Lincoln's spot resolutions. The tone of the speech was angry, and the performance no doubt fiery—one member remembered Jameson as "never sober." [13]

"Will our country ever be in the right?" [14] Jameson asked. In "more than three score years and ten of our national existence, we have never once been in the right." They should "devise any plan by which we may, at some time, be right for once. . . . Cannot their united wisdom devise some way or means by which for one time, we may be in the right?

"The gentleman from Illinois, from the Hardin and Baker district, took a strange position before the American Congress for such a Representative. Yes, sir; look back and see what your Hardin did." And Baker. And Shields. In light of this, "It is astonishing to me how the gentleman could make the speech here which he has." Patriots did not ask whether war was right or wrong, Jameson argued, but rather are we at war?

Eight days after a speech that was allegedly ignored came a response from John Robinson of Indiana. In it he referenced Lincoln's address as being unique and specifically worthy of refutation. "That was a very remarkable statement. He had never ventured to tell the people of Springfield district, Illinois, when electioneering for his seat, that the war was unnecessary and unconstitutional; but after he got here he could venture to declare it! How many gentlemen were in a like predicament, who had gotten here without committing themselves on this question, perhaps the subsequent events of the session would declare. The country, however looked to them to take their position."

Douglas's speech came on February 1. "You [war opponents] voted for it. You voted the men and money. You voted to recognize the legal and constitutional existence of the war. You helped pass the law, and made it the sworn duty of the president to see it faithfully executed. It is your war, as much as his and ours; and you will not be permitted to escape your share of its responsibility, while you participate in the credit which you claim from having given it your support." (Here he is clearly responding to other senators.) But perhaps Douglas was referring to Lincoln when he said, "The precise spot [where war began] is not stated, but the locality is well known to have been on this left bank of the Rio Grande."

The next response to Lincoln came from Howell Cobb of Georgia on February 2.[15] Cobb was held in very high regard, and would serve as Speaker of the House in the Thirty-first Congress. A remarkable twenty-one days after Lincoln's speech, one of the most powerful Democrats in Congress felt the need to take on Lincoln directly. This fact cannot be reconciled with the assertion that Lincoln's speech was little noticed. "I ask him and his party to inform us what particular spot it was that the army first put their foot upon, that constituted the commencement of this unnec-essary and unconstitutional war? Was it when they first entered Mexico ter-ritory? If so, where is that Mexican territory? Was it when they first entered upon the disputed territory? If so, where is that disputed territory? I desire this information, for the purpose of ascertaining the exact time and place, when and where this gross outrage of involving the country in an unjust war was committed." Lincoln pointed out that the troops in Corpus Christi were already in disputed territory, as they were west of the Sabine River. (Cobb would later prove a far more serious antagonist to Lincoln. In 1861, he was directly responsible for leading Georgia out of the Union, an act that precipitated the departure of six other states.[16] It is thought that if he had simply remained neutral, Georgia would have stayed put.)[17]

David Outlaw of North Carolina had gone to watch the Senate on January 12, but wrote that "Mr. Lincoln of Illinois spoke yesterday in the House." While his correspondence was detailed, he never simply recorded a list of speakers, especially those whom he wasn't present to hear. Artemas Hale of Massachusetts wrote in his diary that day, "Mr. Lincoln spoke," even though Hale, too, did not list the names of speakers for their own sake. In fact, one of Hale's Massachusetts constituents, Solomon Lincoln, wrote him: "Our attention has been arrested in this quarter of the country by the able speech of Hon. Mr. Lincoln of Illinois made this session, in the House of Representatives, and it has been a source of gratification to those bearing his name to know that the old stock has not degenerated by being transplanted. On the contrary, it exhibits fresh vigor in the fertile soil of the West."[18]

Back in Illinois, nonpartisan citizen gatherings met to denounce Lincoln. One such meeting "resolved, that Abe Lincoln, the author of the spotty resolutions against his own country, may they be long remembered by his constituents, but may they cease to remember him, except to rebuke him— they have done so much for him, but he has done nothing for them, save the stain he inflicted on their proud name of patriotism and glory, in the part they have taken for the country's cause."

Near Morgan County, home of the fallen war hero Hardin, the people gathered resolved to "express the deep mortification inflicted on us by our representative in Congress, in his base, dastardly, and treasonable assault upon President Polk, in his disgraceful speech upon the present war, and in the resolutions offered by him against his own government, in flagrant vio- lation to the views of a majority of our Congressional electors . . . disgrace so black, so mortifying, so unanswerable. Such insulting opprobrium cast upon our citizens and soldiers, such black odium and infamy heaped upon the living brave and illustrious dead can but invite the indignation of every true Illinoisan, the disgust of republicans and condemnation of men. There- fore henceforth will this Benedict Arnold of our district be known here only as the Ranchero Spotty of one term."

The *Peoria Press* predicted Lincoln's eternal association with this act, say- ing, "The miserable man of spots will pass unnoticed save in the execration that his treason will bring upon his name." Lincoln "displayed the treason of Arnold," and he "will be dead whilst among the living."[19]

But it was always the *Register*, the organ of the Democratic Party, that drove the knife the hardest. It likened Lincoln's beliefs to a disease, and wrote his obituary: "This fever does not prevail to any very alarming extent in Illinois. The only case we have heard of that is likely to prove fatal, is that of poor 'spotty Lincoln' of this state. This 'spotty' gentleman had a severe attack of the 'spotted fever' in Washington City not long since, and fears were entertained that the disease would 'strike in,' and carry him off. We have not heard of any other person in Washington being on the 'spotted list' and it is probable that the disease died with the patient. What an epitaph: 'Died of the Spotted Fever.' Poor Lincoln!"

The *Sangamo Journal* referred to Lincoln's speech as "an able one ... listened to by the House with marked attention."[20] The *Missouri Republican* called the speech "one of great power, and replete with the strongest and most conclusive arguments. He commanded the attention of the House, which none but a strong man can do; and this speech, together with a happy and effectual off hand speech he made the other day on the subject of the controversy between the postmaster general and the Baltimore and Richmond Railroad Company, placed him in the very first rank in the House. This, however, is not more than what his friends, who knew him, expected, and the people of his district and indeed of the state may well feel proud of such a representative."[21]

Back home, the *Journal*, which had long been making similar charges against Polk, defended Lincoln. It dared the *Register* to print the speech unedited, as it had done on February 10, to let its readers see something more than its sinister spin. "The speech is an able one," argued the *Journal*, "and was listened to with marked attention. The *Register* has denounced this speech in all the set styles with which the editor is familiar—will he do the member justice to publish his speech? Or does he fear to have it go to his readers?"[22]

The *Register*'s lame response was an offer to print Lincoln's speech in total, if the *Journal* would print Douglas's remarks on the Ten Regiment Bill. The *Journal* pointed out that it would publish it in a second if it thought it would hurt Douglas and the Democratic Party.[23]

CHAPTER 10

WAR AND PEACE

Outside the grand eastern entrance to the United States Capitol stood two statues by Luigi Persico. Facing the doorway to the Rotunda, *Peace* stood on the left, *War* to the right, in niches carved especially for them. *Peace* held "a fruit bearing branch of the olive, which she is extending towards *War*." *War*, for his part, was "represented in the attitude of listening to *Peace* . . . his head inclined toward his companion," but with a hand on his sword, and the other holding his shield.[1] Between those two choices, war and peace, the House would do their best to decide in the winter of 1848.

The Ashmun amendment had put the Whigs on the record, but now less symbolic and more substantive measures would have to be considered. One member wrote, "We have solemnly resolved that the Mexican War was unnecessarily and unconstitutionally commenced, we believe that it is now prosecuted, not as is pretended to obtain an honorable peace, but for conquest, and yet we do not have the moral courage to arrest it, and save the country from the consequences."[2]

The consequences were potentially terrifying, not limited to more dead and wounded, or more money spent. Polk had abandoned the negotiating position he had when he sent Trist south the previous April. If taking California and New Mexico was no longer Polk's price for peace, then what exactly would satisfy him?

In January, Whig senator William Mangum of North Carolina called on the president for that answer. He offered a resolution asking for "estimates, places, etc. for accomplishing the objects of the present war, and to name those objects."[3] This seemingly benign measure was defeated on party lines, 22–20.

To the House would fall the responsibility of reining the president in. One of the primary ways in which they accomplished this was through their oversight power, making various inquires of the administration on the origins and conduct of the war. The first of these asked for "any instructions which may have been given to any of the officers of the army or navy of the United States, or other persons . . . issued in January 1846, for the march of the army from the Nueces river, across the 'stupendous deserts' which intervene, to the Rio Grande."[4]

On the day of Lincoln's spot resolutions speech, the Speaker presented the House with a message from the president.

"The customary and usual reservations contained in calls of either House of Congress upon the Executive for information relating to our intercourse with foreign nations has been omitted in the resolution before me. The call of the House is unconditional . . . it has been a subject of serious deliberation with me, whether I could, consistently with my constitutional duty and my sense of the public interests involved and to be affected by it, violate an important principle, always heretofore held sacred by my predecessors, as I should do by a compliance with the request of the House. President Washington, in a message to the House of Representatives of the 30th of March, 1796, declined to comply with a request" for instructions and correspondence related to the Jay Treaty, which had already been ratified.

But the House had a member who also had some institutional knowledge. John Quincy Adams said, "The state of my voice is such that it is not in my power to make to this House the observations which I should otherwise have felt it my duty to make upon this case." He believed the House entitled to the information, and that this refusal was without precedent. In Washington's example, the call for information had a built-in exception. He also remembered that the House had formally declared against President Washington. "The very memory of Washington, by everybody in this country, at this time (and by none more than myself), is revered next to worship—the President was wrong in that particular instance, and went too far to deny the power of the House; and as to his reasons, I never thought they were sufficient in that case." He even remembered that the Democratic Party opposed this move of Washington's. "I should say much more, sir, if I had the power."

As February began, there was a serious fear that the United States would swallow all of Mexico.[5] Democratic congressmen Stanton of Tennessee and Hannegan of Indiana were openly in favor of taking the entire country.[6] Senator Rusk of Texas had encouraged Polk, early in the new year, not to rule out the annexation of all of Mexico.[7] Polk assured him that his present position, which was open to that possibility, had not changed and would not change.[8]

Even some Democrats were alarmed at the "All Mexico" movement. Isaac Holmes of South Carolina, fearful that America intended to swallow Mexico whole, introduced a resolution calling for American forces to retreat from the Rio Grande.[9] Holmes's Senate colleague from the Palmetto State, John C. Calhoun, introduced a resolution in the Senate stating that conquering all of Mexico "is inconsistent with our principles and war aims."[10] Calhoun argued that the "avowed objects for which the war has been prosecuted . . . are well known not to be the real objects."[11] While people such as Giddings wanted no land from Mexico, because they thought it unjust or feared slavery might be introduced there, Calhoun agreed with them for the opposite reason: he and others proceeded from racist concerns about permitting millions of Mexicans to become Americans ("We have never dreamt of incorporating into our Union any but the Caucasian race").[12]

One constituent wrote Congressman George Marsh of Vermont, "The idea of conquering and colonizing all Mexico is utterly preposterous," and declared, "I would not take a foot of land if it is to be cursed with slavery."[13]

Alexander Stephens gave a speech that left a strong impression upon his fellow Young Indian and close friend, Abraham Lincoln. "There is no getting over it, or around it, or under it; and until history shall falsify the events of the past, there can be no mistake as to the real paternity of this war, gentlemen seem so anxious to have us believe is now actually in quest of an author, or in search of a father. The true cause lies at the door of your own executive. He commenced it by the exercise of power never conferred upon him, and in a wanton outrage upon the Constitution of his country. Upon his head rests all the responsibility, with all its force and weight, and there it will continue to rest."[14]

Stephens refused to accept that annexation meant war, and argued that Taylor had been moved to the Rio Grande to provoke a war. "Had the President the power rightfully under this Constitution, to do this? I answer in this House, before the American people and in the face of Heaven, most emphatically not."

Lincoln sat in tears well after the speech. He wrote to Herndon specifically for the purpose of saying that Stephens, "a little slim pale-faced consumptive man, with a voice like Logan's, has just concluded the very best speech of an hour's length I have ever heard." If it read as well as it sounded, Lincoln pledged, he would forward a copy.

The friendship between Alexander Stephens, the future vice president of the Confederacy, and Abraham Lincoln is among the most interesting to ever develop in Congress. Stephens would later recall that he was as close to Lincoln as any other member, except perhaps his home state friend Robert Toombs. Despite their differences over slavery, their bond seems to have been forged within the small circle of Taylor supporters in Congress. It was a relationship that no doubt deepened over what they had in common. Lincoln had lost one—and Stephens both—of his parents at an early age.[15] Both had grown up in poverty. Both had tried to scratch out a living in careers that left them dissatisfied before turning to the law. Both men had served in their state legislatures before being elected to Congress. Lincoln and Stephens were both frequently described as men of unimpeachable integrity.

Congressman Stephens was described as a "small, slender man, with stooping shoulders and a pale yellow complexion, a sharp shrill voice, and nothing about him at all remarkable, or which indicates genius, except a very black sparkling eye. He is . . . one of the ablest and most eloquent men in our House, and of pure morals, and a high sense of honor."[16] Horace Greeley remembered him as maybe "the most acute, and perhaps the ablest member of that House."[17]

Stephens lived near Lincoln on Capitol Hill[18] and was known to drop by the boardinghouses of his friends and colleagues.[19] No doubt he and Lincoln passed many a night together discussing their many mutual interests, presidential politics, and the war. As for the war, the president was about to hand his detractors an entirely new reason for outrage. On February 3, a *Sangamo Journal* headline blared, "General Scott suspended from the command of the Army in Mexico," which the article went on to call a "monstrous injustice."[20] Scott had once been sent to Mexico to steal Taylor's laurels. Now the administration, based on the allegations of Polk's political ally, would seek publicly to discredit Scott. Scott had been accused of disrespecting the president, about which the *Journal* noted: "If everybody is to be punished who is wanting in respect to President Polk, there will be the most universal proscription that has been since the times of Nero or Caligula."[21]

The Whigs in the House pushed back, demanding from the president information about the court-martial and issuing a resolution of thanks to Scott and his troops for gallantry. It passed 167–1, with Joshua Giddings the lone "no" vote.[22] On April 17, a demand for certain correspondence between Winfield Scott and Secretary of War William Marcy was passed without roll call, even with a two-thirds majority voting to suspend the rules.[23]

Robert Winthrop, who had previously served as Speaker of the Massachusetts House, knew that doing the job effectively meant building relationships with his members, understanding their priorities and concerns.

Shortly after his contentious selection as Speaker, Winthrop "took a house, engaged a French cook, and began to give two large dinners a week, with smaller ones as occasion served."[24] Winthrop would recall that he "was not one of those, if any there were, who discerned in Abraham Lincoln at that period the promise of exceptional fame; but he liked him personally, finding him shrewd and kindly, with an air of reserved force."[25] Winthrop was a few months younger than Lincoln, and the two could not have been more different in personal and educational pedigree.

At 5:30 p.m., February 2, it was Lincoln's turn to be invited.[26] Winthrop lived "quite in style," remembered Artemas Hale, one of the members invited to dine on the same night as Lincoln.[27] Winthrop entertained thirteen that night, Lincoln included, which was a typical number for his twice-weekly gatherings (his table could accommodate as many as sixteen if necessary).[28] The invitation would have been sent out nine days before, with a response expected.[29]*

One member who dined on a different day recalled they were served "raw oysters, then dough, then roast beef, then oysters ... then boiled turkey, and ham, then venison steak, then macaroni, then partridges or pidgions [sic] ... then duck." Then there was dessert: pumpkin pie, ice cream, apples, oranges, grapes, and figs. Everything was carved by and brought to the table by servants. Half after nine, there was 'the best coffee I have seen in many a day,' Madeira wines and champagne and sherry."[30] This dinner had all the trappings of a marvelous celebration, but the group at Winthrop's that evening did not yet know that they had real cause for rejoicing. For as they feasted and drank champagne, the indefatigable Nicholas Trist had succeeded in his mission to Mexico. That very day, Trist signed the Treaty of Guadalupe Hidalgo, consisting of the objectives set forth by Polk the previous April. But would Polk really send a treaty he now disagreed with, in terms of substance was well as process, to the Senate?

The morning after, Artemas Hale wrote his wife that he had just dined with a future president. Winthrop "is probably looking forward for more and higher stations in the government of the country and I think quite likely he will realize them."[31]

Lincoln had just turned thirty-nine, a few months older than Winthrop. One of these two men would see his political career destroyed at the age of forty-one. Would anyone have guessed it would be Winthrop, instead of Lincoln?

The day after his dinner at Winthrop's, Lincoln probably attended the Whig caucus that set the national convention for Philadelphia in June. One participant left having "great doubts whether we can elect any person; and what is more whether we deserve success."[32]

---

*Those invited that night were Hugh White, Joseph Mullin, William Lawrence, Orlando Kellogg, and former member Henry Seaman of New York, John Crowell and David Fisher of Ohio, John Farrelly of Pennsylvania, John Crisfield of Maryland, Elisha Embree, "Mr. Lincoln of Ilinois," Charles Hudson and Artemas Hale of Massachusetts, all Whigs.

A February 7 advertisement in the *National Intelligencer* proclaimed a "National Birth Night Ball," to be held in Jackson Hall in celebration of Washington's birthday. The funds would be used to build a new monument in the capital to honor the first president. Each state had a member from the House and Senate; for Illinois, they were Lincoln and Douglas.

Meanwhile, the House had to grapple with the president's request for a loan. Polk was certain the Whigs were trying to block the financing, in order to ruin the public credit or force withdrawal from Mexico.[33]

While only a handful of members had voted to cut off funding for the war at any given time, increasingly voters and members were beginning to agree with the man who wrote his congressman: "Withholding supplies is the only means certain in my opinion to secure peace."[34] Albert Gallatin, secretary of the Treasury under Jefferson and Madison, wrote Congressman Marsh of Vermont that they had "but one efficient power, that of refusing supplies."[35]

Samuel Vinton of Ohio moved to reduce the amount requested, from $18.5 million to $16 million.[36] In the previous year, the House had been told that their authorized loans and appropriations would not only be enough, but in fact leave a surplus. Now they were asked for a remedial appropriation as well as this loan.[37] Vinton offered that any questioning in the last session would have resulted in accusations of wanting "to impair the public credit" and "give aid and comfort to Mexico."[38]

Democrat Albert Brown of Mississippi argued for a blank check to the president. "I will vote for a loan, I will vote for treasury notes, and for a tax on tea and coffee; I will vote for men, regulars and volunteers; in short, sir, I will vote for anything and everything that may be needed to prosecute this war to such a conclusion as the government can accept without dishonor."[39]

During the days of debate, Lincoln's housemate John Strohm wrote, "We are doing very little here, except talking about the war—what will eventually be done it is impossible to foresee, but I am afraid that we shall not be able to stop the war and that it will continue another year at least." He noted wryly, "It will take a long time before the country will recover from the injuries inflicted by the administration of James K. Polk."[40]

When Polk's supporters tried to end debate on the measure and force a vote, Lincoln cast three votes in opposition.[41] In two unrecorded votes,

Polk's request was chopped down to $16 million,[42] while another amendment made clear that this was not a blank check, but rather all funds from the loan would be first appropriated by Congress.[43]

Whig John Palfrey of Massachusetts said, "Fighting seemed to many people a very agreeable thing, as long as they were not made to feel how expensive a luxury it was . . . there was many a constituency in this country, now very greedy for blood and glory, who would not receive more than one visit from the collector before they would be sending instructions to their Representatives here to put a stop to the war without delay."[44] At the end the vote was 192–14 in favor of the loan request as amended.[45]

President James K. Polk was the only one of Lincoln's predecessors whom Lincoln had the chance to watch up close. Observing the House tap the brakes on his war efforts, boxing Polk in, Lincoln took to heart the necessity of a good relationship with Congress and maintaining public opinion for the war. Polk had prosecuted his war with two Whig generals, whom he fought with incessantly, with the results sometimes being made public. Lincoln, by contrast, would embrace his Democratic generals, making sure that they, and therefore their constituencies, were happy. Lincoln would also appoint a number of officers who represented different ethnic, geographical, and partisan backgrounds, many of whom were not well qualified for their positions, but who helped Lincoln avoid the fate of Polk.

CHAPTER 11

NOT A SINECURE

"If you knew what a mountain of labor and anxiety I have been opposed by . . . nobody can conceive the amount of toil and trouble which I have been obliged to encounter. . . ."

—Robert C. Winthrop

D espite the fights over the war, slavery, and the presidency, Congressman Lincoln was primarily concerned with the unglamorous duties of office.

Like any other member, then or now, he served as an ombudsman between his constituents and the national government. Lincoln probably received twenty to thirty letters a week and sent out roughly the same number,[1] some from his fifty-five thousand constituents,[2] others from Whigs throughout Illinois, owing to his special status as the only representative of their party in the House. Lincoln reported receiving three hundred letters in the first two months of the second session (a number that may have been higher than average, in light of Taylor's incoming administration and the crush for jobs). During debates on the House floor or back at Sprigg's, where he had more room, Lincoln would respond to the requests and inquiries of those he represented. Some members had an orderly system for responding to constituents. It is likely that Lincoln did not. Working in Lincoln's favor was the lack of places he could lose paperwork. The Lincoln and Herndon law office "had no filing cabinets and no files," and an unwieldy stack of papers, on top of which Lincoln wrote, "When you can't find it anywhere else, look in this."[3]

"I groan at the sight of my mail," wrote George Marsh.[4]

David Outlaw said, "The whole system of doing business is artificial and complicated instead of being what it ought to be, plain and simple."[5] He recorded, "I have so many letters to write, it occupies a good deal of my time. The office of representative is no sinecure, and many of its duties is the most tiresome drudgery,"[6] and once referred to himself as "a mere laborer, who is to be occupied so many hours a day."[7] Outlaw wrote that "a man has no leisure here. When he is not engaged on committees, or in the House, he has to be either writing letters to his constituents, or franking documents to them, and when he has gotten through with this miserable drudgery, ten to one, if someone who is provoking about does not hop in upon him." As he wrote that letter, a constituent from Norfolk had just left his room after an unannounced visit.[8]

Members would perform very basic constituent services, which today would be handled by the most junior staff or even interns. For instance, Lincoln might personally visit the pension office to hand in paperwork on behalf of a constituent.[9] In one instance he wrote to the government auditor on behalf of the father of a fallen soldier, seeking compensation.[10]

When the bureaucracy was not responsive, claims from citizens were presented directly to the House of Representatives (for only Congress could appropriate money). These claimants could range from a citizen who felt that a pension or bounty land claim had been unjustly denied, to a government contractor who felt the terms were not being fulfilled, to someone injured by the government. Most bills introduced in that Congress began "A bill for the relief of . . ."

Congress spent hours evaluating claims, though members were in the worst position to do so. The member presenting the petition had a perverse incentive to see it fulfilled; even if the claim wasn't meritorious, it would represent only a small debit to the national government, while earning the member the gratitude of a constituent. Though the Committee on Claims would review the cases and make recommendations, the average member did not have the information necessary to cast an intelligent vote. But the stakes were high; voting yes might mean unjustly rewarding an illegitimate claimant, but voting no might mean denying someone his due, in many cases crippling him financially.

Lincoln successfully pressed the case of Anson Henry, an Illinois friend who had loaned money toward the state's war effort and now sought reimbursement. Lincoln also pushed for the claim of William Fuller and Orlando Saltmarsh, contractors with the Post Office who were owed money,[11] as well as for John Dawson, who had served as Illinois pension clerk during Tyler's administration and had not received his salary.[12]

Congress would soon create the U.S. Court of Claims to evaluate cases and then make recommendations, but it was President Lincoln who successfully proposed giving the court the opportunity to resolve them. The result was thousands of hours of congressional work time saved, citizens allowed to have a fair presentation to a neutral magistrate, and decisions made independently of political influence.

Letters from constituents spanned every subject under the sun, from inquiries on what could be done with Continental money,[13] to how weights and measures were determined,[14] to reimbursements for a constituent who had lost a horse in the war.[15]

Congressmen were the point of contact for dealing with any federal agency, including the patent office. One constituent sent his representative a patent for a new plow,[16] while another asked a member to see if there was a patent on making starch from corn.[17]

Since the American Revolution, wars had been financed in part by land bounties for soldiers. With so many returning from Mexico, gaining access to their reward became a frequent reason for recourse to their member of Congress.

Though not all articulated it quite like this, one of Embree's constituents summed up the general sentiment: "As one of your 'respected and enlightened constituents' I have of course a chartered right to be as troublesome in bothering you with letters, requests, commissions, & etc, as I may, in my sovereign leisure incline."[18] Some certainly took these letters very seriously. One of Embree's Indiana colleagues wrote a twenty-eight-page response to a constituent when asked about his viewpoints on various topics.[19]

Hardin had received a letter a month before his swearing in, pointing out, "You are the Representative of the Whigs of Illinois and must expect to need the shoulders of Atlas."[20] Lincoln now occupied the same spot. While numerous letters to Hardin appeared to apologize for the difficulty they knew he was under ("We are well aware of the great burden which your position as the only Whig member from Illinois imposes"),[21] Lincoln never received any such disclaimer.

But far and away the most common request was for a position with the government. The American attitude toward public employment had turned toward entitlement, or an act of charity, or a reward for service to the political party. Very few made a pretense of office seeking on the merits. This system burdened and at times paralyzed the national government of the United States.

These job seekers sought positions in the military, posts in the diplomatic corps, various local posts, and people who would take anything.[22]

Polk wrote, "I sincerely wish I had no office to bestow."[23] "In every appointment which the President makes he disappoints half a dozen or more applicants and their friends, who . . . will prefer any other candidate in the next election, while the person appointed attributes the appointment to his own superior merit and does not even feel obliged by it."[24]

No job was considered beyond politics: Caleb Smith recommended a midshipman to the secretary of the navy, pointing out, "There has not been a midshipman appointed from that district for the last fifteen years."[25]

Robert Winthrop, with the most jobs to give out after Polk, wrote, "If you knew what a mountain of labor and anxiety I have been opposed by, for a week past . . . nobody can conceive the amount of toil and trouble which I have been obliged to encounter at the threshold of my new dignity. . . . If I had been president of the United States I could not have been more constantly beset by applicants for office."[26]

Winthrop continued, "All the women want to sell apples and cake in the Rotunda or under the Committee Rooms." Then there were the "besieging and beseeching orphans and widows" who "have clustered around me like bees, and where they could extract no honey have left a sting." Finally, he felt "literally compelled to lock myself up in my room, and turn a deaf ear to the incessant raps at my door. . . ."[27]

Another member said, "The business of office seeking to the extent to which it is carried on here is not only disgusting but alarming." Men seemed "determined not to fulfill the curse of God upon man by curing their bread by the sweat of their brow if they can help it."[28]

One senator told the story of how he was once creatively courted to support John Spencer for the Supreme Court. Spencer was then the secretary of the Treasury, and his nomination was in trouble in the Senate. A young man wanted a job in Spencer's department, and was assured of this if he could deliver one more senator. The young applicant's beautiful sister was introduced to the senator, "dishabille" ("the state of being partly or scantily clothed"), and told him "if he would vote to confirm the nomination she could deny him nothing."[29] Polk was more repulsed by female emissaries than anything, calling it "disgusting that women are sent to me to seek office for their worthless relations."[30]

Polk was normally unfailingly polite, but one can trace his rapidly accelerating anger with the process throughout his term. "The people of the U.S. have no idea of the extent to which the President's time, which ought to be devoted to more important matters, is occupied by voracious and often unprincipled persons who seek office,"[31] he wrote. He believed it such a great crisis that he was determined to pen a book on the subject during his retirement. If Polk had lived to publish his thoughts, perhaps the outrage could have prompted civil service reform a generation earlier, freeing his successors and preventing the assassination of President James Garfield by a disappointed job seeker.

Polk thought them a "herd of lazy worthless people who come to Washington for office instead of going to work and by some honest calling making a livelihood."[32]

Polk called "the rage for office . . . the besetting evil of the times."[33] He noted, "Every president must be greatly weakened because he cannot gratify the craving desire of his professed political friends for office."[34] If he could fit ten people in every position in his government, he still wouldn't make everyone happy.[35]

It was not atypical for Polk to spend much or most of his day interacting with job seekers, which, as the president of a republic, he was expected to be available to do. He would find himself "perfectly overrun" with people "seeking offices for themselves ... enough to exhaust the patience and destroy the good temper of any man on earth, to bear the daily boring which I have to endure."[36] The requests were "daily and unceasing," and limited Polk's ability to get his already difficult job done.[37]

Many members of Congress felt the same way. Outlaw likened the seekers to "a man addicted to strong drink, they require ... public employment."[38] Wentworth complained that "[f]ew persons who have never visited Washington can form any conception of how much of the time of the executive is consumed with applications for office."[39]

Some of the requests centered on military appointments. These bewildered Lincoln "more than most any thing else." Even if the president had such appointments to give out, he noted, "He could hardly be expected to give them to Whigs, at the solicitation of a Whig member of Congress."[40] Polk didn't understand them either, taking notice of "very great ... press by members of Congress and others for small offices, chiefly in the army."[41]

The serious, professional Polk increasingly lost his patience (and nearly his mind) over the never-ending hordes of seekers, the "throng of persons who flock to Washington to get office instead of going to work and making a living by honest industry. Much of my time is taken up in this way and I am sometimes exceedingly worried by it." And the problem was seldom that Polk didn't have the jobs to give; it was the quality of the seekers: "A large proportion of those who thus trouble me are unworthy, and unfit for the places they seek, and many of them are mere loafers who are too lazy to work and wish to be supported by the public."[42] By the end of his term, he'd decided the office-seeking class "are certainly the most contemptible race on earth."[43] Unless he was feeling charitable, he referred to them simply as "the most contemptible of our race."[44]

When the marshal of the District of Columbia grew ill, it triggered a half dozen applications to Polk for his job, just in case he died.[45]

The constant aggravations and political pressures meant social outlets were needed in equal measure. It was said the "parties, during the winter months, are numerous and well attended.... The people of Washington are distinguished for their hospitality and courtesy. All who visit it, if they have any claims to respectability, are invited to their evening or dinner parties."[46]

The Washington diplomatic corps was a fixture on the party circuit; at the time the young capital featured seventeen representatives, from Europe and Latin America.*

Colonel William W. Seaton, mayor of Washington and publisher of the *National Intelligencer*, had a party at his mansion Friday, February 18, 1848, on E Street for journalists and Whig members of Congress.

"The first homage of nearly all, as they entered, was paid to John Quincy Adams, who sat on a sofa, and was the first person to be greeted by nearly every guest, 'his form slightly bowed by time, his eyes weeping, and a calm seriousness in his expression.'" Here it is very likely that Lincoln and Adams met. Unfortunately, this most fascinating relationship of the Thirtieth Congress is one we know virtually nothing about. John Quincy Adams was the living link between the Founding Fathers and Abraham Lincoln. Surely Lincoln, as an eager student of history, wanted to know of Washington, Jefferson, Madison, Franklin, and the others. He would have had questions on the Revolution, or the founding of the constitutional republic. On a less lofty note, Lincoln might have mentioned that he'd once lived on Adams Street, or that Adams had signed his father's land patent for "west 80 acres of land in Posey County, Indiana."[47] Adams embraced his elder statesman role in the House, and was free with assistance or advice to those who sought it. Surely Lincoln did, and surely he was obliged, and it is regrettable that we have no idea what was said.

One time the Illinois delegation was gathered on the House floor disagreeing about the correct pronunciation of their state's name. They enlisted the wisdom of Adams, who remarked that based on his observations, the proper way to say it was "all noise." But that event, and Adams's presence at the entrance to Seaton's party, are the only two incidents in which we can be reasonably sure they met.

Seaton's affair had a tension of joy and sadness. Daniel Webster was absent, learning that day of the death of his son Edward, a major in the army, of fever. But Clay was present with "kind words and pleasant smiles for all

---

*These were Russia, the Argentine Confederation, France, Spain, Chile, Peru, New Granada (Colombia), Portugal, Prussia, Belgium, Denmark, Austria, the Netherlands, the Kingdom of the Two Sicilies, Sweden, Great Britain, and Brazil.

his friends."[48] There was a "sumptuous collation, with much drinking of healths and many pledges to the success of the Whig cause."[49]

Outlaw remembered it "composed entirely of gentlemen . . . a perfect squeeze. Many of the most distinguished men in the country were there, and some of them did ample justice to the good things which our host had provided and especially his champagne."[50] After a night of partying with his colleagues, he said, "These politicians. These politicians. Heaven favor the republic if entrusted to their keeping."[51]

The day following this drunken revelry, cannons were fired "all the morning" in celebration of Buena Vista.[52] Perhaps many who had been at Seaton's covered their heads with a pillow and tried to get more rest.

In a badly divided Washington, a momentous event would soon come to pass that would bring them closer together, but so would one that would ultimately tear them apart.

On February 19, James Buchanan came to the White House, Trist's treaty in hand. The same Nicholas Trist who had been instructed in April, who had been recalled in December, and who had continued apace throughout the winter, breaking only to stick his thumb in Polk's eye, had secured a treaty consistent with the president's original terms.[53] The cabinet met in emergency session on the next day, a Sunday. Polk did not want to send it for ratification. He wanted to continue the war to some unspecified goal, of gaining more than California and New Mexico. While four members of his cabinet believed he should send it to the Senate for ratification, two felt he ought to reject it. These were no less than Buchanan and Treasury secretary Robert Walker, whose objections Polk had to take seriously even if they weren't aligned with his own.[54]

The next day, John Quincy Adams collapsed in the House of Representatives. The *Intelligencer* ran side-by-side columns, one on Adams's attack and the other on the arrival of the treaty of peace with Mexico.[55] "We can at least rejoice at one thing. . . . May it be perpetual!"

That paper also carried a frantic advertisement from the caterer of the Birth Night Ball, which would now have to be canceled. Addressed "To Families, Hotels, Etc," they were desperately hawking their perishables such as "ice cream, jellies, charlotte, meats, and oysters."[56]

That day, Polk convened the cabinet, discussing the possibility of dismissing the treaty.[57] The House "is opposed to my administration," Polk said. "They have falsely charged that the war was brought on and is continued by me with a view to the conquest of Mexico."[58] If he were now to reject a treaty that accomplished his April guidelines, he believed the House would stop sending him men and money. Polk, as stated in his message to Congress, estimated a loan of $20.5 million would be needed if the war lasted beyond June 30, 1849.[59] As enlistments expired, the hold that America now had on California and New Mexico might also be lost. Polk also admitted his worry about how this would affect the presidential election. If the Democrats lost, he believed, the Whigs would forfeit every advantage of the Trist treaty. Buchanan now argued for acquiring everything south to the Sierra Madre mountains, which Polk reminded him was a massive shift from the recent position. Buchanan, it seemed, had concluded that continued war favored him in the upcoming presidential contest. Polk was going to have to increasingly rely on his own counsel in this momentous hour.

The next day, the president resolved to send the Treaty of Guadalupe Hidalgo to the Senate for ratification.[60] The House Whigs had succeeded in forcing his hand, and ultimately an end to the war, one that did not put troops in danger, one that added millions of new acres to what was now a Pacific power, one that resolved the claims of American citizens against the Mexican government that had for too long been disregarded. The Whigs succeeded by a responsible application of their constitutional powers; the intense scrutiny of the loan bill, the modest downward adjustment from the president's request, the demands for documents and records, and the Ashmun amendment, along with all of the other bills introduced and speeches made in favor of ending the war. They had done it.

On February 22 and 23, the House met for five minutes, with Winthrop announcing the condition of Mr. Adams, and then adjourned.[61]

At 9 p.m. on February 23, Sergeant at Arms Nathan Sargent was summoned by Winthrop.[62] He believed the end was near for Adams and wanted all the officers of the House to be present. It was a rare moment of unity for the Speaker and his least favorite member, Joshua Giddings. Giddings was holding a vigil over Adams, no doubt aware that the cause of antislavery was now his to shoulder. "No more shall I receive aid and encouragement from his lips," he noted somberly.[63]

The weather in Washington the day before had been "bright and beautiful," but was now "cloudy, damp, and cold."[64] On February 24, Winthrop announced the death of Adams in the House.[65] That day, there was a joint meeting of the House and Senate. Present were Abraham Lincoln, Jefferson Davis, and their future vice presidents, Hannibal Hamlin of Maine, Andrew Johnson of Tennessee, and Alexander Stephens of Georgia, all gathered to make arrangements to bury a president.

Adams's seat would remain empty, and along with the hall was draped in black cloth for thirty days.[66] This included Clio, Muse of History, except for her hands, tablet, and pen, "whose alabaster whiteness" stood out against the dark drapery.[67]

A new era had begun. That very day, the *Communist Manifesto* was first being printed in London.[68] Revolutionary fervor was sweeping Europe, as events "in rapid succession drove Metternich from Vienna, the Hapsburg emperor from his throne, and the pope from the Vatican."[69] And in America, that last surviving connection to the Founding Fathers had left the government, even as the infant republic most needed his counsel, on the verge of a massive westward acquisition.

On February 26, Adams's funeral service was held in the House. The room was jammed with people, and spectators tried to crowd in wherever they could. Congressman Donnell threatened to sit on a woman who had commandeered his desk.[70] The crowd included "every body in the city, men, women, and children," and many from other cities, a crowd larger than either of the ones that had greeted, and later saw off, William Henry Harrison.[71]

Polk and his cabinet arrived around noon. He assumed the spot reserved for him on the dais, to the right of the Speaker, with Vice President George Dallas to Winthrop's left.[72] Every seat was full. Among those present were the Supreme Court, the uniformed officers of the army and navy, the diplomatic delegations of foreign nations, and dignitaries such as Dolley Madison. Reverend Gurley, the House chaplain, gave the eulogy. The funeral car was led by six white horses.[73] The procession included carriages, horsemen, and people on foot, the military, Odd Fellows, and the Fire Company.[74] It went to the congressional burying ground, one and a half miles east of the Capitol. Inside the ten acres, guarded by a "substantial brick wall," were "fine avenues and smaller walks, ornamented with trees and shrubs."[75]

The vault inside, which would keep Adams until his final journey to Massachusetts, was surrounded by a "neat iron railing" to protect against "resurrectionists" (a contemporary name for grave robbers who would sell bodies to doctors and medical schools).[76]

One writer described the surroundings as "mute but eloquent memorials of mortality, where the 'bitterness of hatred, the insatiability of avarice, and the fire of ambition' no longer exist. . . . We feel, in looking around us, that all is indeed vanity; that we are but ciphers in this beautiful world and that in a few fleeting years we too shall become a kneaded clod . . . and perhaps rest amid the very mouldering heaps over which our eye now coldly but pensively wanders."[77]

The death of John Quincy Adams triggered more introspection than would accompany that of the average octogenarian.

The *Sangamo Journal*, quoting from Thomas Gray's "Elegy Written in a Country Churchyard," reflected, "The paths of glory lead but to the grave."[78] Daniel Barringer wrote that in his entire life, he had never been "more forcibly and deeply impressed with the uncertainty of life and the empty vanity of all earthly glory."[79]

One of Lincoln's colleagues kept a journal that included his favorite quotations. Among these can be found, "I shall die and be forgotten and the world will go on just as if I had never been—and yet how I have lived! How I have longed! How I have aspired!"[80]

Charles Ingersoll of Pennsylvania wrote his daughter that this was "a useful lesson on the vanity of human wishes."[81]

Perhaps Lincoln felt a similar wistfulness. No one had experienced a fuller life than John Quincy Adams. It was not for that reason that his colleagues waxed philosophical, but for what Adams represented: a chance to make a permanent name for themselves in Clio's book, to have a life that would trigger a similar outpouring of affection at their own death.

Sargent thought of Adams as a true fixture, "the most attractive and interesting object in the Representative hall, especially to strangers . . . he was the Mont Blanc of the whole group."[82] When visitors to the Capitol realized which member was Adams, "It was followed by a long, scrutinizing look, as if to photograph his appearance on the tablet of memory."[83] Congressman McDowell called him "a living band of connection between the present and the past." McDowell remembered Adams fighting with people young enough to be his grandsons, how he "hour after hour, instructed the present generation by relating the sayings, opinions, and doings of the great lights of the past, with whom he was intimately associated, all ears attentive on such occasions, and every eye fixed upon 'the old man eloquent!'"

Lincoln was appointed to the Committee of Arrangements to oversee the funeral, which had one member from every state.[84] While this was certainly an honor, the committee size was found to be unwieldy, and power was delegated to a subcommittee of which Lincoln was not a member. It is sometimes erroneously reported that he played a major role in the funeral preparation, or even that he was a pallbearer, but this is incorrect.

During the short recess that followed the funeral, Lincoln spent two hours at Mount Vernon, which he described as very pleasant.[85] At the time, Mount Vernon was owned by John Augustine Washington, the first president's nephew.[86] Washington's gardens and greenhouse and his library were still the same as he left them.[87] Like the other tourists who visit this place, Lincoln would have wandered the grounds and paid his respects at the vault with Washington's grave. Having just concluded the funeral arrangements for one president, Lincoln's time spent at Washington's home reinforced the improbable greatness of the American story, impressed upon him the importance that it must continue, and provoked him to consider his place within it.

James K. Polk was also ready for a trip. No sooner did he send the treaty to the Senate than he learned that Buchanan and Walker, his secretaries of state and war, were whipping against him, encouraging a vote for rejection.[88]

The rest of the news was equally bleak. The Committee of Foreign Affairs in the Senate was likely to recommend rejection, with the appointment of a bipartisan committee to settle the war,[89] instead of ratification. A powerful coalition, North and South, was preparing to oppose the treaty. Daniel Webster was against any acquisition of territory, and would be voting no. Joining him was alleged to be Senator Hannegan, who wanted Polk to take all of Mexico,[90] along with a dozen Democrats who wanted more land than the treaty provided.[91] With such a disparate group combining for its defeat, the treaty was in grave trouble.[92]

Polk would soon note in his diary: "This day closes my third year in the presidential office. They have been years of incessant labor, anxiety, and responsibility."[93] Polk believed that the presidential question was interfering with governing and putting the treaty in peril. Nobody watching the White House through these days would have disagreed.

While the Senate considered the treaty, the House was back to resolutions on slavery and the presidential campaign.

On February 28, Harvey Putnam of New York offered a resolution calling for the new territories to remain free, to keep in place Mexico's ban on slavery. Lincoln voted to advance the resolution, but by 105–93, it was tabled.

That same day, Giddings took the floor to predict the end of the Whig Party. "I now hazard the declaration that on this principle of opposing all attempts of the Federal Government to extend and uphold slavery ... beyond that which is provided for in the Constitution, is now based a party, or the germ of a party, that will at no distant day become dominant in this nation...." Here Giddings was absolutely right. Eventually, a new party would be founded, primarily on the issue of limiting slavery, and which would within twelve years become the majority party in Washington. "Both Whigs and Democrats are in favor of General Taylor," Giddings continued, "not because they know his political sentiments to be right, but because they don't know whether they are right or wrong. They support him, not because they know his views, but because they don't know them."[94]

An Indiana Whig wrote Caleb Smith that in the event the Conscience Whigs ran a third-party candidate, if they were "capable of such folly the sooner the party is dissolved the better. You know very well that Taylor is not my first choice—but I am for him before Locoism."[95] Truman Smith, an original Young Indian who would mastermind Taylor's campaign apparatus, felt the general was the only candidate who could win. "I had rather have a sudden extinction of the party than a lingering death," Smith recorded, in response to people's fears.[96]

Even Barringer, who did embrace Taylor's candidacy, had a powerful expression of sympathy for Clay missing from Lincoln's correspondence. "If I had the power to make Clay President and to command for him majorities in both houses of the national legislature," he would do so. But short of that, he believed Clay a sure loser. Barringer also felt that Clay's lifetime of old scores to settle and enemies would weigh upon him as president.[97]

It may just have been as simple as Lincoln's next missive on the election. He explained his position on the presidential contest to fellow Whig congressman and Young Indian Thomas Flournoy* of Virginia.[98]

"In answer to your inquiries, I have to say I am in favor of General Taylor as the Whig candidate for the Presidency because I am satisfied we can elect him, that he would give us a Whig administration, and that we can not elect any other Whig."

Lincoln was also enticed by the prospect of Taylor coattails boosting Whig candidates up and down the ballot. In Illinois, Taylor "would <u>certainly</u> give us one additional member of Congress, if not more; and <u>probably</u> would give us the electoral vote of the state. That with him, we can, in that state, make great inroads among the rank and file of the Democrats to my mind is certain."[99]

Back in Illinois, Lincoln responded to his friend Usher Linder (with whom he'd tried the Matson slave case), a candidate for the legislature, on which presidential candidate to support. "In law it is good policy to never <u>plead</u> what you <u>need</u> not, lest you oblige yourself to <u>prove</u> what you <u>can</u> not. Reflect on this well before you proceed." If Linder would "simply go for General Taylor," he would "take some Democrats, and lose no Whigs." But if he favored the other nominee, "you will take some Democrats" but "lose more Whigs, so that in the sum of the operation you will be the loser."[100] Lincoln knew that this was simply a game of addition.

Giddings, not quite coming to grips with the current status of things, wrote his wife to "have no fear of General Taylor being the Whig candidate." For there to be any hope of that, he would need to come out boldly in favor of the Wilmot Proviso."[101] But he pointed out that "if Taylor is nominated, it will be our duty to revolt."[102]

It did seem to some that Taylor was losing steam. Clay had just arrived

---

*Flournoy would later serve as a member of the Virginia Convention, which voted for secession from the Union, and served as an officer in the Confederate army, at times under the command of Stonewall Jackson.

in Washington amid much fanfare. There was an "immense throng to hear him" argue a case before the Supreme Court.[103]

While Lincoln was in the throes of presidential politics, he did not ignore his duties in the House.

The Committee on the Post Office and Post Roads reported a bill establishing new routes throughout the United States. If passed, it would stitch together thousands of new miles of postal routes, creating new migration and business opportunities for many Americans. Lincoln's handwriting is all over the legislation, not only for Illinois but elsewhere. This strongly suggests that he was conferring with other members, trying to see what the needs were in their home states and trying to secure their support for the bill. The bill itself was revised many times to reflect these concerns, with little scribbled amendments written on scraps of paper stuck to the page, lines crossed out by hand, sections covered over with paper that changed their language. Lincoln was careful to pay attention to the petitions of his constituents on the subject. At their request, the bill created a new route that originated in Virginia, Cass County, where Lincoln's first letter in his 1843 congressional bid was sent, and ended in Petersburg, Menard County, where he was nominated for the House over three years later.[104] The bill faced a number of procedural setbacks, however, and it was returned to committee, with its fate very uncertain.

While the world waited for word, the Senate debated the terms of the Treaty of Guadalupe Hidalgo behind closed doors.

But despite the warnings of doom that Polk heard, the treaty had unifying characteristics, in its favor as well as against. As the war was pursued and commenced for different reasons, so was it concluded. The *Intelligencer* recommended ratification "as it is, to avoid a greater national evil."[105] Though it had spoken out strongly against the acquisition of land, it realized that this was not a possibility. A protracted war in Mexico would have as its obvious consequence more expense, more death, and as its probable outcome, the accumulation of more territory, if not the end of Mexican sovereignty. Those in favor of more acquisition, such as the president, realized that to lose the treaty might mean a withdrawal from Mexico and a gain of nothing. Constituents were eager for information from their congressmen. One, impatient at the pace of peace efforts, wished Polk and Santa Anna "could meet at Washington with each a good rifle well loaded at a distance of ten feet."[106] It was not clear that he had a preference as to the victor.

At this moment, the maps of the United States and of Mexico were incredibly malleable. In fact, the United States nearly acquired the Yucatán state of Mexico during this time. Remarkably, the Yucatán had stayed neutral during the war. Now under Indian attack, it pleaded with the administration for assistance. In exchange, it would pledge its fidelity to the United States. It seemed that only the danger of scuttling the general peace prevented this from coming to pass.[107]

In the first week of March came reports from state conventions meeting to endorse Taylor, in Virginia, Louisiana, Alabama (which also recommended they skip the convention phase and simply back Taylor), and most strikingly, Clay's home state of Kentucky, which instructed its delegates to back Taylor.[108]

March 3 was the new date of the Birth Night Ball, which had been postponed on account of Adams's death, to raise money for the Washington Monument. Lincoln and the rest of the managers pulled off a successful event, with well-known chef Gautier serving up supper until 11 p.m.[109]

On March 9, Lincoln reported House Bill 301 from the Post Office Committee. Although it never passed, it was a worthwhile attempt to allow newspapers and other periodicals to be sent free of charge through the mail, to allow all citizens the chance to be empowered by knowledge, irrespective of their monetary circumstances.

The next day, Polk learned of the Senate's ratification of the Treaty of Guadalupe Hidalgo, 38–15, late the night before, with some minor amendments. It would now go back to the Mexican Congress for further consideration. Attorney General Nathan Clifford, one of Polk's most trusted aides, was sent to Mexico to sell the amended treaty.[110] Peace, it seemed, was at hand—for Mexico and the United States, anyway. The same could not be said for Congress. The day the treaty was ratified by the Senate, Lincoln and his colleagues were treated to a fight on the House floor.

It was "a regular boxing match," wrote one observer, "between Mr. Haralson of Georgia and Mr. Jones of Tennessee, both fortunately loco focos," which knocked a desk over.[111] "We permit the hall of legislation for a great nation to become a theatre for a boxing exhibition," observed one member.[112]

The House was worried about what to do, and considered a committee to inquire into the matter, when Stephens offered an amendment to strike the committee and to simply accept their apology. Lincoln voted with a slim majority to accept.[113]

Speaking of fights, Lincoln was eagerly strategizing on the course Taylor should pursue to the presidency.

"The question of a national bank is at rest," Lincoln wrote. Taylor should neither urge its reconstitution nor veto it if Congress should see fit to do so. The tariff should be increased to pay down the national debt incurred by the war. Some territory would be taken, but, it was to be hoped, not so much to raise the slavery question.[114]

Lincoln received a letter from a man in Magnolia, Illinois, who knew of ten men who preferred Clay who would not under any circumstances vote for Taylor.[115]

Lincoln understood his thoughts, but felt "I go for him, not because I think he would make a better president than Clay, but because I think he would make a better one than Polk, or Cass, or Buchanan, or any such creatures, one of whom is sure to be elected, if he is not."[116]

Meanwhile, Taylor had once again committed an unforced error. He wrote a letter disclaiming party affiliation, or a willingness to support a nominee, and made the remarkable statement that "my opinions, even if I were the president of the United States, are neither important nor necessary."[117]

Daniel Barringer received a letter from one of his constituents calling it "a great blow to the hopes of his friends and . . . to the hopes of a Whig triumph."[118] Caleb Smith likewise received a letter from Indiana bemoaning the fact that "'Old Zack' had it in his own hands—no man ever had a better start—no man had in his power more of the elements"[119] necessary to win. But he "fooled it away."

Also unclear was the effect that the end of the war, which now looked likely, would have on the presidential contest.

On March 29, Lincoln spoke on a bounty land bill in the House. The amendment was ruled not in order. Lincoln proposed a fix for the problems with the bill: one, that enlisted men who had been promoted through their own merit would not lose their bounty land; two, that War of 1812 veterans should be given the same benefits; and three, that bounty land could be redeemed in parcels instead of in one body.[120] Though it went nowhere, it is one more example of Lincoln as a thoughtful problem solver who could grasp the intricacies of legislation.

In Mexico, the U.S. Army was still waiting for the treaty to go back and forth. Ulysses Grant remembered bullfights every Sunday,[121] as well as touring different cities.[122] They explored great caves on the road to Acapulco,[123] the hill above Cuernevaca, and the tomb of an ancient king.[124]

In Mexico, Grant had forged relationships with many of the officers who would serve on both sides in the Civil War. Grant felt the most important thing he learned was about his counterpart in that war. Lee had been venerated, "but I had known him personally, and knew that he was mortal; and it was just as well that I felt this."[125]

On April 12, 1848, Lee went to Our Lady of Remedios, the place where Hernando Cortes retreated during the Noche Triste. Near the entrance of the church were wax representations of hands, feet, and other limbs the Madonna was credited with curing.[126]

With the peace process on the right track, Congress and Washington were about to be split apart once again.

On April 15, a ship known as the *Pearl* left Georgetown and after dark took on board at Greenleaf's Point seventy-seven slaves. When the escape was detected, the slaveholders tracked the ship down, capturing the *Pearl* at the mouth of the Potomac.[127]

The crew of the *Pearl* would be defended by a new member of Congress, elected to the seat of John Quincy Adams. Lincoln had many prestigious colleagues in the Thirtieth Congress, and one of them was this new member: Horace Mann. Known as the father of American public education, Mann was a gifted lawyer and abolitionist who had temporarily taken his focus off state education to serve in Congress. The legal saga of the *Pearl* defendants would play out over many months and numerous trials and retrials.

Eventually, those convicted were pardoned by President Millard Fillmore, following a four-year incarceration.

Meanwhile, Lincoln was missing his family. After a few months in Washington, an experience on which she'd built such high hopes, Mary retreated with the children to her parents' home in Kentucky. The day after the *Pearl* incident, Lincoln wrote, "In this troublesome world, we are never quite satisfied. When you were here, I thought you hindered me in attending to business; but now, having nothing but business—no variety—it has grown exceedingly tasteless to me. I hate to sit down and direct documents, and I hate to stay in this old room by myself."

Lincoln went on to give an indication that at Mrs. Sprigg's, as with the Globe Tavern, Mary was not always a good fit for group living. "All the house—or rather, all with whom you were on decided good terms—send their love to you. The others say nothing." [128]

Lincoln had spent the evening before looking for "little plaid stockings" for Eddie, unsuccessfully. What a sight he must have been, searching the stores of Washington for socks for his absent son, lonely and alone in the city.

Lincoln had a dream that something had happened to his son, and he could not shake it until he received a letter from Mary indicating everything was all right. "Don't let the blessed fellows forget father." [129]

The time apart from family weighed heavily on Lincoln, as well as on his colleagues. Robert Schenk of Ohio lamented that his girls were growing up so fast that they no longer believed in Santa Claus. [130] Fathers who had spent time ensuring their children's education were now limited to reproving their grammar in letters (a "necessary part of a good education"). [131] Back home, children were going sleighing for the first time, their fathers left to hope "they will enjoy it rationally and have compassion on the horses if not on themselves." [132] One member noted that he would rather spend a half hour with his daughter than all the politicians in Washington for a week. [133]

The separation from families was nearly unbearable.

David Outlaw wrote his wife: "I have never left you since we were married with more reluctance, and feeling greater anxiety about you. You in fact are better off than I am, for you have all our children with you, whilst I shall be thoroughly entirely arriving stranger." [134] In another letter he requested: "Tell them how much I miss them, though they did sometimes annoy me when I was in bad humor, with their noise."[135] While "a seat in congress may be very pleasant to some men . . . it has but little attraction for me—and I feel more like a man going to a funeral, than to enjoy a political triumph."[136] He wrote to his wife "to assure you that daily and hourly you are remembered as the supremest object of my earthly affections."[137] After reading *Tales of the East*, a book similar to the *Arabian Nights*, he said, "If I had the power of some of those genies of whom I have been reading how soon would I transport myself to your dear arms and press you to my bosom."[138] "How much I wish I would transport myself with the rapidity of the telegraph so that I might be in your room in a few moments."[139]

Barringer wrote his wife that he wanted to "shower your future path with flowers," and failing that, "by devoting my heart and mind to the cherished and sacred purpose to free it from the thorns of life."[140]

As part of the fallout of the *Pearl*, on April 20, Washington City was buzzing about a riot set to occur that night, with the object of destroying the printing press at the *New Era*, the abolitionist newspaper.[141]

Palfrey took the House floor to introduce a resolution regarding the "lawless mob" that had assembled "for two nights passed . . . menacing individuals of this body."[142] With only fifteen constables patrolling at night, Washington City could easily tilt into complete anarchy.[143]

With another divisive event at hand, and the city of Washington teetering on riots, Polk's mind was elsewhere. The death of Senator Ashley of Arkansas, a close friend of the president, ensured a fifth straight month of black armbands. Quoting Edmund Burke, Polk lamented to his diary, "What shadows we are and what shadows we pursue,"[144] he wrote, with thirteen months to live.

CHAPTER 12

THE GALLOWS OF HAMAN

"No man can be true to freedom and at the same time vote for General Taylor. To serve God and mammon would not be half as difficult."
—A constituent to Congressman James Wilson

On April 30, heading into the Whig national convention, Lincoln wrote his friend Elihu Washburne: "My hope of Taylor's nomination is as high—a little higher—than it was when you left"[1] "My prayer is that you let nothing discourage or baffle you; but that, in spite of every difficulty, you send us a good Taylor delegate from your circuit."

To his friend Archibald Williams, Lincoln pointed out the math. "Mr. Clay's chance for an election, is just no chance at all. He might get New York," but would need Tennessee as well as the new votes of Texas, Florida, Iowa, and Wisconsin. He also asked Williams to reach out to Orville Browing, another of their friends and a Whig leader in the state, who was said to favor Clay. "If he is, ask him to discard feeling, and try if he can possible, as a matter of judgment, count the votes necessary to elect him."

To Silas Noble, he wrote that he could not support McClean, the most antislavery candidate: Not "that we have anything against Judge McLean; but because we are entirely sure his is not 'a winning card.'"[2]

The Democrats would meet first. Polk accepted many visitors who called on him en route.[3]

On May 22, the Democratic Party gathered at the Universalist church in Baltimore to nominate its candidates for national office. In light of the division that would characterize that gathering, and which would persist through the election, their choice of meeting place was heavily ironic. From the outset there were fights over procedures. During the heated arguments, a bench cracked in the crowded balcony, causing "violent alarm," which rippled through the sanctuary like "an electric shock." Some jumped out windows, or "over the galleries to the floor below," under the belief that the church was falling or on fire.[4]

When order was restored and the convention returned, the committee had to deal with the thorny issue of the disputed New York delegation. The Democrats of that state were badly split into two groups, Barnburners and Hunkers. The former were strongly antislavery, while the latter favored avoiding or minimizing the issue. Both sent delegations to Baltimore claiming to be the official representatives of the party. The chair of the Credentials Committee refused to make a decision until both Barnburners and Hunkers agreed to abide by it. Nothing was decided, and both sides were given an hour to speak the following day.[5]

The Hunkers went first and agreed to submit to the decision of the chair. The Barnburners made no such promises. By a vote of 126–125, both delegations were seated and would share their state's vote. This excruciating attempt at fairness pleased no one. The Barnburners left the convention, while the Hunkers refused to vote.[6]

It was an unfavorable sign as the convention proceeded to choose a standard-bearer. Lewis Cass, the Michigan senator who believed that new territories should decide for themselves whether to permit slavery, came out of the gate strong. He won 125 votes on the first ballot, doubling up Buchanan and Levi Woodbury. He steamrolled through three more ballots, to win with 179.

Anticipating the nomination of Taylor and tracking the popularity of the war, General William Butler, Scott's second-in-command, who had replaced him as head general in Mexico after his suspension, was nominated as Cass's running mate.

The Democratic platform held that Mexico had provoked the war, a "just and necessary war on our part, in which every American citizen should have shown himself on the side of his country, and neither morally nor physically, by word or by deed, have given aid and comfort to the enemy."

Meanwhile, the government of Mexico had been overthrown without ratifying the treaty.[7] Newly nominated Cass paid a visit to the White House, whose current occupant recalled a "pleasant conversation" in "fine humor."[8]

Now it was the Whig Party's turn for some intraparty discord. Taylor's forces met fierce resistance as they attempted to expand his support northward. One observer thought that Taylor's candidacy received "so chilling a reception in the state [Massachusetts], that little more I think will be heard of it."[9]

On May 27, 1848, the *Boston Journal* editorialized: "To contend successfully against this well-organized and powerful party, the Whigs must abandon neither their principles nor their men. To ensure a glorious victory at the next election, the Whigs must nominate a WHIG—a firm, undeviating Whig—known as such by his political opinions and acts throughout the course of his life . . . not the man whose political views in relation to the great questions of the day are yet to be developed—but the man whose whole political course is an embodiment of Whig principles; and whose nomination would give joy to the hearts of the intelligent Whigs of the country, and reflect honor on our people and our institutions."[10]

Senator Daniel Webster hoped the southern delegates would propose a candidate (specifically, him) from the North, where the base of the party lay. On May 31, 1848, he received a letter stating: "Last week several gentlemen from Boston and the towns of the vicinity met and agreed if Taylor should be put in nomination to organize an opposition to him in the state and country if possible . . . A convention will be called for the 4th of July, to repudiate the nomination and to nominate candidates fully committed to the Wilmot proviso. . . . A convention of free states and commit ourselves fully against the election of Taylor."

Thurlow Weed, Whig boss of New York, believed Clay started out with the backing of three in four Whig members in New York.[11] The Whigs had their power base in the North, and without more strength in that region, Taylor was doomed to defeat in the convention.

Whether one loved or loathed the idea of General Taylor for president, his was clearly the candidacy that everyone could not ignore. This is ironic, as one modern observer noted, for if members of the last Whig convention "had been told that four years later their party would nominate Zachary Taylor for president" they "would have been amazed and mystified. Few of the delegates would even have heard of him, and those few would never have thought of him as a presidential candidate."[12]

The day before the convention, the *Intelligencer* noted, "It need not be disguised that there is much division among those delegates who have visited or passed through this city on their way to Philadelphia."[13] Along with Lincoln, "One half of the members of both Houses, or nearly, have gone to Philadelphia."[14]

The City of Brotherly Love was "full to overflowing with people from all parts of the union. Every hotel is crowded, and the citizens have with an unbounded hospitality, opened their doors and spread their tables for the accommodation of the delegates."

Delegates, alternates, and thousands of other Whigs descended on Philadelphia, including a reported ten thousand from just the state of New York.[15] Abraham Lincoln, who had never been farther east than Kentucky before leaving for Congress, was now in Philadelphia, the original capital of the United States. Here the future president of the United States walked in the footsteps of Washington, Madison, and Jefferson as he worked to elect one of their successors.

There were three rallies the night before, for Clay, Scott, and Taylor. Taylor's team met in Independence Square, with an estimated twenty thousand people. It was reported the "scene yesterday evening [June 6] in Chestnut street was animating beyond any thing we have ever had here in Philadelphia since the glorious days of 1776."[16]

Lincoln and the rest convened at 11 a.m., the following day, in the Saloon of the Chinese Museum at Philadelphia.[17] The delegates passed through a *tsoi-moon,* or lucky, door.[18] On either side were tablets with Chinese characters: "Words may deceive, but the eye cannot play the rogue."[19]

The galleries, which could hold three thousand people, were "densely filled" within minutes of the doors' opening.[20] Another thousand were unable to gain admittance, amid feelings of "high hopes and intense energy."

John Morehead, the former governor of North Carolina, was chosen to preside.[21] The Whigs, too, had a seating problem, though it was a picnic next to the Hunker and Barnburner brawl.

The Whigs of Texas, who were allotted thirteen delegates, passed a resolution assigning their proxies to Louisiana in the event they didn't arrive in Philadelphia on time. This came to pass, and a committee was formed to study the issue. In fact, it might not have mattered at all were the Louisiana Whigs not absolutely certain to vote the Texas proxies in favor of Taylor. In the evening, the Credentials Committee decided that Louisiana could vote on behalf of Texas. The floor was opened for nominations. Taylor, Clay, Clayton, Scott, McClean, and Webster were nominated.

Northerners had a majority of fifty-six over southerners at the Whig convention, though the latter were overrepresented because of their Electoral College votes (where they were permitted to claim three-fifths of their slaves).

The delegates voted viva voce from their places on the floor.

On the first ballot, Taylor received 111 votes to Clay's 97, Scott's 43, Webster's 22, McLean's 2, and Clayton's 4. With 279 votes cast, Taylor was short of a majority. Minus the 13 votes of Texas, this would have put Taylor at 98, and given fresh momentum to a faction that had been told, in various ways, that defeating Taylor was futile and they shouldn't try.

One delegate from New York argued that they were there to nominate a Whig, and that anyone who was not a Whig would not receive the sanction of his state.

Judge Lafayette Saunders of Louisiana, a supporter and friend of Taylor's, took the opportunity to present a letter to the convention from the general. Taylor reminded the listeners that he had taken no part "in bringing his name before the American people." With that said, Taylor wanted all to know that he would abide by "the decision and will of the convention," convinced as he was of the need to remove the Democrats from power. If he were not the convention's choice, he would not run.[22]

Truman Smith of Connecticut, an original Young Indian, then read a letter from Taylor promising to the nominee "all the moral influence and support it may be in my power rightfully to exert."[23]

On the second ballot, Taylor's army swelled to 118, with Clay at 86, Scott at 49, Webster 22, and Clayton 4. Though rising, Taylor was still facing serious resistance. But as the Whigs appeared primed to pick a nominee, there was a sudden motion to adjourn. Governor Morehead announced its success. People screamed for division. Others yelled that it was too late to ask for a recorded vote. Confusion reigned, and for a time nobody could tell if the convention was still going on. For that reason, Morehead wisely put it to a division, and the convention did agree to adjourn until 9 a.m.[24] Given the hard feelings sure to follow such a contentious convention, all procedural matters had to be beyond question.

As the conventioneers repaired to their rooms, there was probably little sleep and a great deal of tension. In the morning, the question that they had waited so long to resolve, whose conclusion tonight was stunningly delayed, would be unavoidable.

At 9 a.m. the next day, the Whigs moved immediately to balloting. Now on the third ballot, Taylor rose to 133, Clay dropped again to 74, Scott jumped to 54, Webster 17, and 1 obstreperous delegate voted for Clayton.[25]

On the fourth ballot, Taylor easily crossed the magic number at 171, with Clay collapsing to 32, Scott at 63, and Webster at 14.[26]

Taylor had successful invaded the North, winning with 2 votes from New Hampshire, 1 from Vermont, 3 from Rhode Island, and 4 from New York. It was enough. He had moved from support in 22 states on the first ballot to 24 on the second, 27 on the third, and finally all 30 on the fourth.[27]

When the result was announced to the throngs outside, the crowd erupted.[28]

Inside the hall, there would be some eruptions as well. Some maintained their opposition to Taylor, arguing, "The Whig party is here and this day dissolved. You have put one ounce too much on the strong back of Northern endurance," said one, storming out with at least one other delegate.[29]

Another delegate, Congressman James Wilson of New Hampshire, argued that they were there to nominate a Whig, instead of a man who says "that he will not be bound by the principles or measures of any party," or that he will accept the nomination of either or any party. Wilson would write his constituents that Taylor was "the favorite candidate of the slaveholders, especially of the slave extentionists, and from the very first had been brought forward as the only southern man that could be elected."[30]

At least some Taylor opponents kept an open mind. One argued that the general needed to prove himself. "I am an advocate of free soil and free territory. I cannot be swerved from the position I occupy on this subject by any party machinery or alliances." He then read a poem about the Founding Fathers, to uproarious applause.

Others felt bound to support the nominee. A delegate from New York took the floor to announce that although he'd done more than anyone to try to stop Taylor, he would defer to the will of the convention. He motioned to make the nomination unanimous.[31] Not even this feel-good motion, a staple of all such conventions, could be agreed to.

With the party unable to unite behind Taylor, it was on to the vice presidency.

It was time to find Taylor a running mate. Despite the incredible potential of this job, little thought had been given to it. If anyone would be mindful of John Adams's admonition ("I am Vice President. In this I am nothing, but I may be everything"), it would be the Whig Party. In their entire existence, they had placed but one of their own in the White House. Thirty days into his term William Henry Harrison was dead, his replacement, John Tyler, so disloyal to the cause that the Whigs took the extraordinary step of expelling him from the party.

After a close first ballot, Millard Fillmore won 173 votes to 87 for Abbott Lawrence of Massachusetts on the second, and was nominated.[32]

The convention could not conceivably put together a platform. Governor Morehead offered a valedictory calling for unity in the party: "I too have been defeated in the first wish of my heart. I have not succeeded in the nomination of my favorite candidate—I stand among the vanquished party—but I fall in over the hands of my victor friends, like a conquered damsel into the hands of her lover, and submit kindly to my defeat."[33]

The telegraphs relayed the verdict all across the nation. At a quarter past eleven on June 9, Lincoln telegraphed the *Journal* that "General TAYLOR has received the nomination of the Convention for president of the U. States."[34]

One of Giddings's correspondents may well have spoken for him, claiming to be "stunned, stupefied, outraged, abased, mortified, and enraged to the last degree . . . by the action of the Philadelphia Convention." [35]

Webster was crushed by the result. "These friends, with whom I have been connected, and to whom I have been most warmly attached, personally and politically, for ten or fifteen years, and who have allowed themselves to be called my friends, and with whom I have always consulted, when in power, and out of power, these friends made their movement, last winter, without any consultation with me, and without giving me the slightest notice of their intent." [36]

Henry Clay, who had pursued the presidency for much of his adult life, who had at times had it within his grasp, and now falling short for the final time, "felt a great indignation at the nomination of General Taylor for president, and did not care before whom he manifested it." [37] Clay was very bitter about people he believed had been sent there to support him who had voted Taylor, even on the first ballot, or at their first opportunity. [38] Despite the drama over whether Taylor would support the convention's nominee, Clay never did support the man who had defeated him. [39]

Horace Mann blamed the nomination on "the combined force of slavery and war." [40] One constituent wrote James Wilson, "No man can be true to freedom and at the same time vote for General Taylor. To serve God and mammon would not be half as difficult. I had hoped that whatever the Whigs of other states might do, here they would stand by principle. I have hoped in vain." [41]

While some were in shock or preparing resistance, other Whigs were doing their best to fall in line. George Ashmun wrote a letter to the Whigs of his Massachusetts congressional district, trying to smooth the path for supporting Taylor. "It was not made by the aid of my vote," he pointed out, restating his support for Webster. But "we have a southern candidate fairly nominated in a general convention of the Whig party; and I see no reason why the Whig Party should refuse to sustain him." [42] Ashmun closed by quoting Webster on an earlier occasion: "In the dark and troubled night that is upon us, I see no star above the horizon, promising light to guide us, but the intelligent, patriotic, united Whig party of the United States." [43]

Benjamin French, longtime Democratic clerk of the House, recorded the fallout with glee. "Never have I seen so much discord reign in any party as now distracts the Whig ranks. Northeastern Whigs swear, 'so help them God,' they will not support Taylor, and I am confirmed in my prediction that he will not receive the vote of a single New England state."[44]

John Strohm, Lincoln's housemate, received a letter from his brother in Pennsylvania: "I fear the victory achieved with Taylor will not be worth much, as a Whig victory."[45] Another of Strohm's correspondents told him that "under the present aspect of things, I could not vote for General Taylor . . . as I trust no good Whig would."[46] A New Hampshire Whig wrote, "A very decided majority of the Whigs of the state are opposed to supporting General Taylor for the Presidency."[47] Taylor's selling point was never as a uniter of the Whig Party, but in his crossover appeal. And in that, he seemed to be delivering. Still another of Strohm's supporters told him that their candidate was "promising beyond all expectations. I could name more than a dozen in our neighborhood that never voted a Whig ticket that have declared themselves in support of Taylor."[48]

Meanwhile, a newly reconstituted Mexican Congress had met and ratified the Treaty of Guadalupe Hidalgo as amended. The news was received in Washington on June 22, 1848.[49] The Mexican-American War was over.

From the convention, Lincoln headed to Wilmington, Delaware, to speak on behalf of the Whig ticket. He was introduced to the crowd as the "Lone Star of Illinois." To the hearty applause of the audience, he denounced the high-handedness of the Polk administration and extolled the virtues of Taylor and Fillmore.

Lincoln returned to Washington the following day, and began responding to letters that had piled up in his absence.

He wrote to Herndon, "By many, and often, it had been said they would not abide the nomination of Taylor; but since the deed has been done, they are fast falling in, and in my opinion we shall have a most overwhelming, glorious, triumph." The war issue had been turned against the Democrats— "The war is now to them, the gallows of Haman, which they built for us, and on which they are doomed to be hanged themselves."[50]

Taylor's acceptance and rejection is illustrated well by one of Caleb Smith's correspondents in Cincinnati. "[H]aving advocated the propriety of a national convention, I feel bound to go for Taylor. . . . In other aspects of the nomination I contemplate it with undisguised sadness. The Whigs have sanctioned a bad precedent which will impair, if not finally destroy," the morality "of the party. . . . Many of our best Whigs here say they won't stand it. They will, most of them, finally organize, I think; but not a few will never."[51]

Mary had written to Lincoln wishing to return, and to update him on the family. Bobby had found a kitten while playing outside and brought it back. Eddie brought it water, "fed it with bread himself, with his own dear hands." "How much, I wish instead of writing, we were together this evening, I feel very sad away from you."[52]

Mary proposed the idea of coming back to Washington to visit. "Will you be a good girl in all things if I consent?" Lincoln asked. "Then come along, and that as soon as possible. Having got the idea in my head, I shall be impatient till I see you."[53]

CHAPTER 13

INTERNAL IMPROVEMENTS

"The question of improvements is verging to a final crisis; and the friends of the policy must now battle, and battle manfully, or surrender all."

—Abraham Lincoln

The early days of summer would see the Whigs try to repair their internal defects, the Congress try to build the infrastructure necessary to improve the economy, and the country break ground on a monument to George Washington.

Throughout Lincoln's life in politics, he believed in the idea of infrastructure as a way to grow the economy and create opportunity. Lincoln's service in Congress, in a way, began as a member-elect representing his state at the Chicago River and Harbor Convention. The convention itself was largely in response to Polk's veto of the Rivers and Harbors Bill. Shortly after Lincoln's swearing in, Polk had made the fallout worse by issuing a preachy veto message explaining his action.[1] The recent Democratic convention had approved a platform containing the statement "that the constitution does not confer upon the general government the power to commence, and carry on a general system of internal improvements." For his part, General Cass said, "I have carefully read the resolutions of the Democratic National convention, laying down the platform of our political faith, and I adhere to them as firmly, as I approve them cordially."

On June 20, 1848, Lincoln addressed the House on the subject.

"The question of improvements is verging to a final crisis; and the friends of the policy must now battle, and battle manfully, or surrender all."

Lincoln took the most frequent objections in turn: that internal improvements were too expensive, too regional in their benefit to justify a national expenditure, and unconstitutional.

Lincoln pointed out that the real problem was that members traded their votes for appropriations in their own districts, "and when a bill shall be expanded till every district shall be provided for, that it will be too greatly expanded, is obvious."

Polk's veto message condemned what it termed the profligate spending of John Quincy Adams's administration. According to Polk, total spending under Adams was $1,879,627.01. Congress had been able to discharge this duty in a fiscally responsible way, "and what has been done, it seems to me, can be done again."

Lincoln could not deny that spending benefited certain areas over others, but he did deny that local expenditures could not accrue to the general benefit. Take the navy. The navy was particularly advantageous to Charleston, Baltimore, Philadelphia, New York, and Boston. These were the port cities where ships were built, where they docked, and which they protected. But did the navy benefit only port cities?

Lincoln's next example was the Illinois and Michigan canal. "Every inch of it is within the state of Illinois. In a very few days, we were all gratified to learn, among other things, that sugar had been carried from New Orleans through this canal to Buffalo in New York. . . . The New Orleans merchant sold his sugar a little dearer, and the people of Buffalo sweetened their coffee a little cheaper before—a benefit resulting from the canal, not to Illinois where the canal is, but to Louisiana and New York where it is not. . . .

"An honest laborer digs coal at about seventy cents a day, while the president digs abstractions at about seventy dollars a day. The coal is clearly worth more than the abstractions, and yet what a monstrous inequity in the prices!

"The true rule, in determining to embrace, or request any thing, is not whether it have any evil in it; but whether it have more of evil, than of good."

In a constitutional argument, Lincoln said, "I should not be, and ought not to be, listened to patiently. The ablest, and the best men, have gone over the whole ground long ago."

Polk had quoted from Jefferson's 1806 message to Congress, which asked for a constitutional amendment "to the great purposes of the public education, roads, rivers, canals, and such other objects of public improvements as it may be thought proper to add to the constitutional enumeration of the federal powers." Polk believed this proved that such powers were not in the Constitution.

Lincoln compared this argument in Polk's hands to a gun that fires wide of the mark and knocks the shooter over. Lincoln held up treatises on American constitutional law as proof of his point, and argued that states couldn't afford to make the improvements. How could they? Could they pay for a new improvement from the proceeds of another? Wouldn't that affect Mr. Polk's sense of equality?

"The tendency to undue expansion is unquestionably the chief difficulty," Lincoln said. "I would not borrow money. I am against an overwhelming, crushing system." Instead, Congress should forecast how much could be spent for improvements, then prioritize the most important projects, using statistical data to determine which projects would be more beneficial.

The nation should deal with the larger works, the states the smaller ones, "extravagance avoided, and the wholly country put on that career of prosperity which shall correspond with its extent of territory, its natural resources, and the intelligence and enterprise of its people."

On July 5, the House affirmed the resolutions of the Chicago River and Harbor Convention, 128–59.[2] These resolutions held that the federal government had the constitutional authority and an economic incentive to improve navigation on the lakes and rivers by clearing impediments and constructing harbors, lighthouses, and other infrastructure to facilitate transportation. But so long as President Polk wielded the veto pen, the chance of any such improvement's being signed into law was virtually nonexistent.

Two weeks later, Congressman Lincoln scored his most significant legislative achievement. On July 19, he reported from the committee on post offices and post roads a bill to establish "certain post routes." This was the same bill creating new routes throughout the United States, the one on which he had worked so hard, only to see it run into procedural difficulties and sent back to the committee. This bill, with some changes, was now back on the floor. This time it passed the House of Representatives without a recorded vote, and headed for the Senate. A bill does not get shelved in committee only to return months later and pass without a recorded vote unless there is a substantial amount of behind-the-scenes work. No doubt Lincoln did his share and more to see this important legislation succeed.

Another incident shortly thereafter illustrates that Lincoln was gaining respect among the members of the Thirtieth Congress. President Polk had sent Congress a message urging them to organize the territories in the West. After protracted debate, Lincoln obtained the floor "amongst many competitors."[3] He demurred, saying that he wished to speak on another subject, and that if the House wished to continue discussing the president's message, he would yield. According to the *Globe*, there were cries of "No, no," encouraging him to speak, "go on." Given the endless droning on the House floor that members so often complained about, it is a true compliment that people wanted to hear Lincoln speak, even when he offered to yield. Unfortunately, Samuel Vinton asked if he could continue discussing the present topic. Lincoln graciously gave way, and unfortunately never made the remarks he intended.

But from now on, the presidential question that had dominated the Thirtieth Congress would overshadow nearly everything else.

On June 21, Lincoln attended a caucus of the Whigs to discuss the national race. When he returned, however, he found a letter from Herndon indicating that several prominent Whigs were abandoning Taylor. His response offers an interesting insight into how he viewed his own rise to power. While some senior Whigs may be abandoning Taylor, "You must not wait to be brought forward by older men. For instance, you suppose that I should ever have got into notice if I had waited to be hunted up and pushed forward by older men. You young men get together and form a Rough and Ready Club, and have regular meetings and speeches. Take in every body that you can get."

Judging by most of Lincoln's correspondence, the Illinois Whigs were very happy with the decision of the convention. "[Taylor's] nomination has been received with unbounded applause, whilst that of Cass has fallen still born upon the public. Here in the great Democratic county of St. Clair, there is no enthusiasm, no rejoicing, no demonstration in favor of the 'dough face' [Cass]." With a thousand-vote Democratic majority, there could not be a meeting mustered to ratify the nomination of Cass.[4]

Lincoln sent a constituent a copy of the *Battery*, the new Whig paper, encouraging him to get subscribers. Lincoln signed him up for one copy, which he promised to pay for himself should the constituent be dissatis-fied.[5] Lincoln had sent a great deal of literature back home. Printing con-gressional speeches cost one cent per copy, whether they lasted one minute or one hour.[6] Lincoln spent $132.30 to buy 7,580 copies. Lincoln could mail them for free. Most of them were of his January 12 speech on the spot resolutions.[7] Only six members of the House spent more than $100 on such literature that session.[8]

With July 4 came the celebration of American independence, and in Washington City this year it would have extra significance. The members of the Thirtieth Congress and other dignitaries gathered for the laying of the cornerstone for the Washington Monument.[9] Instead of John Quincy Adams, who as a member of Washington's administration would have given an incomparable speech, Speaker Winthrop addressed the crowd. The day opened with bells ringing out throughout the city and the fire of cannon.[10] At 11 a.m., Lincoln began marching as part of the mile-and-a-half-long procession,[11] which began at City Hall (Washington City Hall is today better known as the D.C. Court of Appeals; a Lincoln statue is in front of the building).[12] Though Adams was gone, the congregants did whatever they could to wrap themselves in the aura of the revolution. Alexander Hamilton's widow was present and onstage, along with Dolley Madison.[13]

Winthrop said: "Just honor to Washington can only be rendered by observing his precepts. He has built his own monument. We and those who come after us in successive generations are its appointed, its privileged guardians. The wide spread Republic is the true monument to Washington. Maintain its independence. Uphold its constitution. Preserve its union. De-fend its liberty. Let it stand before the world in all its original strength."[14]

Lincoln would later have occasion to heed those words. Just as he had helped raise money to build the Washington Monument, he would commit himself to preserving the metaphorical, fantastic Washington monument of Winthrop's speech.

"Seldom if ever has the city of Washington witnessed such a day as that," the *Intelligencer* reported.

CHAPTER 14

THE TROUBLE WITH OREGON

A month after Lincoln was elected to Congress, the British and Americans signed a treaty to prevent a war over Oregon. With Oregon's boundaries settled, now the national government would be responsible for organizing the new territory. But the more territory the United States acquired, the more problems it seemed to have.

There were four distinct beliefs regarding the territories and slavery.[1] Essentially, every member of Congress fell into one of these camps: Slavery should not be allowed to expand beyond its current boundaries; the people of a territory should be free to decide for themselves, a doctrine later known as "popular sovereignty"; the Missouri Compromise line should be extended to the Pacific Ocean, a position favored by President Polk; Congress had no authority to legislate the slavery question in the territories. On this question, offered to the House dozens of times in the Thirtieth Congress, Abraham Lincoln, despite the well-documented feelings of Illinois, voted with the first position at every opportunity.

As the first session of the Thirtieth Congress headed for adjournment, there was an urgency in passing legislation organizing the Oregon Territory. The House version, however, contained Northwest Ordinance language keeping the territory free of slavery. Southerners seemed to have no interest in taking their slaves to far-off Oregon. But it was the principle that was at stake for them, especially those who believed that Congress simply didn't have the power to regulate slavery in the territories. Lincoln cast a number of votes in support of the Oregon Bill, always voting to maintain the Northwest Ordinance language.

Meanwhile, seeking to break the impasse over territorial government, Senator John Clayton of Delaware chaired a bipartisan "Compromise Committee."[2] Their proposal would organize all the new territory of the Union, bringing Oregon in without slavery, while preventing the territorial governments of California and New Mexico from adopting any rules as to slavery. Slaves brought into the territories would be able to sue in federal court to determine their status.[3]

The city was very, very hot, one member recorded, as this explosive bill worked its way through Congress.[4]

On July 27 at 8 a.m., after a twenty-one-hour session of the Senate, the compromise passed, 33–22. Polk recorded that he could not remember a previous all-night session, but it would not be the last one of the Thirtieth Congress.[5]

The hard work and long hours of the Senate would be in vain. In the House, many from North as well as South came away convinced that they were the loser in the compromise. In a way it was not so much a bill as it was a lawsuit, a punt to the Supreme Court, where both sides thought they would lose. Hours after the Senate passed the compromise, Alexander Stephens motioned to table the bill, before it could ever be read, with Lincoln voting in favor. Horace Mann recalled that "when taking the yeas and nays, the House is like Bedlam." But during the Compromise Bill it was "still as a church."[6]

Fear of the bill's unknowns united "every Northern Whig, of about half the Northern Democrats, and of 8 Southern Whigs."[7] Outlaw felt it surrendered "the whole thing to the north."[8] Outlaw protested that "day after day the evils of slavery—its sin—its evils moral, social and political are paraded for our entertainment by men who know nothing of our ... condition, or of the practical bearings of the question which they attempt."[9]

The bill was tabled by a vote of 112–97.[10] If eight House members had changed their votes and then passed the bill, it would have gone to the president, who would have signed it. And nothing about American history would have been the same again.

So who was right? Unfortunately for Stephens, the most powerful southerner in the House, who saw himself as a champion of their interests, it was he. On the day the compromise bill failed, six of the justices who later joined in the *Dred Scott* decision were sitting on the Court, including its author and architect, Chief Justice Roger Taney. The *Dred Scott* decision held that slaves had no standing to bring suit. Even if the Court recognized the validity of the clause in the compromise bill conferring standing on slaves, it still would have proceeded to its central and most devastating holdings: that Congress could not prohibit slavery in the territories, and that the federal government could not free slaves brought to those territories. Such a decision, which enraged the North and precipitated the Civil War, would in all likelihood have happened eight years earlier. Does this mean the war would have come earlier as well? With the exception of Taylor, any of Lincoln's immediate predecessors would have allowed the South to leave without incident. But even if the president had taken Lincoln's eventual path, to preserve the Union, it is unlikely that the North would have prevailed. It was only in the critical 1850s that the North gained the population and industrial advantage that allowed the Union to survive.

With the compromise bill dead, supporters of free soil were determined to organize the Oregon Territory, with language prohibiting slavery. If they couldn't get their way there, in a sparsely populated region bordering Canada, whose soil rendered slavery unfeasible, whose southernmost point was three hundred miles north of the Missouri Compromise line, where exactly could they insist that people be free?

Caleb Smith, as chairman of the Committee on Territories, skillfully managed the Oregon Bill on the floor, decoupling the issue from California and New Mexico.

During debate over Oregon, the South wasn't ready to yield an inch. The fighting over slavery had, in their words, backed them into a corner, requiring them to resist everything. One member said: "I never will vote to exclude slavery from Oregon or any other Territory of the United States as long as I see the north determined to force down upon the south the

Wilmot proviso. I have no idea of the south observing the Missouri compromise while the north repudiates it."[11]

Amos Tuck, Independent Democrat of New Hampshire, argued against "peopling a country with slaves that is now free."[12] In response to southern calls to stop presenting slavery legislation, he said, "One other thing, sir, must be done before we shall realize the universal quiet which is so much desired: it is the abolition of slavery in the District of Columbia. So long as we are doomed to look from the windows of this capitol upon a mart for trade in slaves, the most extensive of any in the world, so long, if liberty survive, will agitation exist in the country."[13]

On August 2, Lincoln voted with the majority to preserve the Northwest Ordinance language in the Oregon bill, 114–88.[14] By a margin of 128–71, with Lincoln voting in favor, the Oregon Bill was on its way to the Senate, with the Ordinance language intact.

Polk continually worried about sectional parties, which he believed bills such as these tended to perpetuate. Later that day, the country would take another meaningful step in the direction of geographical parties.

After Taylor's nomination, the Barnburners of New York, along with antislavery Democrats and Whigs, and members of the Liberty Party, formed the new Free Soil Party, committed to preventing the expansion of slavery. The Free Soil Party nominated former president Martin Van Buren for president, along with Charles Francis Adams for vice president, as well as fielding a slate of candidates for state and federal offices.

Now Giddings, Elihu Root of Ohio, and John Palfrey of Massachusetts announced their departure from the Whig Party and their support for Van Buren.[15]

Meanwhile, Taylor had yet to formally accept the Whig nomination. Surely this was a "crime or accident," said the *Intelligencer*. Yes, surely his acceptance was stolen or mislaid—or perhaps the general was at last heeding the words of the Young Indians and running out the clock.[16] Regardless of the cause, Taylor had not yet accepted the Whig nomination, more than a month after it was tendered. George Pike, Taylor's local postmaster, reported there were two bundles of refused letters, mostly for Taylor, but that the intended recipient had declined to pay the postage.[17]

Regardless of Taylor's acceptance of the Whigs, they had long since

wrapped themselves around him. One of his earliest congressional supporters, Abraham Lincoln, was about to make a full-throated defense of Old
Rough and Ready, and a systematic takedown of his opponents, on the floor
of the House of Representatives.

When the House first met, the presidential question was discussed in
private caucuses, among groups such as the Young Indians, and limited
to whispers in the cloakroom or letters between friends. Now the House
would debate the issue openly on the floor.

Alfred Iverson, a Democrat of Georgia, accused the Whigs of having
deserted their principles, taking "shelter under the military coat-tails of
General Taylor."

Lincoln's response was written on "a few pages of foolscap paper."[18] He'd
gotten permission to speak from a friend's seat, in order to be better heard.[19]
"At first he followed his notes, but, as he warmed up, he left his desk and
his notes to stride down the alley toward the Speaker's chair, holding his
left hand behind him so that he could now and then shake the tails of his
own rusty, black broadcloth dress-coat, while he earnestly gesticulated with
his long right arm, shaking the bony index finger at the Democrats on the
other side of the chamber. Occasionally, as he completed a sentence amid
shouts of laughter, he would return up the alley to his desk, consult his
notes, take a sip of water, and start off again."[20]

Regarding the charges that Taylor was vague on the issues, Lincoln said,
"In their eagerness to get at General Taylor, several Democratic members
here have desired to know" his position on a bankruptcy law. "Can they tell
us General Cass' opinion on this question?"

A voice from the seats interrupted Lincoln. "He is against it."

"Aye, how do you know he is?" Lincoln responded. There was nothing to
indicate this in his platform, or anywhere else.

Taylor would defer to the people on the great questions of the day. To the
Whigs, this seemed to be "the best sort of principle at that—the principle of
allowing the people to do as they please with their own business."

"I am a Northern man, or rather, a Western free state man, with a constituency I believe to be, and with personal feelings I know to be, against the
extension of slavery. As such, and with what information I have I hope and
believe, General Taylor, if elected, would not veto the Proviso."

But "should slavery thereby go to the territory we now have, just so much will certainly happen by the election of Cass," along with new wars and the further expansion of slavery. "One of the two is to be President; which is preferable?

"But I suppose I can not reasonably hope to convince you that we have any principles.

"The other day, one of the gentlemen from Georgia, an eloquent man and a man of learning, so far as I could judge, not being learned myself, came down upon us astonishingly. He spoke in what the *Baltimore American* calls the 'scathing and withering style.' At the end of his second severe flash, I was struck blind, and found myself feeling with my fingers for an assurance of my continued physical existence." Iverson "eulogized Mr. Clay in high and beautiful terms, and then declared that we had deserted all our principles, and had turned [him] out, like an old horse to root. This is terribly severe. It can not be answered by argument. At least I can not so answer it." Rather, Lincoln asked whether the Democrats had turned any old horses out to root, perhaps a "certain Martin Van Buren . . . and is he not rooting a little to your discomfort about now?" Didn't the 1844 convention have a majority of pledged delegates for Van Buren?

The gentleman from Georgia accused the Whigs of having "taken shelter under General Taylor's military coat-tail. . . . But can he remember no other military coat tail under which a certain other party have been sheltering for near a quarter of a century? Has he no acquaintance with the ample military coat tail of General Jackson? Does he not know that his own party have run the five last presidential races under that coat tail? And that they are now running the sixth, under the same cover?" It had been "clung to with the grip of death by every Democratic campaign since" Jackson first used it.

Lincoln referenced the Democratic campaign literature, "'Old Hickories' with a rude likeness of the old general upon them, hickory poles, and hickory brooms, your never ending emblems; Mr. Polk himself was 'Young Hickory,' or 'Little Hickory,' or something so; and even now, your campaign paper here, is proclaiming that Cass and Butler are of the true 'Hickory stripe.' No sir, you dare not give it up. Like a horde of hungry ticks you have stuck to the tail of the Hermitage lion to the end of his life; and you are still sticking to it, and drawing a loathsome sustenance from it, after he is dead. A fellow once advertised that he had made a discovery by which he could make a new man out of an old one, and have enough of the stuff to make a little yellow dog. Just such a discovery, has General Jackson's popularity been to you. You not only twice made president of him out of it, but you have had enough of the stuff left, to make presidents of several comparatively small men since; and it is your chief reliance now to make still another."

Lincoln pointed out that he would not have chosen to go this route, "but I wish gentlemen on the other side to understand, that the use of degrading figures is a game at which they may not find themselves able to take all the winnings." Lincoln was interrupted from the Democrats' side, when someone shouted, "We give it up!"

"Aye, you give it up," Lincoln continued. "They are weapons which hit you, but miss us."

In Lincoln's notes, the next part of the speech was sarcastically headlined "Military tail of the Great Michigander."

Cass's biographers, Lincoln noted, were "tying him to a military tail, like so many mischievous boys tying a dog to a bladder of beans." While their material was not much, they "drive at it, might and main."

"He invaded Canada without resistance, and 'outvaded' it without pursuit." Today the Democrats credited him with being with General Harrison at the Battle of the Thames, but in 1840, they had charged Harrison with "picking huckleberries two miles off" during the fighting. Lincoln supposed "it is a just conclusion with you, to say Cass was siding with Harrison to pick huckleberries.

"By the way, Mr. Speaker, did you know I am a military hero? Yes sir, in the days of the Black Hawk War, I fought, bled, and came away. Speaking of General Cass' career reminds me of my own." Lincoln was not at Stillman's defeat (a victory for the Indians in the Black Hawk War), he pointed out, but was just as close as Cass was to Hall's surrender (an American defeat in the War of 1812). And like Cass, Lincoln saw the place of surrender soon afterward. "It is quite certain I did not break my sword," Lincoln said, mocking Cass's act of defiance, breaking his sword rather than surrendering it, but he accidentally bent a musket pretty badly. If Cass had picked more huckleberries than he, Lincoln believed he had him beat in wild onions.

If the general had encountered hostile Indians, it was more than he, said Lincoln, but he "had a good many bloody struggles with mosquitos." If the Democrats ever "take me up as their candidate for the presidency, I protest they shall not make fun of me, as they have of General Cass, by attempting to write me into a military hero."

Lincoln then moved on to Cass and the Wilmot Proviso. He read verbatim quotations from the senator, establishing that in 1846 he was for it "at once," in March 1847 "for it, but not just then," and in December 1847 "against it altogether."

Lincoln believed that Cass had retreated in the face of "this great Democrat ox-goad" (a device for whipping oxen into compliance). "Back, back sir, back a little," and Cass obediently "shakes his head, and bats his eyes, and blunders back to his position," but the goad kept at it. "Back I say, further back," to where Cass stands today. "Have no fears, gentlemen, of your candidate. He exactly suits you, and we congratulate you upon it. However much you may be distressed about our candidate, you have all cause to be contented and happy with your own."

The next section of Lincoln's notes was titled "Cass on working and eating." The Lone Star of Illinois had served up red meat, and now it was time for dessert.

General Cass had been distinguished by "splendidly successful charges," Lincoln said, but not upon the public enemy; Cass's charges were instead against the public treasury. Lincoln used public records to skewer Cass for largesse in office. Cass, Lincoln pointed out, had been governor of the Michigan Territory as well as superintendent of Indian Affairs.

"They show that he not only did the labor of several men at the same time, but that he often did it at several places, many hundreds of miles apart, at the same time. And, at eating too, his capacities are shown to be quite as wonderful." During one period, Lincoln pointed out, Cass ate ten rations a day in Michigan, ten in Washington, and five dollars' worth a day on the road between them. "By all means, make him President, gentlemen. He will feed you bounteously, if there is any left after he shall have helped himself."

Lincoln next responded to the issue of the Whigs, the antiwar party, nominating Taylor. By opposing the war as "unnecessarily and unconstitutionally" begun, the Whigs had spoken out and agreed and put forth their reasons. "The marching of an army into the midst of a peaceful Mexican settlement, frightening the inhabitants away, leaving their growing crops and other property to destruction, to you may appear perfectly amiable, peaceful, unprovoking procedure; but it does not appear so to us."

But the Whigs voted for supplies, and more than that, Whigs had filled the ranks of the war, offering "the blood of our political brethren in every trial, and on every field. The beardless boy and the mature man—the humble and the distinguished, you have had them. Through suffering and death, by disease, and in battle, they have endured, and fought, and fell with you. Clay and Webster each gave a son, never to be returned." Lincoln pointed out the heroism from his own state, including Hardin's, "and in the fall of that one, we lost our best Whig man." Of the five high officers who died at Buena Vista, four were Whigs.

"But the distinction between the cause of the President in beginning the war, and the cause of the country after it was begun, is a distinction which you can not perceive. To you the president, and the country, seem to be all one.

"We are content with our position, content with our company, and content with our candidate ... in their generous sympathy, [Democrats] think we ought to be miserable, we really are not, and ... they may dismiss the great anxiety they have on our account."

Lincoln was clearly enjoying himself when he realized that he had but three minutes left to finish. He raced to touch on his remaining points. While the Whigs might have dissent in their ranks, were the Democrats truly united? Lincoln likened the New York Democrats to a story he'd heard, of a drunken fellow hearing the indictment against him for hog stealing. The clerk read "ten boards, ten sows, ten shoats, and ten pigs," to which the drunkard exclaimed, "Well, by golly, that is the most equally divided gang of hogs I ever did hear of." Lincoln argued if there were a more equally divided group of hogs than the New York Democrats, he had yet to hear of it. With that he concluded his speech.

He later moved to suspend the rules to submit a report on Cass's compensation versus Taylor's, which of course failed to get the two-thirds necessary.[21]

Many Democrats joined the Whigs in congratulating him on a fine speech. William Sawyer was one who complimented the speech, yet joked, "I hope he won't charge mileage on his travels while delivering it,"[22] a reference to Lincoln's incessant pacing during the address.

Amos Tuck remembered Lincoln "created much amusement by the aptness of his illustrations, walking around in front of the Democratic members, singling out individuals especially responsible for unsound and inconsistent doctrines."[23] Lincoln was "good natured, enjoyed his own wit, heartily joined in the amusement he excited in others, and sat down amid the cheers of his friends."[24] Lincoln and Tuck became close in the House, a friendship that remained for the rest of his life.[25]

Polk, meanwhile, was frustrated by the campaigning in Congress, raging to his diary that the House was making violent party speeches "on the merits and demerits of the presidential candidates. They seem wholly to have forgotten that they have any public interest to transact, and have converted the Ho. Repts. into an arena for making violent party speeches."[26]

Herndon wrote that anyone who "reads it [the speech] will lay it down convinced that Lincoln's ascendency for a quarter of a century among the political spirits in Illinois was by no means an accident."[27]

Finally, on July 31, Taylor accepted the nomination of the Whigs. "Looking to the composition of the Convention, and its numerous and patriotic constituency, I feel deeply grateful for the honor bestowed upon me, and for the distinguished confidence implied in my nomination by it to the highest office in the gift of the American people." That was it. No mention of policy whatever.

The Whig members formed an executive committee to steer their election efforts "to supply every section of the country with useful information."[28]

Lincoln wrote to James Smith, a Presbyterian minister in Springfield, "It is believed that all that is necessary to secure the election of General Taylor is for correct information to reach the mass of the people."[29] Lincoln asked for a list of people, divided between active Whigs, rank-and-file Whigs, and "the more moderate of our opponents," who might be persuadable.

Though active in the presidential contest, Lincoln never took his eye off his responsibilities to Illinois. On August 2, Lincoln and Jacob Collamer of

Vermont tried to pass a bill for a railroad connecting the Mississippi River with the Great Lakes. Though they failed, this would have been a boon to Lincoln's state. When the Chicago & Rock Island Railroad came into being a few years later, it represented a massive economic gain and helped increase the population of the northern part of Illinois.

In the midst of this, Lincoln had to grapple with the news that Stephen Logan, his friend, close political ally, former law partner, and desired successor in office, had been defeated. Logan and Thomas Harris, his opponent, had made numerous joint appearances early in the canvass, but Harris had ceased in favor of traveling the district with the circus, guaranteeing for himself a more significant crowd than may ever have attended a political speech.[30] The *Journal* made fun of Harris, comparing him to a loco who attended a hanging and then attempted to address the crowd from the scaffold (once the man had been cut down, of course).[31]

The editor of the *Boston Daily Atlas* asked Lincoln how this had happened.[32] "I would rather not be put upon explaining how Logan was defeated in my district," Lincoln wrote. He had yet to learn the particulars. Several Whigs who preferred not to vote for Logan had written Lincoln before the canvass. In addition, "Harris was a Major of the war, and fought at Cerro Gordo, where several Whigs of the district fought with him. These two facts and their effects, I presume, tell the whole story." Lincoln did not believe he was the cause.

The *Journal* indirectly blamed Logan, pointing out that Baker would have won in the Seventh.[33] A year later, the Democrats were concerned about a possible Lincoln candidacy for Congress in 1850, making it even less likely that he was responsible for Logan's loss.[34]

Logan was a notoriously bad dresser, so much so that he bought a brand-new hat and suit for the campaign, only to be accused by crowds of purposely dressing down to win over the voters.[35] Logan's extreme wealth was an issue, causing resentment among some voters. During the campaign, a German broadside accused the Whigs of hating foreigners, which also had an effect.[36] Furthermore, those who would blame Lincoln's record on the war for Logan's loss failed to note that he and Logan were in agreement. In the legislature, Logan had voted no, along with all but five Whigs, on a resolution endorsing the war.[37] And yet despite all this, Harris won by the narrow margin of 7,201 to 7,095.[38] In the 1848 election, Edward Baker returned to Congress by moving to a district based in Galena that the Whigs had never won before. People on the ground were sure that Baker would have held the Seventh.

On August 5, Polk had an end-of-session dinner for all of the members of the House of Representatives.[39] The fighting between the House and the president had been barely restrained since the opening minutes of Congress, and one wonders what the atmosphere was like.

By August 7, one member noted that his colleagues had begun leaving for home.[40] For several days thereafter, the House met until eleven or twelve at night.[41]

Meanwhile, the Oregon Bill had been altered in the Senate and was on its way back to the House. Stephen Douglas, chairman of the Committee on Territories, had reported out an amended Oregon Bill. His plan would extend the Missouri Compromise to the Pacific, opening millions of new acres to slavery.[42] On August 11, the Senate version was defeated in the House, 121–82, with Lincoln voting no.[43]

The following day in the Senate, border state senators, led by Thomas Hart Benton, more interested in organizing Oregon than making a point, carried a vote receding from the Missouri Compromise Amendment 29–25.[44] By backing off from their amendment, restoring the language that already passed the House, they ensured that the bill was sent to the president. But what would he do with it?

On August 14, Polk sent the House a signing statement on the Oregon Bill. It was a preachy historical lecture on the wisdom and accommodation of the Founding Fathers, along with a history of the Missouri Compromise. "And it is because the provisions of this bill are not inconsistent with the terms of the Missouri compromise . . . that I have felt at liberty to withhold my sanction. Had it embraced territories south of that compromise, the question presented for my consideration would have been of a far different character, and my action upon it must have corresponded with my convictions."[45]

That same day, Polk signed "an act to establish certain post routes," HR 599.[46] Lincoln had worked hard on this bill in committee and had navigated it through rough waters on the floor, working with members from other states to win their support. Lincoln did not give up when the bill was sent back to committee or again faced trouble on the floor. And now it was signed into law by the president of the United States. Thousands of Americans would benefit from the ability to send and receive letters and packages through the mail, and thousands more would be able to move to new towns. It might not have the excitement of the questions of war and slavery, but this is a concrete example of Congress doing real good for real people. And it was a major accomplishment for the freshman congressman who ran point on the bill.

On the last day of session, the *Globe* reporter noted, "The intense excitement, hurry, and confusion attendant upon the closing hours of the session, which had prevailed to some extent during the entire morning, here seemed wrought up to the highest pitch, and at the call by the Clerk of each member, the hands of the clock—now rapidly moving forward, and just upon the hour of twice—were intently watched."[47] At midnight, Winthrop stood in his chair and announced that pursuant to the joint resolution, the House was now adjourned sine die.[48] Lincoln had finished his first session as a member of Congress.

And the president finally managed to take a vacation. He and his wife went to Bedford, Pennsylvania, where his gracious hosts informed him that he was the first president to visit since George Washington had come to put down the Whiskey Rebellion.[49]

CHAPTER 15

LINCOLN THE YOUNG INDIAN

"I had been chosen to Congress then from the Wild West and with hayseed in my hair I went to Massachusetts, the most cultured state in the union, to take a few lessons in deportment."

—Abraham Lincoln

Lincoln spent the recess hard at work on behalf of Zachary Taylor. A group of congressmen worked at the Central Rough and Ready Club in Washington City. Lincoln worked closely with Truman Smith of Connecticut, a fellow Young Indian who was spearheading the campaign apparatus. Or, as the Democratic press called him, the "principal schemer, spokesman, and general circular letter writer for the Whig party . . . the franker general of their documents" ("franking" being a reference to the power of congressmen to send and receive documents through the mail free of change).[1]

The leaders of the Taylor campaign corresponded frequently with supporters throughout the country. Lincoln wrote to Thaddeus Stevens, whom he had met at the Philadelphia convention, to learn the state of things on the ground. "I desire the undisguised opinion of some experienced and sagacious Pennsylvania politician, as to how the vote of that state . . . is likely to go."

Stevens noted that Pennsylvania was an odd place, owing to the complex combination of Free Soilers, Whigs, and Native Americans that populated Pennsylvania politics.[2]

Lincoln was impatient to return to Illinois, but wanted to stay in the fight where he could help Taylor win. Shortly after the session ended, Smith returned to Connecticut for the Whig state convention, hoping to head off any attacks against Taylor. During this time, he essentially left Lincoln at the helm.[3] As Smith wrote, "Our friends [Jasper] Brady of Pennsylvania and Lincoln of Illinois are now there [Whig headquarters] but Mr. Lincoln can not stay long and Mr. Brady is not sufficiently familiar with the whole field of national politics to make it safe to have it all in his hands."[4] By contrast, Smith is saying that Lincoln did have the skill and ability to oversee a presidential campaign, a valuable insight as to how Lincoln was perceived by his peers. Smith does not appear to have returned to Washington until September 7.[5]

On September 9, reunited with Mary Todd and the boys, who had come east to join him, Lincoln engaged on a campaign swing throughout Massachusetts on Taylor's behalf.

Lincoln had stayed at Central Committee longer than all but two of his colleagues, Jasper Brady, his neighbor on the House floor, and Truman Smith of Connecticut, and left only to press Taylor's case in Massachusetts.[6] By the end, Smith was the only member left in the Whig Congressional Conference Room.[7] Smith recorded that "for the last three weeks [we have sent] from 15 to 20 thousand documents right and left and in carrying on an extreme correspondence with all parts of the country . . . we are making Uncle Caves mail bags absolutely groan," he said, referencing Cave Johnson, Polk's postmaster general.[8] The campaign literature included speeches on behalf of Taylor by Clayton, Toombs, and Stephens, and biographies such as the *Life of Taylor*, available in English and German, as well as the *Moral and Intellectual Character of Taylor*.[9] These were carefully sorted and coded for easy distribution. A "T" in the upper left-hand corner was a copy of the *Life of Taylor*, which could easily be pulled and distributed as needed.

The Central Committee focused its distribution on influential supporters in key states who could then frank mail to opinion leaders and undecided voters. Elisha Embree was sent a thousand packets by the Central Committee, which he could then forward as needed throughout Indiana.[10] That state had gone for the Democrat in the previous two elections, but Taylor's popularity, recent congressional gains, and successful defense of Fort Harrison (near Terre Haute) in the War of 1812 made Indiana a ripe pickup target. During that battle, Taylor was reported to have held off four hundred Indians with sixteen men.[11]

Similarly, Smith asked Artemas Hale in Massachusetts for "a list of as many Whigs within the delivery of every poll in your district who would be willing to act as district volunteers."[12] Hale, who sometimes scribbled notes on his correspondence, wrote the words "zealous Taylor supporter" on Smith's letter, which may have been an understatement. It was not just the specter of Free Soil terrorizing Taylor in the Bay State. Hale and the rest of his congressional colleagues, some of whom represented what used to be safe districts, were campaigning for their lives.[13] Lincoln's friend Charles Hudson, a moderate antislavery man, would be defeated by a Free Soiler.[14]

The campaign hit another bump when Taylor "thankfully accepted" a nomination by a meeting of Democrats and independents in South Carolina.[15] To make matters worse, this gathering had nominated General Butler, Cass's Democratic running mate, for vice president.[16] Fillmore's New York supporters were incensed, and calls were made for Taylor to be removed from the top of the ticket. "Half an hour after the telegraph brought the news to Albany a call was out for a mass meeting to be held in the hall of the capitol building."[17] Only the stature and skill of Thurlow Weed succeeded in calming down the angry crowd.[18] Taylor would soon mitigate some of the damage by praising Fillmore, calling him qualified to be president himself.[19] Richard Wallach, president of the Central Rough and Ready Club, believed that letter had "knocked the last prop from under the Clay Whigs (as well as all the other ultras)."[20]

Wallach may almost have been on the mark there, had he counted the "Clay Whigs" and "ultras" who had remained in the Whig Party. As Lincoln took leave of central headquarters and headed out for the stump, he would find a very different story on the ground in Massachusetts. While Lincoln set out to harvest what he could for Taylor, his housemate Joshua Giddings, now a Free Soiler, had been busy salting the fields.

Giddings had arrived at the invitation of Charles Sumner,[21] and addressed the Free Soil convention in Worcester.[22] In Massachusetts the movement is well, he reported to his son.[23] "You should not fear going wrong if you stand by the principle of free territory," he told him.[24] When he spoke in Boston at the Tremont Temple, "cheers followed upon cheers" for Giddings. Crowds from Lowell to Lyman held him in "breathless attention,"[25] and he took the stage to chants of "Giddings! Giddings! Giddings!"[26] In "some parts" of Massachusetts, Giddings reported, "Taylorism is already dead."[27] A meeting in Bridgewater, assembled to ratify the decision at Philadelphia, "turned out to be a perfect failure."[28] By the end of the month, Giddings had learned of the bitterness his course had left among his Whig friends, but at the same time was being discussed as the vice presidential candidate of the Free Soil Party.[29] Charles Sumner gleefully reported, "Many of our friends are sanguine that we shall carry Massachusetts . . . the people everywhere are with us."[30]

To reach the Bay State, the Lincolns traveled by rail to New York, then by steamer to Norwich, Connecticut, and then by rail to Worcester.[31]

Earlier that summer, Lincoln had the chance to first visit the city of Philadelphia, and many sites critical to the independence and founding of the United States. Now he was in Boston, where one historian imagines "the giant form of our Illinois statesman was seen strolling on Boston Common, or exploring our historic buildings, or gazing upward at the new granite shaft of Bunker Hill."

Lincoln would remember, "I had been chosen to Congress then from the Wild West and with hayseed in my hair I went to Massachusetts, the most cultured state in the union, to take a few lessons in deportment."[32] He had his work cut out for him. Horace Mann believed "there is no state that will suffer so much as Massachusetts" in the division over Taylor.[33]

It was a critical time in Lincoln's development as a politician. For all who reach high office from a low starting point, there must come a time when they are familiarized with the ways of the elite. For Lincoln, this began with the River and Harbor Convention, deepened during his time in Congress, and expanded with his campaign swing through Massachusetts. The 1850s would see Lincoln deliver a number of important addresses to influential audiences, which would ultimately propel him to the presidency. It was on this campaign swing in support of General Taylor that Lincoln would first learn how to connect with the audiences that were so vital to his future success.

The Whigs of Massachusetts "claimed all the decency, refinement, wealth, and cultivation of the state, if not of the United States."[34] Whigs in Massachusetts were divided between two camps, "Cotton" and "Conscience." One dictated cordial relations with the southerners and the preservation of their valuable economic ties. The other found this secondary to the moral concerns of slavery. Or as one historian noted, "Few converts were obtained by the abolitionists in Boston countingrooms."[35]

While in Boston, Lincoln is said to have stayed at Tremont House, the most modern hotel in the United States.[36] Here he would have a chance to reflect on how far he'd come from his first public speech, campaigning unsuccessfully for the Illinois House in 1832. Then, Lincoln had taken advantage of a crowd gathered at a public sale in Pappsville, eleven miles west of Springfield. From the crude platform, Lincoln observed a fight break out, and one of his friends being assaulted. Lincoln interrupted his speech, pushed his way through the crowd, and grabbed the assailant by the neck and the seat of his pants, tossing him in the air a distance of twelve feet, one witness insisted.[37] Resuming at the speaker's stand, Lincoln said: "Fellow citizens, I presume you all know who I am. I am humble Abraham Lincoln. I have been solicited by many friends to become a candidate for the legislature. My politics are short and sweet, like the old woman's dance. I am in favor of a national bank. I am in favor of the internal improvement system and a high protective tariff. These are my sentiments and political principles. If elected I shall be thankful; if not, it will be all the same."[38]

Now Lincoln would give a much more sophisticated speech to a far savvier and more discerning audience.

On September 12, Lincoln spoke at Worcester City Hall. The *Boston Atlas* called it "one of the best speeches ever heard in Worcester," and the *Boston Herald* thought Lincoln "a tremendous voice for Taylor and Fillmore."[39]

The next day, Lincoln attended the Whig convention and dined with Governor Levi Lincoln and George Ashmun as well as Rufus Choate.[40] A former senator and state attorney general, Choate was also a celebrated lawyer who was famous for acquitting a man, caught red-handed for murder, by arguing a sleepwalking defense. Perhaps he regaled Lincoln, a fellow trial lawyer, with this story.[41]

On September 14, Lincoln spoke again in New Bedford.

Next Lincoln addressed a crowd in Boston's Washingtonian Hall. The venue was the home of a temperance society, but his audience that night was the Whig Club of Boston. The hall was sparse, with plain benches for seats and "coarse beds for the poor victims of man's inhumanity, turned into the streets by the merciless rum-seller." Lincoln ascended the speaker's stand on the north end by a staircase of "boards rudely put together."[42] On the wall was a portrait of John Hawkins, a temperance leader, and pictures "illustrative of the drunkard's progress. . . . Sober business is done here, and elegance is not expected."

The *Daily Advertiser* described Lincoln as "a very tall and thin figure, with an intellectual face, showing a searching mind and cool judgment." Lincoln began by expressing how humbling it was to be talking to an audience in Boston, as the people where he was from believed everyone there was "instructed and wise." Lincoln "spoke in a clear and cool, and a very eloquent manner, for an hour and a half, carrying the audience with him in his able arguments and brilliant illustrations—only interrupted by warm and frequent applause."

Lincoln revisited his earlier remarks on behalf of Taylor, that it was a Whig principle to defer to the legislature (the *Illinois Register* remarked that the party out of power being against executive influence "is not very wonderful"),[43] and then moved on to slavery. "All agreed that slavery was an evil," Lincoln said, "but that we were not responsible for it and cannot affect it in states of this union where we do not live. But the question of the extension of slavery to new territories of this country is a part of our responsibility and care, and is under our control." Lincoln believed the Free Soil Party was working against their sole object. They had no other platform—if they did, Lincoln reasoned, it was like a pair of pantaloons "large enough for any man, small enough for any boy." The people had a decision to make: Either Taylor or Cass would be elected president. Free Soilers had "hitched themselves on the skirts of the artful dodger of Kinderhook [Van Buren]," and could only spoil the election.[44]

The Free Soilers charged they would do their duty, leaving the rest to God, which Lincoln argued was an excuse "for taking a course that they were not able to maintain by a fair and full argument."

At the end of what the *Advertiser* called a "truly masterly and convincing speech," he received three cheers for Illinois, and three for himself, the Lone Whig Star.

Up next was Lowell City Hall, on September 16. The Worcester *Daily Journal* recorded a speech "replete with good sense, sound reasoning, and irresistible argument, and spoken with that perfect command of manner and matter which so eminently distinguishes the western orators."[45]

September 18 was a speech in Dorchester, followed by addresses in Chelsea the following day, two speeches on the twentieth, in Dedham and at Cambridge City Hall, followed by Taunton on the twenty-first.

But the most critical event of Lincoln's Massachusetts swing may not have been any speech he made, but one he heard. On September 22, Lincoln was scheduled to speak at Tremont Temple, a Baptist church in Boston. The rally was originally intended for the square behind city hall, but inclement weather forced it indoors. At the time, the temple was exhibiting Rembrandt Peale's *The Court of Death*, a massive painting of 312 square feet featuring twenty-three different figures.

The principal speaker that evening was William Seward of New York. Seward was everything Lincoln was not. A Phi Beta Kappa graduate of Union College, Seward had come to the Whigs from the Anti-Masonic Party, and served two terms as the governor of his state.

Seward's speech was focused on slavery.[46] He argued that Taylor could be trusted on the issue of slavery's expansion, and argued "the time will come, and that not far distant, when the citizens of the whole country, as well as Massachusetts, will select for their leader a freeman of the north, in preference to a slaveholder." Seward no doubt had himself in mind, but in truth it was the other man on the podium, the freshman congressman from Illinois.

Lincoln followed Seward with a "powerful and convincing speech" of "about an hour," which ended with three cheers for "Old Zack," three for Seward, and three for Lincoln.[47] The *Atlas* recorded it was one of "the best meetings ever held in this good Whig city."[48]

Seward, Lincoln's principal rival for the Republican nomination in 1860, who went on to serve as his secretary of state, had a chance to visit with Lincoln back at the hotel they shared.[49] Seward insisted "that the time had come for sharp definition of opinion and boldness of utterance."[50]

Lincoln agreed with him. "Governor Seward, I have been thinking about what you said in your speech. I reckon you are right. We have got to deal with this slavery question, and got to give much more attention to it hereafter than we have been doing."[51]

Lincoln had much time to consider Seward's speech and their subsequent conversation as he and his family made their way home. He traveled through Albany, where he paid a call on Thurlow Weed, who would later manage Seward's 1860 campaign. Before Lincoln departed, they would pay a visit to Millard Fillmore, New York comptroller and vice presidential nominee. Lincoln would return, twelve years later, to visit former president Fillmore on his way to Washington to serve as president. For now, the Lincoln family traveled from Albany to Buffalo by rail, then boarded the steamer *Globe* en route to Chicago.[52]

On September 28, Lincoln had the chance to experience Niagara Falls, which inspired him to start a poem he never finished.[53] "It calls up the indefinite past. When Columbus first sought this continent, when Christ suffered on the cross, when Moses led Israel through the Red Sea, nay, even when Adam first came from the hand of his Maker, then as now, Niagara was roaring here. The eyes of that species of extinct giants, whose bones fill the mounds of America, have gazed on Niagara, as ours do now . . . the mammoth and Mastodon [*sic*], now so long dead, that fragments of their monstrous bones, alone testify that they ever lived, have gazed on Niagara. In that long, long time, never still for a single moment. Never dried, never froze, never slept, never rested."

But this fragment of a poem was not the only inspiration Lincoln found aboard the *Globe*. While steaming up the Detroit River, Lincoln saw another boat that had run aground.[54] To save it, the captain of the grounded vessel "ordered his crew to collect all the empty barrels, boxes, and loose planks on the ship and force them under the sides to buoy the boat over the shallow water."[55] As Jason Emerson points out in *Lincoln the Inventor*, it must have brought to mind Lincoln's arrival in New Salem, when his boat had become stuck.[56] What if there were a device, Lincoln wondered, to help rescue boats that were stranded?[57] On each side of a boat would be inflatable pouches that could be filled with air as necessary to boost the vessel over tough spots.[58] During the recess and after his return to Washington,

Lincoln would work diligently preparing his invention for submission to the patent office.

On October 5, the *Globe* arrived in Chicago and Lincoln registered at Sherman House. The next day, on six hours' notice, Lincoln was asked to speak to a Whig assembly. By October 9, Lincoln was back on the campaign trail on behalf of Taylor, with a speech at the Peoria Courthouse.

The *Register* welcomed him home: "We are pleased to observe that his arduous duties since the adjournment of Congress in franking and loading down the mails with Whig electioneering documents, have not impaired his health. He looks remarkably well."

While Taylor's nomination strengthened the Whigs of Illinois, it put the careers of some of Lincoln's northern counterparts in jeopardy. Many of them now faced Free Soil challenges, or grassroots revolts and attempts to replace them by their own party. George Marsh of Vermont felt the Taylor nomination "may prove so unpalatable to my constituents that my support of it may put an end to my political life. This, however, would constitute a most insignificant part of the regret I should feel at the election of General Cass."[59]

On October 21, Lincoln debated in Jacksonville.[60] His opponent was Murray McConnell, a Morgan County lawyer and Democratic legislator. McConnell argued that Lincoln would not vote, thanks to General Taylor, until the Ashmun amendment had first been adopted. He asked whether Lincoln knew he was misrepresenting his constituents.

"No, I did not know it," Lincoln answered, "and don't believe it yet."

McConnell blamed Logan's defeat on Lincoln. The *Register* reported that "Lincoln has made nothing by coming to this part of the country to make speeches. He had better have stayed away."

Lincoln would do anything but stay away from the campaign trail. He continued to Petersburg, where he had won the Whig nomination, to Metamora, and Magnolia, Hennepin, and Lacon. Perhaps nobody had worked harder to advance Taylor's candidacy than Abraham Lincoln. With Election Day here and the case submitted to the people, all Lincoln could do was wait. At least with regard to the election. Lincoln otherwise used his recess to build a small scale model of his flotation device, using the tools of Walter Davis, a mechanic in Springfield.[61]

The *National Intelligencer* had arranged with different states to receive information by telegraph. Its front page on November 7, Election Day, read, "The deepest solicitude, as well as the highest hopes, are centered on the great act to be performed by the American people this day."

Information was scarce and scattered. The American people had made their decision, but what had they decided? Partial results appeared in newspapers, skewed toward cities closest to telegraph machines. On Friday, November 10, the result was anybody's guess. But the next day, the *Intelligencer* proclaimed, "We are without words fit for expressing our sensations on this glorious event."[62]

For the first time, the Electoral College was selected on the same day.[63] The popular vote was 1,360,099 (Taylor) to 1,220,544 (Cass) to 291,263 (Van Buren), with the state of South Carolina choosing its electors through its legislature rather than by popular vote. Taylor won 163 electoral votes to Cass's 127, with none for Van Buren.[64]

On November 8, Polk reacted somberly to the news that he would be replaced by Zachary Taylor. "Should this be so," he said, "it is deeply to be regretted."[65]

Led by the Young Indians, the Whigs had completed one of the most cynical acts in American political history, nominating a popular figure from a war they opposed, a slave owner whose thoughts on the major issues were unknown and probably inchoate. But that doesn't mean they were wrong. In fact, the closeness of the results supports Lincoln's thinking. The election, it seems, would have been won only by Taylor or some Democrat in the mold of Polk. "We have escaped as by fire," Winthrop thought. "Nobody but Taylor could have carried us through."[66]

On November 26, Lincoln left for Washington for the second session of Congress. In a few short months, Polk's administration would be out— Taylor's would be in. As the lone Whig of Illinois, Lincoln was strongly prevailed upon by job seekers. ("As the only Whig," wrote one, "you must expect to be harassed by us without measure."[67])

One of these he obliged, three days before leaving Springfield. He probably thought little of it, recommending Cyrus Edwards for the position of commissioner of the General Land Office. But this position, and his initial letter in favor of Edwards, would before long return to haunt Lincoln.

CHAPTER 16

MILES GONE BY

On December 4, 1848, the Thirtieth Congress returned for its second session, with 178 present at the roll call. Lincoln, along with two others from Illinois, was still making his way east.[1]

Horace Mann wrote: "Now when we have a southern man and a military man at the head of government, is the time to see whether the Union is a rope of sand, or a band of steel. . . . The great question of freedom or slavery is the only one that would keep me here."[2]

The next day, President Polk submitted his fourth and final Annual Message to the House. The clerk was interrupted by a stampede of "members rushing forward" to get copies.[3]

Lincoln arrived on December 7, realizing quickly that he wasn't missing anything, as the day was lost to a fight over printing.[4] Committee assignments in the Thirtieth Congress were made for the session, not for the entire two years, but Lincoln was reappointed to the same he'd had before.[5]

Lincoln's box in the House Post Office was no doubt filled with letters. One was from an autograph seeker, and Lincoln responded as follows: "Your note, requesting my 'signature with a sentiment,' was received and should have been answered long since, but that it was mislaid. I am not a very sentimental man; and the best sentiment I can think of is, that if you collect the signatures of all persons who are no less distinguished than I, you will have a very undistinguishing mass of names. Very respectfully, A. Lincoln."[6]

But Lincoln was about to move closer to one important distinction: possession of a United States patent for his invention. Upon arrival in Washington, Lincoln showed up at the office of patent attorney Zenas Robbins holding a wooden model of his device.[7]

Robbins recalled Lincoln's visit. "He walked into my office one morning with a model of a western steamboat under his arm. After a friendly greeting he placed his model on my office table and proceeded to explain the principles embodied therein that he believed to be his own invention, and which, if new, he desired to secure by letters-patent. During my former residence in St. Louis, I had made myself thoroughly familiar with everything appertaining to the construction and equipment of the flatbottomed steamboats that were adapted to the shallow rivers of our western and southern states, and therefore I was able speedily to come to the conclusion that Mr. Lincoln's proposed improvement of that class of vessels was new and patentable, and I so informed him. Thereupon he instructed me to prepare the necessary drawings and papers and prosecute an application for a patent for his invention at the United States patent office."[8]

Taylor was expected in Washington at the end of February. "I expect the old gentleman does not intend to give the office holders much time to annoy him," thought one member. Washington was obsessed with who would be chosen for the cabinet.[9]

Everyone was angling for position. In New York, where Taylor had faced strong resistance, the politicians were "most ridiculously contending for the honor of having been original Taylorites."[10]

Though Lincoln and the Taylor Whigs had triumphed, Giddings and the Free Soilers believed that they were the true winners. One of his supporters wrote: "We survive the conflict and though outnumbered we are not beaten—the Cass party is whipped—the Whig party is dead on the field of battle, the Taylor party have run off with the spoils . . . the Free Soil party are in possession of the field of battle with heads and hearts and principles all safe and sound and ready for future battle and victory."[11] He predicted that Taylor would come out against the Wilmot Proviso, swelling the ranks of the new movement and discrediting Taylor's supporters. "God's wheels of providence are great ones and seem to move very slowly to us, whose days are as a hands breadth, but they never get out of gear, and all will come out right, by and by."

In the second session of the Thirtieth Congress, a new distinguished member would be joining the House. Horace Greeley, the editor of the *New York Tribune* and one of the most influential newspapermen in America, arrived to take a seat left vacant by a disputed election.

Greeley remembered Congressman Lincoln as "personally a favorite on our [the Whig] side . . . quiet good natured man, did not aspire to leadership, and seldom claimed the floor. . . . He was one of the most moderate, though firm, opponents of slavery extension, and notably of a buoyant, cheerful spirit."[12]

Greeley did not remember his time in Congress as fondly. He remembered his brief tenure in the Thirtieth Congress as "little that was achieved or the much that was said."[13] The situation was not helped by "the last sands of an administration already superseded."[14]

Greeley was also shocked by the hypocrisy of Congress. After one committee hearing, which saw passage of a law ending the grog ration (free alcohol given to sailors in the navy), one member said to another "that was a glorious vote we have just taken . . . let us go and take a drink on the strength of it."[15]

On December 22, Greeley and his *New York Tribune* lobbed a grenade into the House chamber; unlike the previous firefights that had dominated the House, this one would have a unifying effect. That day the paper published a "Congressional Mileage Expose."[16] It was accompanied by a chart with a list of all the members of the House, the distance from their homes to Washington by the shortest post route, followed by what they actually billed for mileage, along with what they were reimbursed versus what they would have been given along the shortest route.[17] The total cost to the taxpayer, Greeley argued, was $73,492.60, and the "excess of miles traveled was 183,031, making a distance something greater than the circumference of the earth seven times measured."[18] Lincoln billed the House for 1,626 miles, rather than 780 miles (calculated using the distance between post offices).[19] It should be noted that members were not required to take the most direct route, and that for many legitimate reasons they could not. Members often had to travel far out of their way to reach a train or boat. But at the same time, there were clearly those who were working the system to their own benefit.

The mileage reimbursement made up a significant part of a member's compensation. Lincoln and his colleagues earned $8 for every day Congress was in session (which would add up to $2,744 for the Thirtieth Congress).[20] They were reimbursed 40 cents per mile to travel between Washington and home.[21] To put this number in perspective, a congressional committee clerk might make $4 a day.[22] The principal teacher of a school in Washington City made $800 per year in 1848.[23] Most of Lincoln's fees for the time preceding his service in Congress were for $10; simpler tasks were less, more complicated jobs more, for instance, $3 to draft a power of attorney and $100 for a lengthy Supreme Court case. The average Supreme Court case was $20.[24] Between 1840 and 1850, "Lincoln's annual income from the law was probably between $1,500 and $2,000."[25] The Illinois governor's salary was $1,200, and allowed the governor to maintain a very high lifestyle.[26] A maid might make $1.50 a week in Springfield.[27]

The public outcry was enormous. "I think no act of the Roman Senate was ever more corrupt," wrote a constituent to one of Lincoln's colleagues.[28] Congress felt compelled to act on the issue and, a mere five days after the story's publication, spent the day in debate.

Suddenly, the normally sedate Committee on Mileage was the center of attention. A package of three resolutions was considered. First, Thomas Turner of Illinois asked the committee to report whether anyone received more than they ought, how mileage was computed, and what evidence was necessary to substantiate a claim.[29] A second resolution directed the committee to consider whether these allegations added up to fraud.[30] A third allowed the committee to call for witnesses and compel the turning over of documents.[31]

Lincoln moved for division, with the first two resolutions adopted and the third rejected.[32]

Lincoln's roommate Elisha Embree was caught up in the scandal and attacked by the Democratic *Clarion* of his district. He demanded a retraction, sending the paper a letter from Greeley himself in hopes of clarifying the issue.[33] Hoping to survive politically, Embree later tried to add an amendment to the Civil and Diplomatic Appropriations Bill, to link mileage to the shortest mail route between a member's home and Washington.[34] It would not be enough, and Embree would ultimately lose his bid for reelection.

Needless to say, the article and the ensuing furor made Greeley a bit unpopular. "The rage manifested against Mr. Greely [*sic*] by the members of the House was generally in proportion to their 'excess' mileage."[35] Outlaw thought him "a low dirty scoundrel, who ought to be kicked out of the House."[36] It was noted, however, that in later years, the routes traveled by members became much more direct.[37]

There was a meeting in the Capitol of the worst mileage abusers to think of a solution. At the meeting, someone proposed a resolution simply to expel Greeley. It would take a two-thirds vote, but the attendees were feeling pretty good about their chances.[38] John Wentworth, in attendance, explained that this would make Greeley the president of the United States, upon which it was rejected.[39]

This scandal appears to have greatly burdened the members of the Thirtieth Congress, but they would have miles to go before they could rest.

CHAPTER 17

THE VALIANT DEMOLISHER OF WINDMILLS

"We hold these truths to be self-evident, that all men are created equal. . . ."
—Declaration of Independence

In later years, John Wentworth of Illinois remembered: "When a man enters Congress and looks around for some man who is to become president at some day, he must forecast the future predominant question and then look for the man who can command the most confidence for his identification with it."[1] In antebellum America, this "future predominant question" was easy to predict. But the man who would later be most identified with it was not. Yet here in the second session of the Thirtieth Congress, the man in question would take a powerful, irreversible step in that direction.

In 1860, Joshua Giddings sat to write a letter. Abraham Lincoln, the Republican nominee for president of the United States, had been denounced as "the slave hound of Illinois" by a prominent abolitionist. There was a real question whether the true believers should trust this man. Giddings had an answer for them: "Paul was an apostle at Corinth and at Rome, although he had been a persecutor at Damascus," he began. "The consciousness of every man compels him to judge those around him by their present opinions and not by those which they have discarded . . . it is due to truth that those who have labored in the cause of humanity should understand the part which

Mr. Lincoln performed in that closing session of the 30th Congress."[2] What follows is that story.

The question of what Abraham Lincoln believed about slavery, and when he believed it, has been the subject of a great deal of controversy. But Lincoln's voting record cannot be disputed. Charles Hudson, a Massachusetts Whig who had recently been defeated by a Free Soiler, recalled that Lincoln "has always regarded African servitude as a moral and political evil, degrading the slave, and corrupting the master, and so proving a curse to both races."[3] He remembered his friend's "incorruptible integrity,"[4] and recalled that "his firmness is not so much the result of an indomitable will, as of an unwavering integrity."[5]

Among the members of the Thirtieth Congress, there was a diversity of views on the subject.

Dromgoole Sims, who died before taking his seat but spoke for many of his colleagues, believed, "No man who reads the Bible and who is Christian can denounce slavery as immoral."[6]

Abolitionist Amos Tuck viewed it this way: "The south had [seen the] steady growth of population and wealth of the north far outstrip that of the south through many years, in spite of all measures to counteract the growing inequality. The last great enterprise to maintain equality...by annexation, war, and conquest, was becoming less and less hopeful of securing its object."[7] Southern politicians won office "mostly on promises to vindicate slavery, fortify its power, and extend its domain," and were "eager to distinguish themselves by violence of language, in which they attacked the institutions, conduct, character, and policy of the north, without discrimination."[8] "Why was it not realized that violence in deeds must soon break forth, where such overflowing violence in feeling was constantly exhibited?"[9]

Richard W. Thompson of Indiana believed that "no practical good, but much of harm will be produced by an agitation of the question in Congress.... Why agitate the country with a subject which arouses so many of the bad passions of our nature and strikes at so many political relations of the most delicate character?"[10] Thompson's ultimate vote on the issue "excited much talk in the district and motivated people to run against him."[11]

Robert Winthrop argued the South had "really no right to complain at the proposition to abolish the slave traffic in the District. They do not permit it in many of their own states. It is certainly a . . . disgrace to the country, that the seat of government should be one of the principal slave markets, where human beings are assorted into cargoes, without regard to family relations, and shipped off to the south."[12] But he believed northern agitation prolonged the issue.

David Outlaw saw the slavery resolutions as "not only unnecessary but unfortunate, inasmuch as they will inflame the public mind."[13] Outlaw believed the object was "to irritate and inflame the south and north." He opposed "geographical parties, or any thing which tends to form them."

Members also heard from constituents and politicians back home.

States such as North Carolina reacted with resolutions, protesting that slavery had been "maturely considered" at the Philadelphia convention, and that "we view with deep concern and alarm the constant aggressions on the rights of the slaveholder by certain reckless politicians of the north; and that the recent proceedings of Congress on the subject of slavery are wrought with mischief well calculated to disturb the peace of our country." Any act limiting slavery in the District of Columbia would be not only a "gross injustice and wrong," but also unconstitutional.[14] John McDowell of Virginia was accused by a constituent of sitting silently as the administration was attacked by Whigs and abolitionists.[15]

Each member's position was a product of his upbringing and experience.

When Lincoln was born in Hardin County, Kentucky, there were 7,500 residents, including 1,000 slaves.[16] His parents had been members of churches that advocated abolition, and in one instance the issue of slavery had caused their church to split apart. When the South Fork Baptist Church separated, the Lincolns followed the path of antislavery.[17]

One of Lincoln's childhood neighbors was a politician who had opposed slavery.[18] One biographer pointed out that the Lincoln farm faced the Cumberland Road between Nashville and Louisville, and that the young boy might well have seen men and women herded like cattle, heard the clanking of the heavy iron chains, the moans of the damned as they were marched to their fates along the great western road.[19] On flatboat trips to New Orleans in 1828 and 1831, Lincoln saw "negroes chained—maltreated—whipped—and scourged . . . his heart bled."[20]

In Illinois, where Lincoln had lived since he was twenty-one, and Indiana, where he grew up, "Food, speech, settlement patterns, architecture, family ties, and economic relations had much more in common with Kentucky [where Lincoln was born] and Tennessee than with the northern counties of their own states."[21] The southern Northwest was referred to as "a sort of belt or break-water between the extremes of the north and south."[22]

While Illinois was technically a free state, covered by the protections of the Northwest Ordinance, it permitted a scheme of "indentured servitude."[23] By simply marking an X on a contract they often couldn't read, blacks would find themselves "hired" as servants for the rest of their lives.[24] If this wasn't slavery, the distinction was a nicety lost on the signer.

In 1841, while a passenger on a steamboat, Lincoln observed slaves chained six together, "like so many fish upon a trot-line. In this condition they were being separated forever from the scenes of their childhood, their friends, their fathers and mothers, and brothers and sister, and many of them, from their wives and children, and going into perpetual slavery where the lash of the master is proverbially more ruthless and unrelenting."[25]

Illinois had on the books oppressive "black laws," which required free blacks entering the state to "post a $1,000 bond."[26] The Illinois Constitutional Convention of 1848 referred to the people a referendum on whether the legislature should have the power to ban blacks entirely from their borders.[27] It passed with 70 percent of the vote.[28] The *Liberator*, the national abolitionist newspaper, called Illinois "to all intents and purposes, a slave-holding state"[29] and took note in 1837 that of the 607 antislavery organizations in the United States, there were 3 in Illinois.[30] At the end of that year, a mob attacked and murdered Reverend Elijah Lovejoy, an antislavery advocate and publisher.[31] In the year Lincoln first ran for Congress, wild mobs had prevented abolitionist meetings from gathering in central Illinois, and the year he was elected to Congress one of those mob leaders was placed on the state Supreme Court without incident.[32]

In light of these sentiments, it's no surprise that when Lincoln arrived in Springfield in 1837, blacks made up only 5 percent of the population, many of these no doubt indentured servants.[33]

As a state legislator, Lincoln was seldom called upon to vote on slavery.

But there were some notable exceptions. In 1837, the Illinois legislature considered three resolutions, condemning the antislavery movement, expressing "deep regard and affection" for slave owners, and denouncing the effort to abolish slavery in the District of Columbia.[34] Lincoln unsuccessfully offered an amendment to the latter section, that Congress should consider removing slavery from D.C. if her residents asked for it.[35] Lincoln's modest amendment went nowhere. On the resolutions, the Illinois House voted 77–6 in favor, and the Senate 18–0.[36] "Thus, only six members of the legislature voted no. One was Lincoln."[37]

Lincoln attempted to explain his vote for the record. He and fellow legislator Dan Stone offered their explanation in writing.[38] They wrote that while "slavery is founded on both injustice and bad policy," the abolition movement was making things worse.[39] Congress, they reasoned, had no power to interfere with slavery where it existed, and while they did believe it had the power to abolish slavery in the District of Columbia, it should only do so at the behest of the citizens therein.[40]

In 1839, Lincoln "helped defeat a resolution in the Illinois legislature declaring that slavery should be preserved in Washington D.C., that more slave states should be allowed to enter the Union, and that any move to grant Illinois blacks equal rights was 'unconstitutional.'"[41]

This was a good measure of Lincoln on slavery, in substance and temperament, until he left for Congress.

Lincoln's Illinois was an incredibly hostile place to blacks, profoundly supportive of slavery, and violently opposed to dissenting opinions. Even in 1863, when Lincoln issued the Emancipation Proclamation, a resolution passed the Illinois legislature in opposition.[42] Lincoln would frequently be called to vote on slavery during the Thirtieth Congress, and had a nearly perfect record of opposing the institution. With no political upside, these votes and, later, his first ever measure to limit slavery, could only have proceeded from convictions of the heart.

Lincoln always voted to accept and refer antislavery petitions,[43] and in the second session referred one himself, a petition from Hardin's home county of Morgan asking that slavery be abolished in the District.[44]

In the waning days of his presidency, Polk was worried that the territories within the Mexican cession would be lost to the Union if territorial governments could not soon be organized.[45] He felt this especially true in California. After the discovery of gold at Sutter's Mill in 1848, the territory had been flooded by many smart, entrepreneurial types, searching for riches or for profits from doing business with those that were. Surely these were just the type to form their own country and strike out alone.

John Palfrey, who along with Giddings and Tuck had caused so much excitement at the beginning of the first session, would unleash a tempest upon the second. On December 13, he introduced a bill to repeal all acts maintaining slavery in the District of Columbia.[46] But by a vote of 82–69, Palfrey was denied leave to introduce the bill.[47]

Later that day, Elihu Root moved to instruct the Committee on Territories to create governments for the Mexican cession that specifically excluded slavery therefrom. A motion to kill the proposal was defeated, 107–80, with Lincoln supporting the majority.[48]

On December 16, the breakfast table at Mrs. Sprigg's would become a microcosm of the struggle over the new territory. John Pollock announced that he would vote for a bill organizing California and New Mexico, even without Northwest Ordinance language. Giddings denounced the plan, pointing out that the southerners would ensure enough people would migrate in order to tilt the vote in favor of slavery.[49] This concept, of course, would return as the euphemistic "popular sovereignty," the idea of letting white settlers in the territories determine whether they wanted to permit the slavery of black people within their borders. And once adopted in the Kansas-Nebraska Act, this is precisely what happened, and for years thereafter the blood of slaveholders and free soilers watered the fertile fields of the Great Plains.

But as Giddings tried to rally his messmates to action over the breakfast table, at least one had had enough. Pollock called him an agitator, making trouble over nothing. Giddings in turn signaled his unwillingness to have his "motives impugned by a miserable doughface who had not mind enough to form an opinion nor courage enough to avow it."[50]

Unsurprisingly, this did not resolve the situation. Pollock jumped to his feet and "sprang from the table as he sat on the opposite side and marched around" to where Giddings stood, ready for him. Dickey and McIlvaine prevented this miniature civil war from getting violent, and eventually the two sat back down. Giddings came away thinking Pollock "a miserable scamp." These feelings were not limited to the breakfast table at Lincoln's boardinghouse, but extended throughout the Whig caucus. Giddings thought them never "as bitter as they are now."[51]

On December 18, Giddings introduced a bill to hold a referendum in April in the District of Columbia on whether to permit slavery.[52] It was a fascinating way to pose the question; it was, after all, the doctrine of popular sovereignty, on which Lewis Cass and the Democrats had campaigned in the election previous. But it was Patrick Tompkins, who had moved out of Sprigg's between sessions, who asked him a question that effectively terminated the measure. Tompkins noted that the bill allowed all male inhabitants over the age of twenty-one and with one year's residency to participate in the election. Did this mean blacks as well as whites? Tompkins wondered. Even slaves?[53]

Giddings replied that "when he looked abroad upon the family of man, he knew no distinctions. He knew of no persons in this District that did not come from the same creating hand that formed himself, or the gentleman from Mississippi."[54]

The bill was laid on the table, 106–79, with Lincoln voting yes.[55] Enfranchising blacks was still an extremely controversial topic, unsurprisingly in a Congress that had to fight so long to stop the spread of slavery to places like Oregon.

Why did Lincoln, who had consistently voted to refer antislavery petitions, and voted dozens of times for free soil, vote to table? As to the question of slavery in the District, Lincoln was preparing a bill of his own. It would not be tackling issues such as black suffrage, as Giddings wanted, or instant abolition with no compensation to owners, as Daniel Gott of New York wanted.[56] Lincoln wasn't interested in symbolic defeats, at least not when a concrete victory could be obtained. He wanted a bill that could pass—something that would actually expand liberty to real people.

Lincoln knew that such a bill must be narrowly tailored in order to pass. He was a constant witness to the fury of slaveholders and their defenders, both inside and outside of Congress, and he knew that triggering their unified opposition would be fatal to the bill. Giddings received numerous threatening letters from the South. One, written by "Joseph J. Slaveholder," observed that "your course in the Congress of the nation is to be viewed with pity rather than indignation by the slave holders of our country. You have spent your life thus far, in the vain attempt to eradicate an imaginary evil from our social system; and your efforts will be about as fruitful as those of the illustrious conquerors of the peaceful fold, and the valiant demolisher of windmills."[57]

Another pointed out, "Till your brethren undertook to sell them they were contented and happy. It is you and your associates who have caused this distress on the poor ignorant negroes." For good measure, the writer added that "your heart is so black, yes so black, that if it was rubbed against the devil's chimney sweep it would not be injured." This particular cowardly correspondent withheld his name, he says, "for fear you might be honored by being rebuked by me."[58]

The next great row over slavery occurred over an unlikely subject. Louis Pacheco spoke multiple languages, from French to Seminole, and studied classical languages from an academic perspective. Because of the circumstances of his birth, Pacheco was also a slave, owned by Antonio Pacheco, who could do none of those things. At the end of it all, Winthrop would ask: "Was there ever such a chapter of accidents as the history of the Antonio Pacheco case?"[59]

In 1835, American forces were preparing to drive the Seminoles from Florida.[60] One hundred men under the command of Major Francis Dade were positioned in preparation for armed conflict.[61] Needing a guide and interpreter, the army hired Louis Pacheco, a slave, from his master for twenty-five dollars a month.[62] It was perhaps naïve to trust that Louis would assist the army in driving the Indians from their land. At any rate, he was able to convey to the Seminoles the route by which he planned to take the army. The ambush was so complete that Major Dade and all one hundred men under his command were killed.[63] It is even thought that Pacheco, racing to join the enemy during the firefight, took up arms against the men he had been trusted to lead.[64] Despite this setback, the Seminoles were defeated two years later.[65] As a condition of peace, the Seminoles were allowed to take their slaves with them.[66] An Indian chief named Jumper claimed Pacheco as his own, and was allowed by the army to relocate with him to Indian Territory.[67]

Now, the heirs of Pacheco's owner demanded the government compensate them for the value of the slave.

James Wilson of New Hampshire cited seven previous cases in which Congress had refused to honor a claim made for a slave.[68] Armistead Burt of South Carolina argued that in all of these cases, the master had voluntarily put his slave in danger. Wilson had already anticipated this argument and cited others, including one in which a slave had died while working for the federal government in building the defenses of New Orleans.

The rejoinder was that the Constitution provided no property rights for "corn . . . breadstuffs, or in any article of merchandise."[69] The government had hired Pacheco from his owner, did not return him, and when his owner presented his claim, ordered him removed from Florida. Burt argued that in previous cases in which Congress had refused to honor a slave claim, there was no evidence the slave had been impressed, rather than volunteered.[70] Burt pointed out that the federal government had levied a tax on slaves specifically (thus recognizing a property interest).

Lincoln voted to table the Pacheco claim, but by a margin of 66–88, it failed.[71]

Giddings argued, "At the foundation of this government great truths were laid down, which every man here this day either adhered to or rejected."[72] The federal government was founded, he argued, on the self-evident principle "that all men are created equal. . . . Let them tell him not that they held to this important and fundamental truth, and yet undertake to legislate for the oppression of their fellow men, and involve his people and the people of the whole land in the payment for immortal souls." There was no one in the House, he said, who could "lay his hand on his breast, and before his God declare that he believed" in life, liberty, and the pursuit of happiness who could support this bill.

"I cannot sleep at night," Giddings recorded, the lack of rest "visibly affecting my health."[73]

Debate on Pacheco resumed January 6. The bill was now up for a vote. Giddings entered the Hall of Representatives "trembling with fear of failure," the slaveholders looking on "solemn and perplexed."[74] A majority of 90 to 89 favored the bill, Lincoln voting no. But under the Twelfth Rule of the House, wherever he may make the difference, the Speaker is permitted to cast the deciding vote. If he voted no, the bill would fail, 90–90. All eyes looked to Robert C. Winthrop, mutually distrusted by both sides. Winthrop prefaced his vote with a professorial explanation, saying that he did not concur fully with the principles of either side, when he was interrupted by the clerk, who handed him a sheet of paper.

A tense moment ensued, as Winthrop declared to the House that a mistake had been made in the way the vote was announced, and that 91 votes were in favor and 89 against. The news was received with "varying expressions of amusement, applause, or gratification."[75]

Burt of South Carolina took the floor, when Palfrey tried to get his attention. The Speaker ruled his question out of order. "Under the extraordinary circumstances under which that bill has been passed—"

"I do not yield the floor," Burt said.

"I ask the gentleman—" Palfrey pleaded.

"I trust the gentleman will not interrupt—" Burt said.

At this point Lincoln stood up and said, "I have had information brought to me in relation to the record of my vote on the bill which has just been passed. I desire to be informed by the Clerk how my vote is recorded."

The clerk responded, "The vote is recorded in the negative."

"That is right," Lincoln said.

After a number of desperate attempts to stall or force a revote, the House moved on to the next order of business. Many clamored for the floor, and during debate Giddings had to ask the Speaker to gavel the House into order, for he could not hear.[76]

On January 8, Winthrop addressed the House and explained that there had been an error in the tabulation of the previous vote. The original announcement had been 90–89, and he had been prepared to decide the question when the clerk informed him that the vote had truly been 91–89. Since Saturday, it had been discovered that both of these counts were wrong. In reality, the vote stood at 89–89. This would require him to break the tie, and he prepared to do so.

Before he could, however, he was again interrupted. John Farrelly, Whig of Pennsylvania, stood and asked how his vote had been recorded. Winthrop answered that his vote had not been counted.

"I voted 'no,'" Farrelly explained. This made it 89–90, killing Pacheco's claim. Given the confusion, the clerk read the call of the roll to see if there were any other errors. It was correct—the bill had been defeated.[77]

Giddings remembered it "among the happiest moments of my life," the crowning event of "a great day for freedom."[78]

But on January 19, the Pacheco matter was back. There was a motion to reconsider the vote by which the bill had been rejected. By 98–92, it passed, with Lincoln voting against.[79] Then by a vote of 101–95, the bill passed, with Lincoln again voting no.[80] It was one thing to vote consistently, on dozens of occasions, to keep slavery out of the territories. Some proslavery advocates believed as much, and Lincoln believed his constituents wanted that. It was another when Lincoln tried to eliminate slavery where, as a congressman, he had the power, in the District of Columbia. But his votes against the Pacheco claim affirm his belief that slaves were people, not property, and that the federal government would not be neutral on the issue.

The day after the vote, a relieved Winthrop wrote, "You ought to congratulate me on my escape from the clutches of Antonio Pacheco."[81] He wrote: "I don't think this bill would have received 50 votes, if Giddings had not rallied the whole south blindfold to its support, by attacking a principle so vital to their security."[82]

Winthrop believed Calhoun and Giddings "are the positive and negative poles of the same magnet, which is threatening to draw the country from its true constitutional centre. They almost deserve to be drawn themselves, and quartered too."[83] But "Boston and Baton Rouge will belong to the same country as long as Old Zack is at the helm."[84]

Back at Mrs. Sprigg's, both Lincoln and Dickey were working on bills affecting slavery in the District of Columbia. Giddings encouraged their efforts. That evening, Giddings heard a knock at the door. He opened it, to see Lincoln there holding a copy of his proposed bill. He discussed it with Giddings, asking for his feedback, which was freely given.[85]

Lincoln spent the next day working on the bill. With every piece of legislation, especially at the federal level, there are a number of stakeholders with different constituencies and motivations, often at cross purposes with one another. One of the major things that Congress would take into account was the opinion of the District's residents—even Giddings's bill had acknowledged as much. Lincoln visited Mayor Seaton, presenting him with his final draft. Seaton believed the bill so palatable to all sides that he suggested Giddings must disapprove. Lincoln, believing this mistake to be useful, did not disabuse him of the notion. And he once again called on Giddings, reading him the final product.

On January 10, Lincoln read his proposal to the House. The carefully crafted bill had eight sections.

Section one guaranteed that any person currently outside the District of Columbia could never be held in slavery within the District. This would put an end to the slave traffic coming into the District, and prevent any new slaves from being added within its borders.

Section two provided that anyone presently in the District, or anyone who would ever be born in the District, could never be held as a slave outside of its borders. This would have eliminated the outgoing slave traffic. In order to ensure its passage, Lincoln included an exception for officers of the government who brought their slaves with them to Washington for a temporary time.

Section three pertained to the children of slaves. After January 1, every child born in the District would be free. To render this acceptable, these children would owe an apprenticeship to their parents' owner until reaching a certain age, at which point they would be "entirely free." To ensure these children could be self-sufficient as free persons, this provision required the masters to provide for their education.

No bill that deprived current owners of their slaves could ever pass. Lincoln's proposal was one for graduated emancipation. But to increase the bill's impact, section four provided that any slave owner in the District could apply to the government at any time and receive full fair market value in exchange for freeing any of his slaves.

Section five empowered the municipal officials of the District to arrest and deliver any fugitive slaves resided within its borders. If Lincoln or anyone else would create a new legal route for emancipation, they would need to address the persistent southern complaint over runaway slaves.

Section six required a referendum of the free white males over the age of twenty-one and living in the District for a year in order for the act to take effect. This, of course, was nothing more than the "popular sovereignty" the Democrats loved so well.

Section seven confirmed that involuntary servitude following a criminal conviction was not covered by this act, and eight expanded the bill's effect to the entire District.

After reading his proposal, Lincoln said that of "about fifteen of the leading citizens of the District of Columbia to whom this proposition had been submitted, there was not one but who approved of the adoption of such a proposition." Lincoln wanted to be clear: this did not mean these citizens would vote for emancipation, only that they favored a public referendum.

"Who are they?" "Give us their names!" came the shouts from the crowd. Lincoln did not react—his assurances were no doubt real, but he almost certainly had not secured permission to share the names.

Despite Lincoln's hard work, this thoughtful, reasonable measure went nowhere. The kind of balanced legislation necessary to pass a badly divided Congress was more likely to get crushed by both sides, rather than embraced.

On the evening of the eleventh, all of the housemates at Mrs. Sprigg's remained after tea in the dining room, talking about Lincoln's bill.[86] "It was approved by all," Giddings remembered, no small feat for a house and housemates that had nearly been treated to a side of violence with their breakfast a few weeks earlier. Giddings believed it was the best bill that could be passed, and he was willing to swallow compensating slave owners if it meant freedom.[87]

Lincoln's future running mate, vice president, and successor, Andrew Johnson, ran for reelection to Congress in Tennessee campaigning against Lincoln's bill. On May 26, addressing a crowd at Evan's Crossroads, he warned of civil war. Speaking first on other bills, Johnson said it was a "great unfairness this proposition comes from a Northern man, when we consider whose blood and treasure was poured out in acquisition of those territories. The south sent to the battle field of Mexico 45,600 volunteers, while the North only sent 23,034 . . . nearly 2-1 in numbers, and three to one in proportion to the population of the north and south, and now if he proposes to emigrate with his property to the soil he purchased with his blood and his treasure, he is told by the northern men, no—you must stay where you are." Johnson closed by explaining the bill introduced "by Mr. Lincoln, a member from the state of Illinois. . . . If this is done in the District of Columbia, it will be followed up in the states. If Congress keeps up the agitation, and commences legislation upon this momentous question, the friction will be so great, the excitement become so intense, diffusing itself from the center along the great arteries of the union, until the whole body politic will wax so hot, that this mighty Union will melt in twain . . . cling to it [the Union] as the mariner clings to the last plank, when night and the tempest close around him."[88] Little could Johnson have known that he'd be the running mate of Mr. Lincoln, on the Union ticket, in 1864. Lincoln's bill was clearly taken seriously by southern members, no doubt because it alone had a realistic chance of becoming law.

In addition to being campaign fodder, Lincoln's bill influenced the Address of the Southern Delegates in Congress.[89] John C. Calhoun, giant of the Senate, had called a bipartisan meeting of southern members. The southern Whigs came under pressure by southern Democrats to join them in a new political party. This was just as the northern conscience was being pricked by the Free Soil movement, Giddings noted.[90]

A number of southerners thought the meeting ill-advised. Alexander Stephens and others refused to sign the petition calling for the meeting.[91] They then showed up for the purpose of thwarting it. On December 23, seventy members showed up. Calhoun offered a number of resolutions condemning perceived violations of the constitutional rights of southerners. He called for the immediate unification of southern whites into a single political party, and threatened disunion if the northern agitation on slavery did not cease. Stephens moved to refer the resolutions to a committee, with each southern state represented, and to regroup on January 15 to report.[92] The next day, it was all anybody seemed to be talking about. But what would come of the meeting remained to be seen.

It was not always easy being the housemate of Joshua Giddings. It seemed the other members, perhaps some who didn't relish a confrontation with Giddings himself, might accost his housemates with their concerns. This may have led to some friction at Sprigg's, for Giddings reported his fellow boarders were showing him "much more kindness than they did a few weeks since. Mr. Dickey in particular defends me and quarrels with my persecutors."[93] Benjamin French, the former House clerk, plainly told Giddings that "no one member [had] one half of the influence upon the House that [he] did."[94] Maybe so, but isolation is frequently the price of leadership. A week later, Speaker Winthrop threw a party, inviting all the members, North and South, Whig and Democrat—except for Giddings.[95] Giddings's desk on the House floor became a tourist attraction, with members introducing their friends to the new celebrity. "There seems to be some curiosity to make my acquaintance," he noted.[96]

Stephens had bought time against ill-considered southern meetings, but now they would reconvene. Everyone was nervous for the results. Giddings had a member in the room who promised to come back to him with word. Finally, after midnight, there was a knock on the door.[97]

Thankfully, Calhoun's report was rejected along party lines in the southern meeting.[98] "Almost all the Whig members and a number of leading Democratic members . . . refused to sign it."[99] The idea of a unified South threatening disunion was tabled—for now.

With the slavery issue at a fever pitch, Polk was determined to organize the Mexican cession. He lobbied Congress hard, especially Stephen Douglas, who as chairman of the Senate Committee on Territories wanted to bring in California and New Mexico as a single territory. Polk strongly advised against it, trying to convince Douglas to separate California and New Mexico.[100] Polk also believed that New Mexico, which included the interior of the Mexican cession, was less likely to be lost to the Union than coastal California.

As the southern members met, Polk had intelligence of mass chaos and anarchy in California due to the gold rush. He believed the only answer was to admit California directly as a state.[101] He tried to enlist Stephens's help, but was rebuffed. Stephens was still at this late hour opposed to bringing California and New Mexico into the Union.[102]

Polk furiously tried to lobby Congress on California. He turned the tables on the job-seeking congressmen, using their meetings to twist their arms over California.[103]

Congressman Lincoln had seen the intense emotions on both sides of the slavery question, and taken a side, and surely felt good for having done so. More so than in his reliable votes, he had tried to lead against an evil that had pained him as long as he'd witnessed it. For the slaves along the Cumberland Road, on the block in New Orleans, in the pens of Washington City, for the waiter from Mrs. Sprigg's who had paid the price in his hopes for the future, Lincoln had not just cast a vote, he had acted.

Lincoln had made good on his comments to Seward at Tremont Temple. It was time to take sides, to stand up and be counted. Michael Burlingame, who analyzed 175 speeches between 1854, when Lincoln returned to politics, and 1860, shows that Lincoln was a "one-issue man" who was "almost a monomaniac on the question of slavery in politics from 1854 forward." [104] In the last year of his life, Lincoln would recall, "I am naturally anti-slavery. If slavery is not wrong, nothing is wrong. I can not remember when I did not so think and feel." [105]

Orlando Ficklin, who had served with Lincoln in the legislature and U.S. House, and against whom he'd tried the Matson slave case, believed Giddings's influence was the key. Ficklin believed, "In this company his views crystallized, and when he came out from such association he was fixed in his views on emancipation." [106]

In closing his 1860 letter defending Lincoln, Giddings wrote: "I speak not for Mr. Lincoln; I have no authority to do that, but I speak of him as he stands historically connected with that cause which is dear to you and me.

"He had been bred among slaveholders, educated in the belief that slavery was just, proper, and necessary. He was the only Whig representative from Illinois, and while at home was surrounded by a pro-slavery sentiment but little modified from that of Kentucky." But by his actions in Congress, "he took his position with those who were laboring in the cause of humanity. He avowed his intention to strike down slavery and the slave trade in the district, to strike from our statute book the act by which freeman were transformed into slaves, to speak and act and vote for the right. He cast aside the shackles of party and took his stand upon principle.... I view it as one of high moral excellence, marking the heroism of the man. He was the only member among the Whigs proper of that session who broke silence on the subject of those crimes.... In that hour of freedom's danger, Abraham Lincoln was with them."

Those who accuse Abraham Lincoln of insincerity, opportunism, or tardiness on the slavery issue substitute their judgment for that of Joshua Giddings, the most prominent abolitionist in America, a man who lived and worked closely with Lincoln.

By the close of the Thirtieth Congress, Lincoln's head and heart were aligned on the slavery issue. There would be no turning back.

CHAPTER 18

WITH MALICE TOWARD SOME

"I am heartily rejoiced that my term is so near its close."
—President James K. Polk

Amid the din of the slavery questions, Samuel Vinton of Ohio rose to make a solemn speech. He pointed out that the House had perhaps thirty working days remaining, but no appropriations bills had been passed.[1] This would be difficult under any circumstances, he said, but if the cholera epidemic continued to worsen in Washington, it would be impossible to keep Congress together.

The Civil and Diplomatic Appropriations Bill was one of the essential annual acts of the national government. It covered everything from the salaries of numerous government officials, to the cost of the paper they used in the course of their work, to the firewood that heated government buildings, as well as the entire cost of embassies and consulates overseas. If it stalled, the government of the United States would simply go out of business. Now, this typically noncontroversial bill would be tied up and threatened by a process that was anything but civil or diplomatic.

On January 16, the debate over the bill devolved into speechmaking on mileage.[2] As the days dragged on, the House managed to fight over the bill's minutiae. Henry Murphy of New York demanded that a different paper merchant be used. He and Thomas Henley of Indiana got into an exchange on the floor about it, with Henley defending the paper's quality.

"I say that the paper now used is a disgrace to Congress and the country," Murphy said.

Henley replied, "It was difficult to tell what would disgrace Congress; perhaps gentlemen would differ in opinion on that point."[3]

Members offered amendments, and amendments to amendments, and made motions that were ruled irrelevant, then challenged the chair.

There were numerous votes to slightly increase or decrease the salaries of any one of the positions named in the bill.

Stephen Douglas accused the Whigs of creating new jobs, new diplomatic posts, and higher pay in anticipation of Taylor's presidency.[4]

But on January 23, with no warning of the danger ahead, the House was able to send the bill to the Senate without so much as a recorded vote.[5]

That same week, Henry Hilliard of Alabama introduced a bill to allow California to enter as a state, and New Mexico to be given to Texas (thus dramatically expanding the slavery territory of the United States).[6] Lincoln voted twice against allowing its introduction.

Outlaw noted the push to make California a free state was a consequence of the annexation of Texas, which did not succeed in its aims to strengthen slave power. In fact, Outlaw believed it made it weaker, and might yet overthrow it. In looking to the crowded galleries, he thought the spectators "must be surprised at the want of order which proceeds in this great council chamber of the Union."[7]

On February 13, Polk recorded, "It is four years ago this day since I arrived in Washington. . . . They have been four years of incessant labor and anxiety and of great responsibility. I am heartily rejoiced that my term is so near its close. I will soon cease to be a servant and will become a sovereign."[8]

On February 14, a joint session of Congress counted the votes of the Electoral College, officially making Taylor and Fillmore the president and vice president–elect of the United States. As an original Young Indian, Abraham Lincoln was no doubt proud to participate. It was now official. The Whigs would have their first president since 1841, when John Tyler was kicked out of the party. Not counting the thirty-day tenure of William Henry Harrison, Taylor would be the first Whig president ever.

As the Thirtieth Congress raced toward the finish line, these two explo-

sive issues were about to converge. The Civil and Diplomatic Appropriations Bill that had passed the House was being considered in the Senate.
The trouble would originate from Isaac Walker of Wisconsin. Interestingly,
Walker had served with Lincoln in the Illinois legislature before heading
north, becoming one of the first two senators for the new state. He proposed an amendment to the Civil and Diplomatic Appropriations Bill to
allow the president to create a temporary civil government for California
and New Mexico.

If it passed, Polk could unilaterally extend the Missouri Compromise
line to the Pacific. Or if he wished, organize without a mention of slavery.
Once this was done, the South would never permit the land to become free
again.[9]

Some members were simply tired of the slavery issue, especially when it
delayed territorial organization. On February 27, Pollock told the housemates at Mrs. Sprigg's that he was still prepared to vote for California
without the Wilmot Proviso language and that others were ready to do the
same.[10] He didn't want Taylor to be embarrassed out of the starting gate,
and wanted to pass on as little controversial legislation to Taylor's administration as possible.

Controversial did not seem an adequate word to describe things. As ten-
sions increased on the House floor, Lincoln walked over to Giddings and
had a strange conversation with him. "If violence occurred on this side of
the House," Lincoln said, Giddings "should not forget them nor leave [his]
friends there to suffer."[11] Giddings thought Lincoln was worried about
nothing, like the others "too much excited."[12]

At last the final month of the Thirtieth Congress and the Polk administration had arrived. "The city is filling up with strangers," Outlaw noticed,
with "great numbers" en route, "some from curiosity, but a much larger
number to enter into a scramble for office."[13]

On February 28, Lincoln successfully reported a bill from the post office
committee. The bill specified that anyone found to have combined to fix
prices against the post office would lose his right to bid on contracts for five
years, and anyone so doing a second time would be banned for life.[14]

Meanwhile, requests from the job seekers piled up on Lincoln's little
desk—applicants for the registrar of the land office of Vandalia; postmaster

of Palestine, Illinois; U.S. marshal; collector for the Port of Chicago. One applicant would prefer being the ambassador to one of the South American republics, "but is willing to receive any from which more money is to be received than paid out."

Lincoln told one: "You overrate my capacity to serve you. Not one man recommended by me has yet been appoint[ed] to any thing, little or big, except a few who had no opposition."

Seekers would extol their Whig virtues, their personal attributes, their friendship with Lincoln, and occasionally tell a hard-luck story, as though government employment were some kind of charity. Many employed more than one of these tacks.

David Davis, an Illinois lawyer and friend of Lincoln who would go on to manage his campaign for president, suggested that Lincoln should pursue the General Land Office,[15] a powerful subcabinet position overseeing all federal lands.

Was Lincoln already thinking about a post in the Taylor administration? With the Seventh District lost, and a Senate seat out of the question, a place with Taylor would allow Lincoln, who had just turned forty, to remain in national politics and perhaps position himself for future opportunities.

Lincoln responded to Davis: "I have more cause to thank you for it than you would suppose. Out of more than three hundred letters received this session, yours is the second one manifesting the least interest for me personally. I do not much doubt that I could take the land office if I would. It also would make me more money than I can otherwise make. Still, when I remember that taking the office would be a final surrender of the law, and that every man in the state who wants it himself would be snarling at me about it, I shrink from it."

Davis responded on February 21: "What you state shows the infirmity of human nature—all the men who are writing to you are thinking about themselves—and they suppose that you have no need of their aid. My advice is worth nothing, still were I in your place could I get it I would take the land office."

But for now, there were no appropriations for the Land Office. On February 28, Vinton complained that there were two days left to pass legislation, and $20 million in appropriations being held up.[16] On March 1, the Senate adopted the Walker amendment, 25–18.[17] The divisive issue of slavery in the territories was now attached to an appropriations bill vital for the survival of government.

On March 2, Vinton continued his sometimes successful quest to focus the House on the appropriations bills. After dealing with Senate amendments on flogging in the navy, or whether to purchase the papers of George Washington and James Monroe, the real issue came up: whether to agree with the Walker amendment.

Wentworth offered an amendment to the Senate version: "That there shall neither be slavery nor involuntary servitude" in the new territories unless punishment for a crime.[18] The amendment was rejected 89–96, without a roll call vote, but it is nearly certain that Lincoln was present and voted for the amendment.[19]

When the House reconvened for the evening session, Wentworth offered another amendment to the Senate bill, using the Northwest Ordinance language. Alexander Stephens, who was then chairing the House, ruled it out of order, saying that it was the same as the earlier amendment as regards to slavery, and as for the Northwest Ordinance language, inapplicable.[20] The decision of the chair was appealed, and barely sustained, 85–84.[21]

"There was great confusion in the Hall."[22] People shouted that they couldn't hear what was happening.

At this, Democrat Sidney Lawrence of New York moved to modify the Senate amendment to say "that nothing in this act shall be so construed as to extend any law relating to the coastwise slave trade to California and New Mexico."[23]

By 89–82, it was adopted, with Lincoln certainly voting yes.[24]

Washington Hunt of New York then moved to amend the Senate amendment, that "the laws of Mexico abolishing slavery in the said territories shall remain in full force until the same shall have been repealed by the authority of Congress."[25]

There was an objection, but Stephens ruled the amendment in order. He was challenged, and sustained 95–87.[26]

Richard Meade of Virginia offered an amendment stating that nothing in the act would limit the constitutional rights of states and citizens that now existed; he explained frankly that the amendment would make clear that slaves could be taken into the territories. The amendment was rejected.[27]

The House then voted on whether to accept the Senate's amendment. By a vote of 114–100, the Senate's amendment was rejected, with Lincoln voting no.[28]

That evening, the secretary of the Senate appeared and said that they would not recede in the Walker amendment, and asked for a conference committee to resolve their differences.[29]

CHAPTER 19

THE LAST FULL MEASURE

March 3, 1849, was the final day of the Thirtieth Congress. It would be among the most violent and contentious days in the history, before or since, of that institution. But it began on a note of conciliation and harmony.

George Ashmun took the floor, announcing that a bust of their fallen friend, John Quincy Adams, paid for with the private funds of members of both parties, had arrived at the Capitol, and resolved to place it in the Speaker's room. He also added that the artist had transported it from Boston, despite having no obligation to do so, and in so doing bore a cost that would cripple him financially. Ashmun moved to compensate him for his loss. When there was objection to paying the transportation fee, Joseph Grinnell of Massachusetts offered to do so out of his own pocket. Ashmun modified his resolution, and it passed 125–19.[1]

There were a number of bills for which the spadework was done, which passed one by one. There were also some strange eleventh-hour proposals. One, from Greeley, condemned Amerigo Vespucci as a mere follower of Columbus, and therefore moved to change the name of the country to the United States of Columbia.[2]

In the evening, there was a "magnificent spread, free to all members, in one of the committee rooms."[3] It was paid for by House staff, "by a levy of five dollars per head."[4] The food was no doubt magnificent, but the motives were less than altruistic. Years earlier, after a particularly brutal session, House staffers were voted a bonus of $250. Now accustomed to this, the staff made certain to receive it at the end of every session. But to debate the issue at this late hour, they needed a two-thirds vote to suspend the rules, which failed. With so much money on the line (more than two months' salary for the average clerk), the public employees were undeterred. A second bill was offered, to give a bonus to the chaplain, which obtained the two-thirds. After all, who wanted to vote against a bonus to a man of God? But once the bill was brought to the floor, an amendment was offered to give the $250 bonus to all House employees, which successfully passed.[5]

The House would soon revert to the hostile environment in which it began the Thirtieth Congress. On a pro forma resolution thanking Speaker Winthrop, Andrew Johnson moved an amendment to strike the word *impartial,* and inveighed generally against his tenure. By a vote of 161–15, Johnson's amendment failed.

In its final hours, as it faced a government shutdown, as the Missouri Compromise was threatened, all that was needed was a simple striking of a match to set the entire room on fire. Acts of violence were rampant, which could and did begin suddenly, for any reason or for no reason at all. The following incident is firmly in the latter category.

Robert Johnson of Arkansas asked Orlando Ficklin angrily, "Why do you always oppose any motion I make?" Ficklin pointed out that he had just supported his motion. "You lie!" Johnson yelled, and "sprang forward" at him.[6] As if Ficklin had not had enough, Samuel Inge of Alabama rushed him, striking him again and again with his cane, as Winthrop helplessly called for order from the chair.[7] Giddings observed that "many blows were exchanged and some blood was shed." When they were finally separated, Inge said, "Why, I thought that the fight between the North and the South had commenced, and I might as well pitch in."[8] Inge, for his part, was actually an equal-opportunity hothead, fighting a duel with a congressman from North Carolina during the Thirty-first Congress.

While talking to a friend on the Democratic side of the aisle, Giddings was accosted. Greeley believed he "could not have passed quietly through that side of the House between ten and two o'clock of that night without being assaulted, and, had I resisted, beaten within an inch of my life if not killed outright."[9]

Horace Mann believed that "had the north been as ferocious as the south, or the Whigs as violent as the Democrats, it is probable there would have been a general melee."[10]

Some of the members were "generally intoxicated, too much to appear in public," but not too drunk to weigh in on the most critical issues facing a republic in crisis as Clio's clock ticked toward adjournment.[11]

The United States was now a Pacific power, but the broad stretches of western wilderness were as yet unorganized. The House voted to prohibit slavery in the new territory. The Senate disagreed. Held hostage was the Civil and Diplomatic Appropriations Bill. Should that fail to pass, the United States government would soon run out of money. The Thirtieth Congress would end in a matter of hours. But the Thirty-first Congress would not meet until next December. Even if Taylor called a special session, most House members had not yet been elected. Even if they had, it would take weeks to get the message out and then weeks to assemble in Washington. (Even with the outbreak of the Civil War, Lincoln could not reconvene Congress until the Fourth of July.) A government shutdown would prove humiliating for America, and disastrous to her credit. It simply couldn't happen—could it?

At sunset, James Knox Polk looked over his desk, cleared of all business before it. He left the White House for the last time, moving for the night to Willard's Hotel. He then proceeded to the Capitol, as customary, with his cabinet. With him he carried a written veto message regarding the Wilmot Proviso. "I did not hesitate for a moment in my course," he wrote.[12]

That evening, the conference committee disbanded. Charles Atherton of New Hampshire returned to the Senate and Vinton to the House and announced that the committee had met, discussed the issues that separated them, and could not agree.[13]

Daniel Webster pointed out that "important bills connected with the continuance of the administration of the government, which for sixty years have never failed to be passed in time to carry on the government, are now to some degree in jeopardy . . . we are at a crisis of some importance."[14]

But in the House, the Whigs were about to give in.[15] For the first time in American history, millions of new acres would be open to slavery. John McClernand of Illinois moved that the House recede from its disagreement with the Senate amendment, allowing the Senate version to stand and be sent to the president.

The vote on the measure was 110–107, with Lincoln voting against. Lincoln would shut down the government of the United States before he voted for the expansion of slavery.[16]

All appeared lost, when Richard Thompson of Indiana rose to speak. He said that what he was doing was for northern men as well as southern men, and had no sectional feelings in his remarks. He had spent the evening in conference with the Senate, believing the stakes nothing less than a threat to "the integrity and safety of the union of these states."[17] Unless something was done, he said, "they would leave this Hall . . . under a state of excitement that would pervade all parts of the Union."

Thompson's amendment to the Walker amendment added that "the existing laws [of the territories] thereof should remain in force until changed by consent of Congress."[18] Since the Mexican Constitution forbade slavery, this would guarantee freedom in the new territory. The pendulum swung. Greeley noted, "The pro slavery men were now as anxious to expunge the territorial clause as they had been determined to insert it at all hazards."[19]

On the vote for Thompson's amendment, it was 111–105.[20]

It was then observed on the floor that the clock had stopped at 11:15, as if Clio were willing the House to remain until its duty was finished. The motion to reconsider was laid on the table.[21] It was now after midnight. A number of points of order were made, declaring the session over, which the Speaker ignored.

If Richard Thompson had, instead of his amendment, walked across the Rotunda into the Senate chamber and set the drapes on fire, he could hardly have created more trouble.

A number of southerners flocked to Polk's room "in great excitement."[22] Amid the noise and clamor, Polk ordered the room cleared except for his cabinet. The first item was a constitutional question. As it was after midnight, was he even still the president of the United States? At the end of the day, it was argued that Polk had won a four-year term. Since he had not been sworn in until noon on March 4, he still had time left.

The second question: Would he sign the appropriations bill with language banning slavery, or issue the veto letter he held in his coat pocket? Remarkably, Buchanan, Walker, Marcy, and Toucey advised him to sign, pointing out that there was a distinction between preserving existing Mexican policy on slavery and adding the Wilmot Proviso.[23] Only Mason advised him to veto.[24] Having consulted his cabinet, Polk flung open the doors to the vice president's room, without announcing his decision.[25]

Senator Henry Foote of Mississippi was furious over the House amendment preserving existing law. "O my countrymen! Submit to Mexican law; forget the principles of civilization; forget that you have ever acquired knowledge; forget everything you have learned, either at school or elsewhere; and bow down in profound submission to semi barbarism?"[26] Foote also pointed out that discussing elections was forbidden in Mexico, and that none of them had any clue what Mexican law was or what they were voting on.

Finally, Jefferson Davis moved to disagree with the House amendment and appoint a conference committee with an eye toward removing the territorial question altogether, to pass the appropriations bill.[27]

There were a number of competing amendments, and a motion to adjourn based on the session being over, which the chair ruled out of order.[28]

Senator Simon Cameron, a future member of Lincoln's cabinet, called for the question. Foote called him to order, arguing that his term had expired. Cameron made a point of order about whether the language was parliamentary. Foote called it very parliamentary, and Cameron answered that he did not ask his opinion. The *Globe* records that "other words were uttered by both the Senators from Pennsylvania and Mississippi, and something approaching a personal collision occurred."[29]

Andrew Butler of South Carolina added that such an amendment had no place in the Civil and Diplomatic Appropriations Bill. "And whilst we are professing a tender regard for California, I hope we shall not forget a proper respect for ourselves. And I suppose such a thing has never occurred in the history of the government as an adjournment of Congress without passing the bills for appropriating the necessary means for carrying on the government."[30]

Daniel Webster agreed that "it is not usual, it is not wise," when making appropriations for the government, to introduce "a subject so disputatious as that its further progress may endanger the passage of the measure before us."[31]

Meanwhile in the House, Robert Schenk of Ohio moved successfully that they inform the Senate that they were ready to adjourn.[32] If this was aimed at ratcheting up the pressure on the Senate, to push them to acquiesce, it could not have been more perfectly timed.

The Senate then voted on an amendment by John Berrien of Georgia acknowledging that the laws of the conquered country were in effect, insofar as they were compatible with the Constitution.[33] To this the House would not agree—it was simply a resurrection of the Compromise Bill, since no one could agree what the Constitution meant on the issue of territorial slavery.

There were a number of parliamentary objections to the Senate's continuing to meet, and a number of senators refused to vote. One senator condemned it as a mere town hall meeting, with no more power to transact business than any other town hall meeting.

But by 27–21, the Berrien amendment was defeated. Those who believed that midnight ended their service motioned for adjournment, failing by a margin of 33–7.

At 4 a.m., after waiting on the bill, Polk left the Capitol and retired to Willard's Hotel.[34]

Senator Jesse Bright of Indiana said, "We are to decide whether the wheels of the government for the next twelve months shall stop, or shall continue to roll on. If they are to go on, we must strip this bill of all that is incongruous, and pass it in the condition in which it ought to be."[35]

But led by Senator Foote, a group kept attempting to shut down the Senate, protesting that the body had expired, that even the term of Polk had expired, that they must go home.

There was a question about how to untangle this mess. Could the Senate vote down the House amendment, and recede from its own amendment, which would automatically place it before the president? What about a separate amendment to strike out all references to the new territory? Douglas felt that was a worse result than shutting down the government, that it was tantamount to abandoning the people of the territories. Because the

House amendment was not an amendment to the bill itself, but to the Senate amendment, if the Senate receded the whole extraneous question that had divided the houses would disappear.

So the Senate receded from the amendment, by a margin of 38–7, and the bill was passed.[36] In the House, it was announced that the Senate had receded from the Walker amendment. At 6 a.m., a delegation from Congress met Polk at his hotel and presented him with what Congress had passed.

Ultimately, the Senate was "unwilling to take responsibility of stopping the wheels of government."[37] The amendment preserving the antislavery status quo had been stricken, as had the Walker amendment. It was a clean appropriations bill. Polk signed it. "Thus closed my official duties as President of the U. States," he later wrote.[38]

In the early morning hours of the day, Abraham Lincoln concluded his first and only term in Congress, and his last moments in elected office until 1861.

After a tense, violent, all-night session, at 7 a.m. on March 4, 1849, the House adjourned sine die after a speech by Winthrop. "The hour has arrived which terminates our relations to the country, and our relations to each other, as members of the Thirtieth Congress."[39]

We have been associated, gentlemen, during a most eventful period in the history of our country and of the world. It would be difficult to designate another era in the modern annals of mankind, which has been signalized by so rapid a succession of startling political changes.

Let us rejoice that while the powers of the earth have almost everywhere been shaken, that while more than one of the mightiest monarchies and stateliest empires of Europe have tottered or have fallen, our own American Republic has stood firm.

Let us rejoice at the evidence which has thus been furnished to the friends of liberty throughout the world, of the inherent stability of institutions which are founded on the rock of a written Constitution, and which are sustained by the will of a free and intelligent people.

And let us hope and trust—as I for one, most fervently and confidently do—that by the blessing of God upon prudent, conciliatory, and patriotic counsels, every cause of domestic dissension and fraternal discord may be speedily done away, and that the states and the people, whose Representatives we are, may be bound together forever in a firm, cordial, and indissoluble union.

Offering once more to you all my most grateful acknowledgments of your kindness, and my best wishes for your individual health and happiness, I proceed to the performance of the only duty which remains to me, by announcing, as I now do, that the House of Representatives of the United States stands adjourned, sine die.

Some histories, not content to label Lincoln an undistinguished member, go further and argue that he was a little-known member of a do-nothing Congress. This is far from the case.

The Thirtieth Congress made many important decisions that did the public enormous good, sometimes in direct proportion to how little they excite modern historians. Between December 1847 and March 1849, Congress increased the number of examiners at the patent office, for a hungry country that was rapidly innovating, and passed legislation protecting the health and safety of passengers on ships, as well as important proconsumer measures regarding the labeling and safety of medicine. They created new postal routes to the bourgeoning new towns dotting the American map, the cleared forests and prairies where new people came together in community, and a new cabinet-level department (Interior) focused on managing the new broad swaths of the United States. The members of the Thirtieth Congress brought Wisconsin into the Union, organized the Minnesota Territory, as well as that of Oregon, with a guarantee that all who set foot on her soil would be free. While New Mexico and California would have to wait, their place in the Union was strengthened by the new federal presence in the form of postal services and revenue offices. More important, the Thirtieth Congress accomplished the greatest task that any Congress could boast: resolving a war, and doing so on terms incredibly favorable to the United States, and consistent with the honor of those who fought it, now free to return to their fields and farms and homes. That's good work enough for any Congress.

CHAPTER 20

GENERAL TAYLOR'S GRAND TRIUMPHAL MARCH

M arch 4 fell on the Sabbath. General Taylor obtained a legal opinion, and decided to be sworn in on Monday, March 5. "During the week the city began to fill up," noted one observer, "and on Monday last it was *full*."[1] "Anyone who passed through our streets would have supposed that 'all creation' had made Washington their headquarters."[2] It was a crowd "larger than was ever before collected in Washington."[3]

Congress may have been finished, but Lincoln had a busy and unusual week ahead of him. In addition to his inaugural duties, Lincoln would argue a case before the United States Supreme Court and be awarded his patent.

Lincoln served as one of the managers for the Inaugural Ball. The grand event would be held later that evening in a temporary structure in Judiciary Square, just west of City Hall. Twelve years later, Lincoln attended a ball for himself in the same place.[4]

At daybreak, "The strains of martial music resounded along the principal avenues of the city," and the bells "rang out a stirring peal."[5]

At his temporary home at Willard's Hotel, General Taylor donned a plain black suit. Old Rough and Ready, after a lifetime in the military, was now a civilian.

The parade began at half past eleven. A dozen military companies traveled along Pennsylvania Avenue toward the Capitol. In a carriage with four gray horses were Speaker Winthrop and the mayor of Washington. After a stop at the Irving Hotel, Polk climbed aboard for his final act as president, the passing of the baton.[6]

The rooftops "were covered and every window was completely blocked up with heads."[7] The party arrived on the east side of the Capitol. There had been extensive staging constructed on the east portico.[8]

"You will have to climb a tree to see Old Zack pass by," Winthrop told a friend.[9]

Polk was horrified on the carriage ride when Taylor mentioned offhandedly that California and Oregon were too distant to become members of the Union. Polk thought him "a well meaning old man. He is, however, uneducated, exceedingly ignorant of public affairs, and, I should judge, of very ordinary capacity."[10] One wonders if Polk shot a reproving stare in Winthrop's direction, as if to say, "What on earth have you Whigs done?"

Here Lincoln witnessed the final act of a campaign he had begun before his own swearing in for Congress—to use Taylor as a weapon to win back the presidency for the Whigs, and to end the seemingly unbreakable hold of the Democrats on the White House. As a member of the Thirtieth Congress, Lincoln would have had a prime position to savor his triumph. Chief Justice Roger Taney read the oath, in view of twenty thousand people. The new president was saluted with salvos of artillery fire.[11]

Polk grumbled that Taylor's speech was delivered in a "very low voice and very badly as to his pronunciation and manner."[12]

Then presidents twelve and thirteen shook hands. "I hope, Sir," offered Polk, "the country may be prosperous under your administration."[13]

In the evening, Taylor and Fillmore traveled together to all four balls, along with Winthrop and the mayor.

Lincoln attended the Grand Inaugural Ball with a group of friends, including Elihu Washburne. The temporary ballroom was reached "through the corridor of city hall," down a "broad flight of steps, which led down to the dancing saloon." The paper reported four thousand people at the Grand Ball, including members of Congress, foreign ministers, and uniformed military and naval officers.[14] Josef Gungl, one of the preeminent band leaders in Europe, then on a celebrated tour of the United States, provided the entertainment.

The *Intelligencer* said that "the spectacle was in the highest degree impressive," while Washburne remembered it as "by far the most brilliant inauguration ball ever given. Of course Mr. Lincoln had never seen anything of the kind before. One of the most modest and unpretentious persons present—he could not have dreamed that like honors were to come to him, almost within a little more than a decade."

But for tonight the honors were Taylor's, and his party arrived between ten and eleven.[15] Gungl's "celebrated and powerful band were for a minute or two entirely drowned."[16] At half past eleven the Taylor party left for the official banquet in City Hall, but then returned to the dancing saloon, where they stayed until half past midnight. The paper reported that Taylor "was able to receive almost every gentleman," which does not quite seem right given the size of the crowd. But it nearly certainly meant that President Taylor and former congressman Lincoln, the thirteenth and sixteenth presidents of the United States, had a chance to visit in Judiciary Square on this cold inaugural evening.

Lincoln and his friends stayed until 3 or 4 a.m.[17] The coat check was a disorganized mess, but despite this, Lincoln quickly found his cloak, which barely covered his shoulders. But he searched for his hat for an hour. Finally giving up, Lincoln walked out onto Judiciary Square. "It would be hard to forget the sight of that tall and slim man," said Washburne, "with his short cloak thrown over his shoulders, starting for his long walk home on Capitol Hill, at four o'clock in the morning, without any hat on."[18]

After an all-night session to close Congress, and a marathon day of ceremony and celebration, Lincoln had to complete one more major task before leaving Washington for Springfield. On March 7, he would become the first future president to argue a case before the United States Supreme Court.

Lincoln had come a long way since obtaining his law license in September 1834, and a long way from his first case, *Hawthorn v. Wooldridge*. Lincoln's client alleged that Wooldridge beat and kicked him, incapacitating him for six weeks. Lincoln asked for five hundred dollars in damages, and won thirty-six.

In the intervening time, Lincoln had become one of the best lawyers in the state. By the time he was elected to Congress, he'd handled three hundred cases before the Illinois Supreme Court.[19]

Now Lincoln represented the defendant in *Lewis for use of Longworth v. Lewis*.

The facts read like some horrific test question from a law school property law exam. In 1819, one Moses Broadwell executed a deed to William Lewis for a parcel of land in Ohio. Unfortunately, the title was not perfect, and Lewis lost one hundred acres in a subsequent court dispute. Lewis sued Broadwell's estate in 1843.

In 1827, Illinois had passed a law that all cases for breach of contract would have a statute of limitations of sixteen years. But people living outside Illinois could bring a lawsuit within sixteen years of moving to the state. In 1837, the out-of-state exemption was repealed, holding everyone to the same sixteen-year standard. The estate cited the statute of limitations, while Lewis pointed out that he had lived out of state.

The Supreme Court met in the Capitol, beneath the Senate chamber. Sunlight entered from the east and "[fell] too full upon the face of the attorney who may be addressing the Court."[20]

"On the wall, in a recess in front of the bench, is sculptured in bold relief, the figure of justice, holding the scales, and that of fame, crowned with the rising sun, pointing to the Constitution of the United States."[21] The room featured busts of Chief Justices Ellsworth and Marshall.[22] As they do today, the justices wore black robes.[23] Lincoln would have stood squarely in front of Chief Justice Roger Taney—who would write the *Dred Scott* opinion that led directly to his presidency, and who would swear in Lincoln as president twelve years later—and made his argument.

Taney, writing the majority opinion, noted succinctly, "The question is, from what time is this [statute of] limitation to be calculated?" His decision was that the deadline to file a lawsuit began in 1837, when the Illinois legislature removed the out-of-state exemption, and not before, permitting the lawsuit against Lincoln's client to go forward.

Justice McLean, who had been a candidate for president, wrote the dissent and agreed with Lincoln's client, arguing that "when the exceptions of a statute of limitations are repealed, the act stands as though it had been originally passed without them."

The truth was, Lincoln had a hard argument to make, changing the rules in the middle of the game. But the strong dissent from Justice McLean shows that Lincoln advanced his best arguments and served his client well. This case has been cited by federal courts in thirty cases, most recently in 1999, the judges and lawyers probably unaware of the famous attorney who had originally argued it.

On March 10, Lincoln appeared in person at the patent office with his application, having earlier "swore an oath to its originality before a Washington justice of the peace, and paid a thirty-dollar fee."[24]

On March 31, former congressman Abraham Lincoln arrived home in Illinois.

CHAPTER 21

THE COMET AT THE
END OF THE WORLD

The close of the story of Congressman Lincoln would see him as a reluctant, and finally an aggressive, seeker of a position in the administration of Zachary Taylor. He nearly prevailed, and if he had, it would have taken him and the country on a radically different course. The campaign began with Lincoln's friends urging him to seek the seat, followed by a blizzard of correspondence, with Lincoln calling on as many supporters as he could, and Washington insiders updating Lincoln with reports on the state of the race.

The object of his pursuit was the General Land Office, a position "just below a cabinet post in prestige and patronage power."[1] It had previously been a part of the Treasury Department and would now be under the new Department of the Interior.

Judge Richard M. Young of Illinois had served in this capacity under Polk, and the state hoped to maintain the office.[2]

There were several major impediments to Lincoln's appointment. One was that he had recommended another.

Illinois Whig Cyrus Edwards had been elected to the legislature in 1832 and 1840, and had been 926 votes away from winning the 1838 race for governor.[3] As he was a relative of Ninian Edwards—Lincoln's friend, political ally, and the husband of Mary Todd's sister—Lincoln had all the more reason to oblige him. Congressman-elect Edward Baker preferred another, a division that threatened the state's hold on the office.[4]

A number of Lincoln's friends felt Illinois was in danger of losing this post, and that Lincoln must seek it himself. As Anson Henry wrote, "You are the only man in the state that can secure the appointment," and so "it is our earnest desire that you should without delay press your claims upon General Taylor for the office."[5]

On June 1, Lincoln, in Charleston, Illinois, wrote to Pennsylvania congressman Moses Hampton.[6] "At last, I have concluded to take the General Land Office if I can get it. I have come to this conclusion, more to prevent what would be generally bad for the party here, and particularly bad for me, than a positive desire for the office." He asked Hampton to write directly to Taylor.

Now that Lincoln had decided to do it, hoping that things could be smoothed out with Cyrus Edwards, he had one major hurdle to overcome.

Chicago lawyer Justin Butterfield had been working hard for the position since April. Butterfield, a former U.S. attorney for Illinois, was known as an excellent lawyer with a sense of humor to match. He had served as the personal attorney of Joseph Smith, president of the Church of Jesus Christ of Latter-day Saints, during his time in the state. Appearing before Judge Pope on behalf of Smith, in a courtroom full of the latter's supporters, Butterfield quipped: "I am to address the Pope, surrounded by angels, in the presence of the holy apostles, in behalf of the Prophet of the Lord."[7]

Butterfield would do whatever it took to win. He wrote out a sworn statement that he had never opposed Taylor's candidacy,[8] while as recently as April he had written to Lincoln, "We all go for Clay in these parts."[9] Butterfield had once told Lincoln that he had supported the Mexican War after paying a political price for his opposition to the War of 1812. "Henceforth, I am for war, pestilence, and famine," Butterfield decreed.[10]

The *Register* had a field day with Lincoln's candidacy, even penning an original poem for its readers, titled "A Steeple Chase, For the Spoils Cup." It read in part:

Away went Justin, neck or naught
Away went hat and wig;
He little dreamed when he set out
Of running such a rig.
Away went Lincoln, who but he;
His fame soon spread around;
He carries weight! He rides a race;
He's for an OFFICE bound.

Lincoln began a furious letter-writing campaign. Though a reluctant candidate, he was now in with his whole heart. His letters generally carried the same message: it would be either he or Butterfield appointed, and to please write him should he be their preference. "Not a moment of time to be lost." [11]

Lincoln sought help from his former congressional colleagues, to demonstrate national support, as well as those from Illinois, to prove he was the choice of the Whigs there.

Lincoln wrote to William Seward, who appears to have not responded in any way. Ironically, if he could have secured the post for Lincoln, he might well have been the Republican nominee for president in 1860.

Butterfield had a massive advantage in terms of time and, like Lincoln getting the drop on Hardin in 1845, had locked down endorsements that might otherwise have gone to his opponent.

Judge Young, who eagerly wanted Lincoln to succeed him, was holding on in order to buy him time, but in no event could he last past June 30.

Josiah Lucas, an Illinoisan and clerk at the Land Office, provided valuable intelligence for Lincoln. "I do know that Butterfield is trying his best for the place, although not here in person, he is operating through friends." [12] Lucas urged Lincoln to return to Washington to seek it in person. "Otherwise old Butternuts gets it. Who in the thunder wants him?" [13]

In previous administrations, even Lincoln's belated entry should have been enough. From an early hour, he had played a major role in delivering the presidency to Taylor. But Taylor, who had nearly refused to run because of the demands of job seekers, had decided to institute a new process. Taylor would require all applicants to apply to the relevant department heads.

Nothing "can be entertained by the President for any office whatever."[14] This did not simply mean the department heads would get first crack at new applicants—Taylor was so eager to be relieved of the responsibility that had so vexed Polk and his predecessors that he was willing to let the department heads make the final decision, even when their wishes were contrary to his. Witness what happened when one of Taylor's oldest friends asked him for a job. The president replied, "I hope you will get it, sir; and if the cabinet officer has any doubt upon the matter, I will authorize you to refer to me." But his friend was not hired, and that was the end of it.[15]

Cabinet members had different incentives. Rather than reward party loyalty, they were more likely to repay their own political debts, and to build patronage networks from their own states. Unfortunately for Lincoln, Secretary of the Interior Thomas Ewing insisted upon Butterfield, "[a]nd that he is his man." Lucas reported that Ewing anticipated trouble with land titles, and as "the most profound lawyer in the state, especially as a land lawyer," he preferred him. "Taylor is for you, I think. . . . What ever you do, do quickly."[16]

Lincoln also got the same message from William Henderson. "It is said the President is for you, and perhaps a majority of the cabinet, and that Mr. T. Ewing is warmly in favor of friend Butterfield of Chicago." Henderson also urged Lincoln to come to Washington. He would later renew this request more urgently: "Your friends require your presence, delay is fatal."[17] Later, Henderson would encourage him to drop his modesty: "this one time lay it bye, and paddle your own boat."[18]

Despite their broad new patronage powers, cabinet officials could not make their decision in a vacuum; the powerful supporters of each candidate would require a delicate political balancing act.

Lincoln wrote William Preston, secretary of the navy: "Mr. Butterfield is my friend, is well qualified, and I suppose, would be faithful in office. So far, so good."[19] But in 1840, during a "fierce and laborious battle in Illinois," Butterfield was appointed district attorney without spending a dollar or lifting a finger. When "you and I were almost sweating blood to have General Taylor nominated, this same man was ridiculing the idea, and going for Mr. Clay; and when General T was nominated, if he went out of the City of

Chicago to aid in his election, it is more than I ever heard of, or believe. . . . Shall this thing be?"

The presidency of James K. Polk was the only one that Lincoln had the opportunity to watch firsthand. Likewise, the creation of Zachary Taylor's government was the only one that Lincoln witnessed. Though Taylor had good intentions, to avoid being trapped as the job dispenser in chief he created a reformed process that essentially destroyed the Whig Party. What was the point in serving a party with no clear reward system? Just look at the great lengths that Lincoln, who had "sweat blood" for Taylor, was having to go to in order to outmaneuver someone who had not done a thing. As president, Lincoln would fire four-fifths of the government, the biggest turnover in the history of the country.[20] Though its exercise was laborious, patronage was power. Lincoln could offer jobs to maintain congressional relationships, as well as support for the war. And many members knew they'd have a safe landing in the administration if they lost their seats.

In the middle of his quest for the Land Office, Lincoln learned that at least one of his applications had been successful. On May 22, Lincoln was granted a patent for his lifting device to move boats over shoals (U.S. 6,469). His attorney wrote: "It affords me much pleasure to inform you that I have obtained a favorable decision on your application for a patent."

As for Lincoln's other application, Josiah Lucas personally went to President Taylor, showing him letters on Lincoln's behalf. "They informed him that Butterfield was the last man in the state that Whigs would go for, for any office. I told him it would give great dissatisfaction to the people of the state, and that his firm friend Lincoln was the choice. He expressed great partiality for Lincoln and was astonished to find that Butternuts was not their choice." Taylor, Lucas reasoned, "has been deceived."[21]

At the same time, Lincoln received a letter informing him of the "very severe illness of your father." It was serious: "He is very anxious to see you before he dies. . . . I am told that his cries for you for the last few days are truly heart rendering [sic]."[22] The next day, his stepbrother wrote: "Father is yet alive and that is all and he craves to see you all the time and he wants you to come if you are able to get here, for you are his only child that is of his own flesh and blood and it is nothing more than nature for him to rave to see you."

Lincoln decided to visit his father, with whom he never seems to have had a normal relationship. Whatever illness it was had passed, and Lincoln returned to Springfield within a week.

On June 9, Lincoln was awakened by a knock on his door. Standing there was Levi Davis, bearing a letter from Butterfield. The letter requested that both parties refrain from traveling to Washington to lobby for the position. "I therefore propose for your consideration whether it would not be better for us both to remain at home; which I am willing to do, if you are, please send an answer by the bearer."[23]

Lincoln told the messenger that he could not easily find a light to draft a response, but that he was to convey to Butterfield that were it up to him he would cheerfully agree. But he had promised his supporters otherwise, and therefore declined the invitation.[24] The next day, Lincoln was on his way to Washington.

This is reminiscent of Hardin's 1846 proposal to switch to an open primary from a convention and to agree to cease campaigning. Butterfield clearly understood he was ahead, and like Lincoln's erstwhile opponent he also tried to change the rules to suit himself at the eleventh hour. Lincoln was wise to decline.

Unable to get Lincoln to effectively "give up," Butterfield panicked. One of Lincoln's correspondents wrote: "I learn that Mr. B has left this morning for Chicago and from thence to Washington City. I have no doubt of your success, still the true plan is to leave no stone unturned." Lincoln's campaign, though barely off the ground, had already made an enormous impact. "Butterfield is very much alarmed" by what he's been hearing from Washington, it was said.

During this time, a "strictly confidential" communication was sent to Abraham Lincoln.[25]

"We the undersigned believing the facts in our possession to justify the step we here take, and feeling warmly for your personal interest, take the liberty of putting you upon your guard against treachery in the camp." It seemed that some people who Lincoln thought were his friends were really working against him. "If these men have not given you a written line of confidence, be assured it will be given against you. . . . After getting this in your mind destroy the paper." It is curious that Lincoln did not. The whole incident would leave him with an unusual amount of bitterness, and perhaps this letter served as proof that he had been wronged.

David Davis, who had first suggested Lincoln seek the Land Office, wrote him a letter to be passed on to the president. "The appointment of old Butterfield would be outrageous. The party in this state, if such is the policy, is flat. Is it not strange, that the voice of members of Congress from a state is not taken about appointments."

Long before he expected to return, Lincoln arrived back in Washington to press his case for appointment as commissioner of the General Land Office.[26] As his former colleague Richard Thompson encouraged him, "Faint heart never won fair lady."[27]

Lincoln departed from Ransdell's tavern in Springfield in the early-morning hours. On the stage he met a Kentuckian coming from Missouri who offered him chewing tobacco. "No, sir, thank you," Lincoln explained, "I never chew." And the two remained quiet. After hours of silence, the Kentuckian pulled out a leather-covered cigar case, offering one to Lincoln. Lincoln again refused, since he never smoked. As they pulled into the station where the tired horses were swapped out for new ones, the Kentuckian produced a flask of brandy. "Well, stranger, seeing you don't smoke or chew, perhaps you'll take a little of this French brandy. It's a prime article and a good appetizer besides." Lincoln, however, passed on the offer, as he didn't drink. As the Kentuckian transferred to a stage bound for Louisville, he shook Lincoln's hand. "See here stranger, you're a clever but strange companion. I may never see you again, and I don't want to offend you, but I want to say this: my experience has taught me that a man who has no vices has damned few virtues. Good day." Lincoln, of course, took no offense and enjoyed retelling the story.

At Terre Haute, Judge Abram Hammond (the future governor of Indiana) and Thomas Nelson, who would be Lincoln's ambassador to Chile, boarded the stage. Nelson remembered Lincoln as "a long, lank individual, whose head seemed to protrude from one end of the coach and his feet from the other." Lincoln was alone on the stage, and fast asleep.

Judge Hammond woke him up by clapping his shoulder, asking, "Did you charter the stage for the day?"

"Certainly not," Lincoln apologized, moving to the front seat.

Hammond and Nelson eyed him curiously. "A queer, odd looking fellow he was, dressed in a well-worn and ill-fitting suit of bombazine, without vest or cravat, and a 25 cent palm hat on the back of his head. His very prominent features in repose seemed dull and expressionless."

The two made jokes about his appearance, to which Lincoln joined in the laughter. Around noon the stage stopped for dinner at a roadside inn. The two invited Lincoln to eat with them, which he seemed to consider "a great honor." Only half of Lincoln's oversized frame fit on the undersized chair. As the party resumed the trip, conversation shifted to "the comet," a subject of much interest in the scientific community. Lincoln was fascinated by the comet, which his traveling companions seemed well versed in. After hearing their explanations, he asked, "What is going to be the upshot of this comet business?"

Nelson seemed to think "the world would follow the darned thing off!" How insignificant their many struggles seemed to be, in the shadow of a comet that might potentially destroy the world.

The group spent the night at Browning's hotel in Indianapolis. Nelson and Hammond went to their room to clean up from the road. Nelson returned downstairs and saw Lincoln entertaining a group of prominent admirers, some of the biggest names in the state, fixed on whatever "story he was telling."

Who was this man, he asked Browning, the proprietor of the hotel. "Abraham Lincoln of Illinois, a member of Congress."

Nelson was "thunderstruck." He ran upstairs to tell Hammond that the man they'd been mistreating all day was a member of Congress. The two snuck out via the back door, "down an alley to another house" like thieves in the night, to avoid "further contact with our now distinguished fellow traveler."

Nelson would later become "a zealous advocate" of Lincoln's nomination and election as president. As the president-elect was headed east, Nelson was asked to join his party. Meeting them at the hotel dining room in Indianapolis, he scanned the crowded room for Lincoln. He then felt a gangly arm around his shoulder. 'Hello, Nelson! Do you think, after all, the world is going to follow the darned thing off?"

On June 15, Lincoln wrote directly to Zachary Taylor. "Nothing in my papers questions Mr. B's competency or honesty, and I presume nothing in his questions mine." Lincoln pointed to his support in the states most affected by the Land Office. "I am strongly recommended by Ohio and Indiana, as well as Illinois." He pointed out that no one had been appointed from the Seventh District, the only one that had ever sent a Whig to Congress. After reading so many hundreds of letters from job seekers, Lincoln knew the most effective and least effective arguments.

Daniel Stowell, editor of the papers of Abraham Lincoln, has categorized the support received by Lincoln and Butterfield by region. Stowell notes that the twenty-nine Springfield residents, including his own brother-in-law and best man at his wedding, had signed a petition favoring Butterfield, as they were "dissatisfied with the course of Abraham Lincoln as a member of this Congressional district."[28] In a follow-up letter, they explained that the Spot Resolutions speech had been the cause of their frustration, a speech they believed had caused the defeat of Stephen Logan.[29] But Lincoln was still strongest in central Illinois, easily beating Butterfield there, while lacking in support in Butterfield's Chicago-area base. All told, thirty-one of Lincoln's House colleagues weighed in for him in a remarkably short period of time, including Winthrop, as well as four who arrived too late.[30] Yet another testament to Lincoln's standing among his peers.

The total number of supporters on both sides, who signed petitions or wrote letters separately, was 365 for Lincoln and 235 for Butterfield.[31]

But it was to no avail. On June 21, Justin Butterfield was appointed commissioner of the Land Office.[32] After he heard the news, Lincoln went back to his hotel room and "threw himself down on the bed," his long legs sticking over the side.[33] Lincoln lay for an hour "or more," saying, "Well I reckon the people will find some use to put me to yet."[34]

Butterfield's tenure would turn out to be a disaster. Firing the clerks who had been helpful to Lincoln and replacing them with ten of his family members, he was frequently absent due to illness and ultimately resigned in 1852.[35]

Nicolay and Hay, the personal secretaries of President Lincoln, report: "In after days he recognized the error he had committed, and congratulated himself upon the happy deliverance he had obtained through no merit of his own.... If Justin Butterfield had not been a more supple, more adroit, and less scrupulous suitor for office than himself, Abraham Lincoln would have sat for four inestimable years at a bureau-desk in the Interior Department, and when the hour of action sounded in Illinois, who would have filled the place which he took as if he had been born for it?"

Then, of course, there was "the strong probability that the singular charm of Washington life to men who have a passion for politics might have kept him there forever. It has been said that a residence in Washington leaves no man precisely as it found him."[36]

But that was "in after days." For today, Lincoln was profoundly affected by the decision. In what could serve no other purpose than to make him feel better, Lincoln wrote Ewing asking him for written confirmation that had he initially sought the Land Office, he'd have received it. Surprisingly, Ewing did in fact write the letter, saying, "I have no hesitation in expressing the opinion that if you had been, in the first instance, a candidate for the officer of Commissioner of the General Land Office, you would have received the appointment. You were generally and favorably known here." Butterfield, he explained, was initially in line to be solicitor of the Treasury. "The President had determined to give this office to Illinois, and there was no other applicant in the state, however high his merits, who could, under all the circumstances have been presented to the president so favorably as yourself. I also take great pleasure in saying that your bearing throughout has been such as to entitle you to my highest consideration and respect."

But Lincoln was not finished. He wrote again to Ewing, asking him to "please transmit to me the papers on file in your department recommending me for the Commissioner of the General Land Office, if not inconsistent with the rules of the Department."[37]

Congressman Alexander Evans wrote Lincoln, "I remember very well when a small band of General Taylor's friends (30 in number) at Washington, and you one of them, brought about his nomination; since then many have received the credit of that act who are in no way entitled to it, but about your action there is no mistake."

Lincoln wrote to David Davis on July 6. "As to my Washington trip, you know the result. I can not give you particulars in a letter, but will tell you all when I see you. I will only say now, that I am less dissatisfied than I should have been, had I known less of the particulars, and that I hope my good friends everywhere will approve the appointment of Mr. B in so far as they can, and be silent when they can not."[38]

Lincoln wrote to Ewing on July 9.[39] "I was surprised to find amongst them no letter from Hon. R. W. Thompson or Hon. Elishe Embree ... both of these gentlemen had informed me by letters, that they had written the President in my behalf, and had sent me copies of their letters to him." Judge Collamer had written him saying Butterfield "appeared to be better recommended from the public land states than I. I felt sure he was mistaken; yet, never disposed to wrestle with the court after the case is decided, I made no reply." With them, Lincoln had the state of Indiana, but without them Butterfield had it.

Ewing responded that these letters had been considered, but they mentioned other applicants and therefore couldn't be forwarded.[40]

Lincoln did not let things go. Ewing had sent him eight letters that mentioned other applicants. Clearly, Lincoln did not feel he was getting the full story from Ewing.

All had gone wrong for Lincoln. Cyrus Edwards, though his case had been made by Lincoln well past the point at which it was clear that he could not get the office, had written a letter denouncing Lincoln and supporting Butterfield. This was the man on whose behalf Lincoln had engaged in the fatal delay. One of Lincoln's many memorable quotations is, "The better part of one's life consists of his friendships," but it was actually said of Edwards, a heartbroken lament that he had done something to cost him a friend.

Lincoln would later receive, and reject, an appointment as governor of the Oregon Territory. It was a prestigious job, at least on par with the Land Office. It seems Lincoln thought that any future he might have in politics would involve staying in Illinois, rather than the remote and sparsely populated territory.[41]

Yes, he had wanted a position in the national capital, the seat of power. But in this he had failed. Lincoln had much to consider as his train steamed out of Washington City, starting his long journey back to the West. From his earliest days, he was certain that he was bound for great things. But as the endless fields of the West now came into view, that dream seemed farther away than ever before. A train is fixed on its tracks, driven by an unseen engineer, and this one was carrying Abraham Lincoln, a former member of Congress, back to Illinois, where it had all begun, as though nothing had intervened, back to his family, friends, and frontier law practice, toward an uncertain future.

THE EMANCIPATION OF ABRAHAM LINCOLN

Whigs North and South had played a game of presidential roulette with Taylor. He would soon prove to be beyond the greatest hopes of his northern supporters. In August 1849, he said, "The people of the north need have no apprehension of the further extension of slavery."[1] He encouraged California to apply directly for statehood, without corresponding trade-offs for the South.[2] It is unclear whether Taylor's position against slavery expansion, or his reluctance to offer trade-offs to the South, could have caused the Civil War earlier. It is equally possible that Taylor, as a southerner, slave owner, and national war hero, could have arrested any secession movement in its tracks, as Andrew Jackson did. His premature death made this unknowable.

The fire left burning in the aftermath of the Thirtieth Congress was contained, for a time, by the Compromise of 1850. It was not a compromise in the traditional sense, with the North and South coming together. Rather, a group of centrist senators, led first by Henry Clay, then by Stephen Douglas, held the balance of power and voted through a number of measures that both sides wanted.[3] California was admitted on her own terms, which everyone understood meant it would be free, and territorial governments established for the rest of the Mexican cession without mention of slavery.[4] Texas's debts were assumed by the federal government, while it dropped its claims to areas outside of its modern boundaries.[5] A tougher fugitive slave law was passed, while the slave trade was abolished in the District of Columbia. Possession of slaves in D.C. would be permitted for so long as the state of Maryland continued to do so.[6]

During all this, Lincoln was back at his law practice, back on the Eighth Circuit, as removed from politics as he'd ever been. This changed in 1854, when the Kansas-Nebraska Act repealed the Missouri Compromise, adopting "popular sovereignty," the right of the people in those territories to decide the question of slavery. Lincoln found himself "aroused . . . as never before," and decided to reenter politics. The movement that had begun with the founding of the Free Soil Party now culminated in the creation of the Republican Party, formed in response to Kansas-Nebraska.

In 1856, Lincoln was the runner-up to be nominated for vice president for that new party. After the vote had closed, John Van Dyke, Lincoln's neighbor on the House floor, said, "I knew Abraham Lincoln in Congress well, and for months I sat by his side. I knew him all through, and knew him to be a first rate man in every respect."[7] Lincoln's friend wrote him that Van Dyke's speech was "a high compliment and at some length. It was well done and I regret that his remarks in full as to yourself were not published. He did you great credit."

Four years later, of course, Lincoln would again be a candidate at the convention for national office. Besides Illinois, the first state to coalesce behind Lincoln was Indiana, "A key turning point, for it elevated Lincoln above the status of a mere favorite son and made him seem like a truly viable candidate."[8]

David Davis, who managed Lincoln's campaign at the convention, would later push Caleb Smith for a cabinet post, saying, "No one rendered more efficient service from Indiana, at the Chicago Convention than he did . . . without his active aid and co-operation, the Indiana delegation could not have been got as a unit to go for you. And until we had got the Indiana delegation entirely united, we could not properly appeal to the other delegations for votes."[9] Lincoln wrote Smith after the convention that "I am . . .

much indebted to Indiana; and, as my home friends tell me, much to you personally."[10]

Another critical development came when a committee of twelve delegates, three from each of four swing states, met in David Wilmot's room to try to unite on a candidate. Davis and Smith pressed the case for Lincoln, who was considered the most acceptable, if not the first or even second choice of the others.[11]

After he was nominated, convention chairman George Ashmun closed by saying, to tremendous applause: "There never was elected to the House of Representatives a purer, nor a more intelligent and loyal Representative than Abraham Lincoln. You are pledged to his success; humanity is pledged to his success; the cause of free government is pledged to his success."[12]

Giddings, who had been a delegate to the convention, wrote Lincoln to congratulate him, pointing out that he'd won because he was "an honest man," and "not in the hands of corrupt or dishonest men."[13]

When Lincoln won the presidency, Giddings and his allies saw it as the culmination of their life's work.

"After all the struggles of your life," Amos Tuck wrote Giddings, "to form a majority party upon a worthy platform of principles, have been crowned with success!"[14]

Benjamin Perley Poore, a national reporter and a friend of Lincoln's from the House Post Office, recorded that the press corps had remembered Lincoln well and was very satisfied with his choice as president.

But this was not universally the case.

Lincoln and Alexander Stephens, one of his closest friends from the House, engaged in a correspondence on the pending threat to the Union. On December 22, 1860, Lincoln wrote, "I fully appreciate the present peril the country is in, and the weight of responsibility on me. Do the people of the South really entertain fears that a Republican administration would, *directly, or indirectly*, interfere with their slaves, or with them, about their slaves? If they do, I wish to assure you, as once a friend, and still, I hope, not an enemy, that there is no cause for such fears.

"The South would be in no more danger in this respect, than it was in the days of Washington. I suppose, however, this does not meet the case. You think slavery is *right* and ought to be extended; while we think it is *wrong* and ought to be restricted. That I suppose is the rub. It certainly is the only substantial difference between us."[15]

Stephens replied, "Personally, I am not your enemy—far from it; and however widely we may differ politically, yet I trust we both have an earnest desire to preserve and maintain the Union."[16]

Stephens would later oppose secession in the Georgia state convention, losing to the forces of Howell Cobb, their colleague from the Thirtieth Congress. When his state joined the Confederacy, however, Stephens felt compelled to go along, becoming vice president of the Confederate States of America. The two Young Indians and old friends and allies would now lead their respective sides in the Civil War.

Caleb Smith would join Lincoln in the cabinet, as secretary of the interior, and several of his congressional associates received different jobs from Lincoln's administration. Giddings became consul general to Canada (as it was not yet an independent nation, it did not receive its own ambassador). It seems Lincoln was able to reward a friend and satisfy an important constituency, but also have Giddings out of the country during the early phase of the war, in which success demanded Lincoln proceed cautiously on slavery to keep the border states in the Union.

Wherever Judge Van Dyke went during the war, people were full of questions: "It was Judge here and Judge there and what about the war? Would the Union hold? Would we win? And to everyone almost the same answer. We could not fail to win with Lincoln at the helm."[17] As a former bank president, the judge knew how to diversify his portfolio, but he told everyone he met that he'd put every penny he had into Union war bonds.

Toward the end of the war, Lincoln and Stephens would meet again, aboard the *River Queen*, off Hampton Roads, Virginia, to discuss the possibility of peace. Lincoln knew the South would never agree to return, but at least he could cultivate the image of a man earnestly desiring peace, which he was. Despite the dire circumstances, the two laughed and reminisced about their old days in the Thirtieth Congress.

When the diminutive Stephens emerged from a giant overcoat, Lincoln said he had never before seen such a "small nubbin emerge from such an immense husk."[18]

At the end, Lincoln said, "Well, Stephens, it seems we can do nothing for our country. Is there anything I can do for you?"[19]

At a prisoner-of-war camp in Michigan, Stephens's nephew was ordered to be taken to Washington. He knew not why, but he feared the worst. Instead, he was received at the White House, greeted warmly by the president of the United States, and sent home, a federal prisoner to be exchanged in his stead.

By the time he arrived home, Lincoln was gone.

For the first time in his life, the son of John Van Dyke saw his father, the stern judge, with tears falling from his gray eyes as he cast his gaze out the window.[20]

Winthrop wrote, "Was there ever anything so sad and so shocking as the late scenes at Washington! I have no words to express my horror—my real grief for the death of the President . . . the history of the world presents no more awful tragedy. But God rules us all and we must bow to his decrees."[21]

Months after Lincoln's death, Stephens wrote, "My whole consciousness, since I heard of President Lincoln's assassination, seems nothing but a horrid dream."[22]

On February 12, 1878, which would have been Lincoln's sixty-ninth birthday, the House of Representatives gathered to accept, from Mrs. Elizabeth Thompson, Frank B. Carpenter's painting *First Reading of the Emancipation Proclamation of President Lincoln*.

There would be one speaker from the North and one from the South, a fitting tribute to the worth of the life they were there to honor. The first was a former Civil War general from Ohio, Congressman James A. Garfield.

He talked about "the third House of the American Congress [former members who had died], that silent assembly whose members have received their high credentials at the impartial hand of history. Year by year, we see the circle of its immortal membership enlarging; year by year, we see the elect of their country, in eloquent silence, taking their places in this American Pantheon, bringing within its sacred precincts the wealth of those immortal memories which made their lives illustrious; and year by year, that august assembly is teaching deeper and grander lessons to those who serve in these more ephemeral houses of Congress."[23]

This painting, Garfield felt, belonged alongside the paintings that Lincoln had so marveled at when he'd first arrived at the Capitol. This was a new chapter in the history of the American civilization, alongside Vander-lyn's *Landing of Columbus* or Trumbull's *Declaration of Independence*. Garfield thought it the "third great act in the history of America—the fulfillment of the promises of the Declaration."

Garfield acknowledged that not all would agree, but "the lesson of history is rarely learned by the actors themselves, especially when they read it by the fierce and dusky light of war, or amid the deeper shadows of those sorrows which war brings to both," but "the unanimous voice of this House in favor of accepting the gift, and the impressive scene we here witness, bear eloquent testimony on the transcendent importance of the event portrayed on yonder canvas."

Garfield told the story of how Lincoln called his cabinet in and announced his decision. "Without this painting, the scene could not even now be reproduced. The room has been remodeled; its furniture is gone; and Death has been sitting in that council, calling the roll of its members in quick succession. Yesterday he added another name to his fatal list; and today he has left upon the earth but a single witness of the signing of the Proclamation of Emancipation. With reverence and patriotic love, the artist accomplished this work; with patriotic love and reverent faith, the donor presents it to the nation. In the spirit of both, let the reunited nation receive it and cherish it forever."

The next speaker was a southern congressman, recently returned to the House through a circuitous path.

"I knew Mr. Lincoln well," said Alexander Stephens. "We met in the House in December, 1847. We were together during the 30th Congress. I was as intimate with him as with any other member of Congress except perhaps one. . . . Mr. Lincoln was warm hearted; he was generous; he was magnanimous; he was most truly 'with malice toward none, with charity for all.'"

So Lincoln, who carried a heavy burden in his life, must now be free. Right? Lincoln was able to preserve the Union and destroy slavery. If our Founding Fathers brought forth on this continent a new nation, then Lincoln is the American Noah, the common ancestor of the Union. But we must not be so quick to declare victory. Liberty must be maintained by every generation, and freedom is a fragile thing, one that may be lost.

During the mass slaughter of World War I, Vachel Lindsay wrote a poem, "Abraham Lincoln Walks at Midnight," suggesting that in the failure of later generations to follow Lincoln, he was anything but free. It reads in part:

> *It is portentous, and a thing of state*
> *That here at midnight, in our little town*
> *A mourning figure walks, and will not rest,*
> *Near the old courthouse pacing up and down.*
>
> *His head is bowed. He thinks of men and kings.*
> *Yea, when the sick world cries, how can he sleep?*
> *Too many peasants fight, they know not why;*
> *Too many homesteads in black terror weep.*
>
> *The sins of all the war-lords burn his heart.*
> *He sees the dreadnaughts scouring every main.*
> *He carries on his shawl-wrapped shoulders now*
> *The bitterness, the folly and the pain.*
>
> *It breaks his heart that things must murder still,*
> *That all his hours of travail here for men*
> *Seem yet in vain. And who will bring white peace*
> *That he may sleep upon his hill again?*

So is Abraham Lincoln free or does he walk at midnight?

Abraham Lincoln stood for opportunity, for "the right to rise," for the liberty and dignity of all humans, and for peace if it can possibly be obtained without sacrificing principle. Though his successes are unmatched in the history of America, the work goes on, until each generation highly resolves that Abraham Lincoln did not live in vain. Lincoln reminds us that however badly divided we may be, "We are not enemies, but friends. We must not be enemies." Lincoln reminds us that "union is strength," and that "the mystic chords of memory" that bind us are infused with the power to overcome what threatens to tear us apart. "A new birth of freedom" is always possible for our republic. And to remind us of our sacred trust, "that government of the people, by the people, for the people, shall not perish from the earth."

NOTES

PROLOGUE: AN EPISTLE TO THE MUSE OF HISTORY
1. LaGumina, Salvatore John. *The Italian American Experience: An Encyclopedia* (New York: Garland, 2000), 33.
2. *Louisville* (Kentucky) *Times,* Frankfort, March 11, 1891.
3. Sargent 2, 331.
4. *National Intelligencer*, Washington, D.C., February 22, 1848.
5. Watterston, 25.
6. http://artandhistory.house.gov/house_history/index.aspx, 30th Congress.

CHAPTER ONE: THE MOST AMBITIOUS MAN IN THE WORLD
1. *The Collected Works of Abraham Lincoln*, Vol. 1, 7; hereafter CW.
2. CW 1, 7.
3. Burlingame, Michael. *The Inner World of Abraham Lincoln* (Champaign-Urbana, Ill.: University of Illinois Press, 1997), 236.
4. *Inner World*, 237.
5. *Inner World*, 236.
6. *Inner World*, 238.
7. Herndon 2, 263.
8. Herndon 2, 263.
9. Herndon 2, 264.
10. *Inner World*, 236.
11. Peck, William Farley. *History of Rochester and Monroe County, New York*, 63.
12. Peck, William Farley. *History of Rochester and Monroe County, New York*, 63.
13. Holt, 24.
14. Holt, 12.
15. Holt, 69.
16. Holt, 9.
17. Holt, 70.
18. Sibley, Joel H. "'Always a Whig in Politics': The Partisan Life of Abraham Lincoln," *Journal of the Abraham Lincoln Historical Association*, Vol. 8, Issue 1, 1986.
19. Holt, 69.
20. Sibley, "'Always a Whig in Politics.'"
21. Johnson, Allen. *Douglas: A Study in American Politics*, 43.
22. Johnson, 43.

23. Johnson, 44.
24. The Lincoln Log, May 10, 1838.
25. Advertisement in the *Register*, May 15, 1846.
26. Donald, 115.
27. Donald, 115.
28. Donald, 115.
29. Angle, Paul. *Here I Have Lived: A History of Lincoln's Springfield*, map of Springfield opposite page 18.
30. *Register*, October 21, 1842, as reported in the Lincoln Log, October 23, 1842.
31. Riddle, 37.
32. *The Collected Works of Abraham Lincoln*. For the Whig Circular of March 4, 1843, see pp. 309–18.
33. *Sangamo Journal*, March 10, 1843; hereafter *Journal*.
34. Biography from the United States Senate website, accessed June 23, 2012, at http://www.senate.gov/artandhistory/history/common/generic/VP_Richard_M_Johnson.htm.
35. Thompson, Charles Manfred, "Attitudes of the Western Whigs Toward the Convention System," found in *Proceedings of the Mississippi Valley Historical Association* 170; hereafter "Attitudes."
36. "Attitudes," 185.
37. "Attitudes," 171.
38. Holt, 31.
39. "Attitudes," 173.
40. CW 1, 180–81.
41. *Works*, Vol. 1, 318.
42. *Journal*, January 26, 1843.
43. Bioguide.gov. Accessed June 17, 2012. http://bioguide.congress.gov/scripts/biodisplay.pl?index=H000186.
44. Mo Davis to JJH, November 1, 1843.
45. Letter to Mrs. Hardin, December 22, 1843.
46. Hardin to his daughter, November 21, 1843.
47. Hardin to son, probably 1843 at Christmastime.
48. Washburne, Elihu. "Abraham Lincoln in Illinois," *North American Review*, Vol. 141, No. 347 (October 1885), 307–19, at 309.
49. Oates, Stephen B. *With Malice Toward None* (New York: HarperCollins, 1990), 115.
50. Oates 116–17.
51. *Register*, May 31, 1843.
52. Burlingame, Michael. *Abraham Lincoln: A Life*, 633. Note that all citations to this work are from the unedited version, hosted by Knox College online. This exhaustive study of Lincoln's life is a gift to history, and the agreement to print the unedited version, with all of the information acquired by Dr. Burlingame in its compilation, is an incredible service from both him and his publisher.
53. *Register*, February 10, 1843.
54. *Register*, March 17, 1843.
55. Herndon 2, 205.

56. Herndon 2, 206.
57. Herndon 2, 210.
58. Beveridge 2, 14.
59. Beveridge 2, 15.
60. Herndon 2, 213.
61. Herndon 2, 213.
62. Beveridge 2, 15.
63. Beveridge 2, 15.
64. Herndon 2, 215.
65. Herndon 2, 215.
66. Herndon 2, 215.
67. Lincoln and Webster, 310.
68. Herndon 2, 217.
69. Herndon 2, 223–24.
70. Herndon 2, 226.
71. Herndon 2, 227.
72. Herndon 2, 227–28.
73. Herndon 2, 229.
74. Herndon 2, 229.
75. Herndon 2, 229.
76. CW 1, 208.
77. Herndon 2, 233.
78. Simon 295–96.
79. Burlingame, 572.
80. Herndon 2, 231.
81. *Register*, May 12, 1843.
82. *Journal*, March 23, 1843.
83. Riddle, 63.
84. Burlingame, 640.
85. Holland, Josiah Gilbert. *Life of Abraham Lincoln.*
86. *Journal*, March 23, 1843.
87. Burlingame, 644.
88. CW 1, 319–21.
89. CW 1, 319–21.
90. Herndon, 2, 270.
91. Herndon, 2, 270.
92. Letter from Hardin to supporter, April 15, 1843.
93. Letter from Hardin to supporter, April 15, 1843.
94. Letter from Hardin to supporter, April 15, 1843.
95. Letter from Hardin to supporter, April 15, 1843.
96. Letter from Hardin to supporter, April 15, 1843.
97. Letter from Hardin to supporter, April 15, 1843.
98. W. C. Spears to JJH, April 24, 1848.
99. W. C. Spears to JJH, April 24, 1848.
100. W. C. Spears to JJH, April 24, 1848.

101. Tarbell, Ida. "The Life of Abraham Lincoln." Published in *McClure's Magazine*, Volume VI, No. 6, 527–28. Accessed online, February 23, 2012, at http://www.gutenberg.org/files/13304/13304-h/13304-h.htm.
102. Riddle, 71.
103. Riddle, 71.
104. Tarbell, "Life of Abraham Lincoln," 527–28.
105. *Journal*, May 11, 1843.
106. *Journal*, May 11, 1843.
107. *Register*, May 5, 1843.
108. Riddle, 73.
109. Mo David to JJH, November 1, 1843.
110. Kernell, 673, Table 1.
111. Struble, 658.
112. Struble, 666.
113. Kernell, 674.
114. Kernell, 675.
115. Kernell, 675.
116. Kernell, 676.
117. Struble, *Political Science Quarterly*, 654.
118. Struble, 658.
119. Struble, 658–59.
120. *Register*, July 7, 1843.
121. CW 1, 322.
122. The Lincoln Log, August 7, 1843, citing election returns.
123. Burlingame, 648.
124. *Register*, August 11, 1843.
125. Burlingame 648.

CHAPTER TWO: THE RIGHT TO RISE

1. CW 1, 304.
2. CW 1, 332.
3. Merry, 73.
4. Merry, 71.
5. Merry, 71.
6. Merry, 72.
7. Merry, 73.
8. Merry, 73.
9. Hardin's written recollection, March 1, 1844.
10. Merry 66.
11. Merry, 73.
12. CW 1, 334.
13. Burlingame, 667.
14. Lincoln Log, February 21, 1844, citing letter from William Butler to Hardin.
15. CW 1, 332–33.
16. CW 1, 334–35.

17. Lincoln Log, April 3, 1844, citing David Davis Papers, Abraham Lincoln Presidential Library and Museum.
18. Letter to Hardin, May 10, 1844.
19. *Register*, May 24, 1844.
20. Donald, 100.
21. Donald, 100.
22. Donald, 101.
23. Burlingame, 648.
24. Letter from Morgan County to JJH, January 10, 1844.
25. CW 4, 130–31.
26. Oates, 118.
27. Oates, 118.
28. Burlingame, 691.
29. Burlingame, 691–92.
30. Burlingame, 691–92.
31. Burlingame, 691–92.

CHAPTER THREE: TURNABOUT IS FAIR PLAY

1. *Register*, January 2, 1845.
2. CW 1, 349.
3. CW 1, 350.
4. Nicolay and Hay 1, 242.
5. Nicolay and Hay 1, 243.
6. CW 1, 350–51.
7. Letter to Mrs. Hardin, December 22, 1843.
8. Martin L. Morris to JJH, November 19, 1845.
9. Martin L. Morris to JJH, November 19, 1845.
10. JJH to the editor of the *Tazewell Whig*, November 26, 1845.
11. CW 1, 351–52.
12. Daniel Stickel to JJH, January 22, 1844.
13. CW 1, 351–52.
14. Struble, 659.
15. CW 1, 351–53.
16. Ira Fern to JJH, January 23, 1846.
17. Ira Fern to JJH, January 23, 1846.
18. Ira Fern to JJH, January 23, 1846.
19. PU Thompson to JJH, January 12, 1846.
20. Andrew Wardlaw to JJH, January 28, 1846.
21. Letter to JJH, February 5, 1846.
22. Letter to JJH, February 5, 1846.
23. Law Practice of Abraham Lincoln File ID: L03959.
24. CW 1, 353–54.
25. CW 1, 355.
26. CW 1, 356–58.
27. CW 1, 359.

28. CW 1, 359–60.
29. CW 1, 360–65.
30. Burlingame, 693.
31. Hardin, February 3, 1846.
32. Burlingame, 695.
33. *Register*, March 6, 1846.
34. David McKinson to AL, March 11, 1846. Papers of Abraham Lincoln.
35. Merry, 209.
36. Merry, 241.
37. Merry, 211.
38. Merry, 279.
39. Merry, 219.
40. Merry, 219.
41. Grant, Chapter III.
42. Grant, 139.
43. Grant, 139.
44. *General Taylor and His Staff*, 16.
45. *General Taylor and His Staff*, 16.
46. *General Taylor and His Staff*, 21.
47. *General Taylor and His Staff*, 21.
48. *General Taylor and His Staff*, 21.
49. Merry, 241.
50. Merry, 241.
51. Merry, 241.
52. Merry, 241.
53. Findley, 31.
54. Pratt, 100.
55. Nicolay and Hay 1, 246.
56. Herndon, 258.
57. Herndon, 258.
58. Bray, Robert. "Abraham Lincoln and the Two Peters," *Journal of the Illinois Historical Association*, Vol. 22, No. 2 (Summer 2001), 27–48, 40.
59. *The Churches of the Frontier*, 9.
60. Nicolay and Hay 1, 247.
61. Sweet, William W. "Churches as Moral Courts of the Frontier," *Church History*, Vol. 2, No. 1 (March 1933), 3–21.
62. Sweet, 17.
63. Sweet, 17.
64. Nicolay and Hay 1, 248.
65. Tarbell, "Life of Abraham Lincoln."
66. CW 1, 347–48.
67. Polk 1, 382.
68. Polk 1, 384.
69. Polk 1, 386.
70. Polk 1, 386.

71. Polk 1, 388.
72. Polk 1, 388.
73. Polk 1, 390.
74. Sargent 2, 292.
75. Polk 1, 393.
76. Polk 1, 394.
77. Riddle 2, 8.
78. Polk 1, 395.
79. Grant, 148.
80. Ford to JJH, May 18, 1846.
81. Johannsen, 98.

CHAPTER FOUR: LINCOLN FOR CONGRESS

1. Herndon, 258.
2. CW 1, 381–82.
3. Beveridge 2, 85.
4. *Register*, May 8, 1846.
5. Bonham, Jeriah. *Fifty Years' Recollections* (Peoria, Ill.: J. W. Franks and Sons Printers, 1883).
6. Findley, 58.
7. CW 1, 382–83.
8. Burlingame, 709.
9. Burlingame, 709.
10. Burlingame, 709.
11. Burlingame, 709. Though the word "balls" is omitted from Herndon's Informants, I agree wholeheartedly with Dr. Burlingame's interpretation of what Lincoln said.
12. Findley, 41.
13. Nicolay and Hay 1, 249.
14. Beveridge 2, 86, and footnote 5.
15. Findley, 42.
16. Shawneetown, August 20, 1846, *Illinois State Gazette*.
17. CW 1, 383–84.
18. Carwardine, Richard J., 43.
19. Northwest Ordinance, July 13, 1787.
20. Remini, Robert. *Henry Clay: Statesman for the Union* (New York: Norton, 1991), 178.
21. Remini, 181.
22. *Impending Crisis*, 20.
23. *Impending Crisis*, 20.
24. *Impending Crisis*, 20.
25. *Impending Crisis*, 23.
26. *Impending Crisis*, 21.
27. *Impending Crisis*, 22.
28. Dyer, 174.
29. Dyer, 174.
30. Grant, 120.

31. Meigs, William Montgomery. *The Life of Thomas Hart Benton* (Philadelphia: Lippincott, 1904), 363.
32. Wheeler 1, 255.
33. Meigs, 365.
34. *Journal*, February 11, 1847.
35. *Journal*, February 18, 1847.
36. Dyer, 174.
37. Williams, Harry T. *Lincoln and His Generals* (New York: Random House, 2011), 11.
38. Williams, 11.
39. Eicher, John, et al. *Civil War High Commands* (Stanford, California: Stanford, 2001), 210–11.
40. Neely, Mark. "War and Partisanship: What Lincoln Learned from James K. Polk," *Journal of the Illinois Historical Society*, Vol. 74, No. 3 (1981), 213.
41. CW 1, 389–91.
42. White, 145.
43. Nicolay and Hay 1, 255, 257.
44. Smith, Justin Harvey. *The War With Mexico*, Vol. 1, 375.
45. JJH to Stephen Douglas, February 4, 1847.
46. JJH to Stephen Douglas, February 4, 1847.
47. Sargent 2, 303.
48. JJH to Stephen Douglas, February 4, 1847.
49. Smith 1, 385.
50. Smith 1, 388.
51. Smith 1, 389.
52. Written Recollections of Buena Vista, Hardin family papers.
53. Written Recollections of Buena Vista, Hardin family papers.
54. Written Recollections of Buena Vista, Hardin family papers.
55. *General Taylor and His Staff*, 229.
56. Written Recollections of Buena Vista, Hardin family papers.
57. CW 1, 392–93.
58. Johannsen, Robert W. *To the Halls of the Montezumas: The Mexican War in the American Imagination.*
59. Johanssen, 104.
60. Johanssen, 104.
61. Dyer, 269.
62. Hawthorne, 63.
63. Dyer, 266.
64. Lee, 52.
65. Gary, Ralph. *Following in Lincoln's Footsteps*, 342.
66. Lee, 52.
67. Lee, 53.
68. Hawthorne, Julian, Elishu Benjamin Andrews, and James Schoule. *United States from the Discovery of the North American Continent*, Vol. 6, 62.
69. *Journal of Southern History*, 194.

70. Adams, William. "Louisiana and the Presidential Election of 1848," *Louisiana History: The Journal of the Louisiana Historical Association*, Vol. 4, No. 2, 131–43.
71. Walton, 195.
72. Walton, 195.
73. Walton, 196.
74. *The Lincoln Reader*, 135.
75. Williams, 608.
76. Beveridge 2, 89.
77. Pratt, 5.
78. Williams, 609.
79. Williams, 609.
80. Williams, 610.
81. *Daily Missouri Republican*, July 12, 1847, as found in PAL.
82. *Remembrance*, 17.
83. Williams, 610.
84. Findley, 32–33.
85. Burlingame, 696.
86. LL, quoting David Davis to Sarah W. Davis, August 8, 1847.
87. Beveridge 2, 94.
88. Beveridge 2, 94.
89. Beveridge 2, 94.
90. Walton, 196.
91. Papers of Elisha Embree, in the Lucius Embree papers, Indiana State Library, Indianapolis, Indiana, Letter from Conrad Baker to EE, April 27, 1847.
92. Embree papers, May 6, 1847, from numerous supporters.
93. Papers of Elisha Embree, in the Lucius Embree papers, Indiana State Library, Indianapolis, Indiana, Letter from Conrad Baker to EE, April 27, 1847.
94. Embree papers, letter from constituent, July 12, 1848.
95. Papers of Richard W. Thompson, Indiana State Library, Indianapolis, Ind. Letter to Whig Convention, May 17, 1847.
96. Walton, 196.
97. Walton, 199.
98. Walton, 200.
99. Walton, 200.
100. Walton, 201.
101. Dyer, 174.
102. Grant, 147.
103. Grant, 148.
104. Chroust, Anton-Hermann. "Abraham Lincoln Argues A Pro-Slavery Case," *American Journal of Legal History*, Vol. 5, No. 4 (October 1861), 299–308.
105. Beveridge 2, 95.
106. Chroust, 300.
107. Beveridge 2, 96.
108. Beveridge 2, 97.

109. Chroust, 302.
110. Foner, 46.
111. Chroust, 302.
112. Beveridge 2, 97.
113. Beveridge 2, 98.
114. Chroust, 304.
115. Beveridge 2,100.
116. Donald, 115.
117. Donald, 115.
118. *Journal*, October 28, 1847.
119. Riddle 2, 8.
120. Findley, 62.
121. Findley, 63.
122. Findley, 63.
123. Findley, 68.
124. Speech of Henry Clay, November 13, 1847. Accessed online at http://www.henry clay.org/wp-content/uploads/2008/05/1847marketspeech1.pdf, March 5, 2012.
125. Riddle 2, 9.
126. Ohrt, Wallace. *Nicholas Trist: Defiant Peacemaker*, 134.
127. Booth, John Wilkes. *Right or Wrong, God Judge Me: The Writings of John Wilkes Booth*, 36.
128. Booth, Asia. *The Unlocked Book* (New York: G P. Putnam's Sons, 1938), 42–43.
129. Topham, 213.
130. Artemas Hale Diary, Library of Congress, December 1, 1847.
131. Artemas Hale Diary, Library of Congress, December 1, 1847.

CHAPTER FIVE: A HOUSE DIVIDED

1. Sarmiento, 257.
2. Sarmiento, 254.
3. Sarmiento, 256.
4. Sarmiento, 257.
5. English papers, Indiana State Historical Society, Indianapolis Ind., printed in the *Indiana State Sentinel*, December 10, 1847.
6. Hershman, 141.
7. English papers, Indiana State Historical Society, Indianapolis Ind., printed in the *Indiana State Sentinel*, December 10, 1847.
8. Beveridge 2, 101.
9. Beveridge 2, 101.
10. Watterston, 148.
11. Foner, 33.
12. Foner, 26.
13. Watterston, George. *New Guide to Washington 1846*, 9.
14. Watterston, George. *New Guide to Washington 1846*, 9.
15. StreetsofWashington.com. Accessed online at http://www.streetsofwashington.com/2009/12/metropolitan-aka-browns-marble-hotel.html, July 24, 2012.

16. Watterston, 162.
17. Hershman, 140.
18. Watterston, 56.
19. *The Lincoln Reader*, 133.
20. Beveridge 2, 102.
21. Beveridge 2, 104.
22. Outlaw to his wife, December 10, 1847.
23. Outlaw to his wife, January 16, 1848.
24. Beveridge 2, 102.
25. Beveridge 2, 102.
26. Ludy, Robert B. *Historic Hotels of the World: Past and Present*, 240.
27. Smith, Jean Edward. *John Marshall: Definer of a Nation*, 78.
28. Wallis, Michael. *Davy Crockett: Lion of the West*, 204.
29. White, 142.
30. Hershman, Robert R. *Records of the Columbia Historical Society, Washington D.C.*, Vol. 50, (the fortieth separately bound book) (1948/1950), 137–57.
31. Outlaw to his wife, February 23, 1848.
32. Outlaw to his wife, December 10, 1847.
33. Outlaw to his wife, December 17, 1847.
34. *On This Spot: Pinpointing the Past in Washington DC*, 3, 21.
35. Carrier, 24.
36. Evelyn, 21–22.
37. Weld, 884.
38. Donald, 119.
39. Outlaw to his wife, February 7, 1847.
40. Wheeler 1, 286.
41. Wheeler 1, 274.
42. Outlaw to his wife, February 28, 1848.
43. Weld, 883.
44. Wheeler 1, 287.
45. Wheeler 1, 268.
46. Wheeler 1, 269.
47. Wheeler 1, 272.
48. Wheeler 1, 272.
49. Wheeler 1, 284.
50. Wheeler 1, 292.
51. Wheeler 1, 278.
52. Wheeler 1, 278.
53. Wheeler 1, 184.
54. Wheeler 1, 186.
55. Wheeler 1, 186.
56. Wheeler 1, 238.
57. Wheeler 1, 238.
58. Wheeler 1, 248.
59. Weld, 882–83.

60. CW 7, 454, and footnote.

61. Weld, Theodore Dwight. *Letters of Theodore Dwight Weld, Angelina Grime Weld and Sarah Grimke, 1822–1844*. Edited by Gilbert H. Barnes and Dwight L. Dumond, 882–83: Weld to Angeline G. Weld, January 1, 1842. Accessed online April 6, 2012.

62. Weld, 882–83.

63. Weld, 884.

64. Weld, 882–83, http://bytesofhistory.com/Collections/UGRR/Sprigg_Ann/Sprigg _Ann-Weld.pdf.

65. Wheeler 1, 396.

66. Wheeler 1, 392, 396.

67. Wheeler 1, 420.

68. Wheeler 1, 377.

69. Charles Francis Adams to JG, February 17, 1848.

70. Winthrop diary, December 1, 1847.

71. Winthrop diary, December 2, 1847.

72. Winthrop diary, December 3, 1847.

73. Papers of Artemas Hale, University of Michigan, Ann Arbor. Letter from Grinnell to AH, November 13, 1847.

74. Winthrop correspondence dated December 2, 1847.

75. Winthrop correspondence dated December 2, 1847.

76. I arrive at this number by adding the vote total for Speaker, plus Winthrop and Smith, who probably did not vote.

77. Outlaw to his wife, December 5, 1847.

78. Winthrop diary, December 4, 1848.

79. Winthrop diary, December 4, 1848.

80. CW 1, 416–17.

81. Winthrop, 69.

82. Winthrop, 70.

83. *Washington Daily Union*, December 1, 1847.

84. *Intelligencer*, December 6, 1847.

85. AH to wife, January 26, 1848.

86. Outlaw to his wife, January 16, 1848.

87. Watterston, 208.

88. Watterston, 53.

89. Watterston, 208.

90. Outlaw to his wife, February 10, 1848.

91. Watterston, 207.

92. Watterston, 23.

93. Force, *Picture of Washington and its vicinity for 1848*.

94. Force, *Picture of Washington and its vicinity for 1848*.

95. Force, *Picture of Washington and its vicinity for 1848*.

96. Watterston, 24.

97. Watterston, 24–25.

98. French, Benjamin. *Witness to the Young Republic*, 72.

99. For occupational, age, and other biographical information, "The Biographical Directory of the United States Congress," accessed online at www.bioguide.congress.gov, containing such information for every past and present member of Congress.

100. Manning, 4.

101. Manning, 3.

102. Pratt, 100.

103. United States Department of Agriculture: Usual Planting and Harvesting Dates for U.S. Field Crops, December 1997.

104. Accessed online April 1, 2012, http://www.senate.gov/CRSReports/crs-publish.cfm ?pid=%260BL)PL%3B%3D%0A.

105. White, 144.

106. Sargent 2, 330.

107. Sargent 2, 331.

108. *Journal*, December 23, 1847.

109. Beveridge 2, 103.

110. Wentworth, John. *Congressional Reminiscences* (Chicago: Fergus, 1882), 7; hereafter "Wentworth."

111. Findley, 124.

112. Findley, 125.

113. Wheeler, Henry G. *The History of Congress*, 1, 9.

114. Wheeler 1, 26.

115. Tuck, 83.

116. Winthrop, Robert C. *A Memoir of Robert C. Winthrop* (Boston: Little, Brown, and Company, 1897), 71; hereafter "Winthrop Memoir."

117. Charles Francis Adams to JG, December 8, 1848.

118. JG to his son, May 7, 1848.

119. Giddings to Palfrey, May 27, 1848, document in Boston Public Library.

120. *Liberator*, December 18, 1848, in the Papers of Joshua Giddings, Ohio Historical Society, Columbus, Ohio.

121. *Liberator*, December 18, 1848, in the Papers of Joshua Giddings, Ohio Historical Society, Columbus, Ohio.

122. *National Whig*, Friday, December 10, 1847.

123. Wheeler 1, 440.

CHAPTER SIX: LINCOLN'S WASHINGTON

1. *Congressional Globe*, December 10, 1847.

2. Outlaw to his wife, December 6, 1847.

3. Outlaw to his wife, December 8, 1847.

4. *Globe*, December 7, 1847.

5. The President's Annual Message can be found in the *House Journal* of December 7.

6. Outlaw to his wife, December 6, 1847.

7. Donald, 305.

8. Donald, 305.

9. Directory of the Thirtieth Congress, published by the postmaster of the House of Representatives, 1848, found in the Embree Papers, Indiana State Library.

10. Mills, Robert. *Guide to the Capitol and National Executive Offices* (Washington City: W. Greer: 1847–48).
11. Van Dyke, 12.
12. *House Journal*, December 9, 1847.
13. Winthrop papers. Winthrop letter dated December 14, 1847.
14. Winthrop diary, January 6, 1848.
15. AL to Francis Blair and John Rives, January 11, 1848, found in PAL.
16. Outlaw to his wife, December 10, 1847.
17. Outlaw to his wife, December 8, 1847.
18. Correspondence in Hardin Papers dated February 1, 1844.
19. Watterston, 203.
20. *Union*, December 3, 1847.
21. Directory for the Thirtieth Congress.
22. Watterston, 205.
23. *Globe*, December 23, 1847.
24. Directory for the Thirtieth Congress.
25. Outlaw to his wife, December 13, 1847.
26. Outlaw to his wife, December 14, 1847.
27. Busey, Samuel Clagett. *Personal reminiscences and recollections of forty-six years' membership in the medical society of the district of Columbia, and residence in this city with biographical sketches of many of the deceased members* (Washington, D.C., 1895).
28. *Globe*, December 22, 1847.
29. Outlaw to his wife, December 20, 1847.
30. Alexander Stephens, correspondence dated September 20, 1848.
31. Outlaw to his wife, December 7, 1847.
32. Outlaw to his wife, December 13, 1847.
33. Outlaw to his wife, January 6, 1848.
34. Outlaw to his wife, January 7, 1848.
35. Outlaw to his wife, February 3, 1848.
36. Outlaw to his wife, February 7, 1848.
37. Outlaw to his wife, March 3, 1848.
38. Hale diary, December 10, 1848.
39. Hale diary, December 14, 1848.
40. Hale diary, December 27, 1848.
41. White, 149.
42. Outlaw to his wife, February 13, 1848.
43. Outlaw to his wife, February 17, 1848.
44. Findley, 168.
45. Findley, 168.
46. Riddle 2, 78.
47. This can be found in the "yeas" and "nays" book of the Thirtieth Congress, at the National Archives I Center for Legislative Research.
48. *Globe*, April 25, 1848.
49. Watterston, 141.
50. Diary of James K. Polk on the relevant dates.

51. Watterston, 145. See also Abraham Lincoln in the National Capital. Records of the Columbia Historical Society, Washington, D.C., Vol. 27 (1925), 1–174.
52. Winthrop, 77.
53. Winthrop, 77.
54. Outlaw to his wife, February 14, 1848.
55. Watterston, 96.
56. Watterston, 27.
57. *Remembrances*, 217–19.
58. *Remembrances*, 217–19.
59. Watterston, 31.
60. Description of the Library of Congress can be found in Watterston, 28–31.
61. Weld, 887.
62. Washburne, 315.
63. Newspaper Account Book, Thirtieth Congress, Second Session, National Archives I.
64. Van Dyke, 13.
65. Watterston, 102.
66. Outlaw to his wife, February 3, 1848.
67. Outlaw to his wife, December 16, 1849.
68. *Union* advertisement, December 1847.
69. *Intelligencer*, December 4, 1847.
70. For an example of a calling card used by a member of the Thirtieth Congress, see Charles J. Ingersoll Papers, Library of Congress.
71. CW 1, 459.
72. Outlaw to his wife, February 13, 1848.
73. Outlaw to his wife, February 3, 1848.
74. Outlaw to his wife, February 19, 1848.
75. Outlaw to his wife, December 8, 1847.
76. Outlaw to his wife, December 8 1847.
77. Barringer to his wife, February 22, 1847.

CHAPTER SEVEN: THE SECRET QUESTION

1. Nicolay and Hay 1, 263.
2. Busey, *Reminiscences*.
3. Busey, *Reminiscences*.
4. Busey, *Reminiscences* .
5. *House Journal*, December 21, 1847.
6. *House Journal*, December 28, 1847.
7. *House Journal*, December 30, 1847.
8. Foner, 17.
9. *House Journal*, December 30, 1847.
10. Text of Joshua Giddings's resolution on the subject, *Globe*, January 17, 1848.
11. *House Journal*, January 17, 1848.
12. Northup, Solomon. *Twelve Years a Slave*, 39.
13. Northup, 41.
14. Description of slave pen can be found in Northup, 41–42.

15. Northup, 42.
16. Northup, 42.
17. Northup, 44.
18. Northup, 44.
19. Northup, 45.
20. Northup, 47.
21. Northup, 49.
22. Northup, 56.
23. Northup, 56.
24. Northup, 60.
25. Northup, 61.

CHAPTER EIGHT: A GREAT PRESIDENT-MAKING MACHINE

1. Hale diary, December 31, 1847.
2. Hale diary, January 1, 1848; see also Papers of Charles J. Ingersoll, Pennsylvania Historical Society, correspondence dated January 1, 1848.
3. Hale diary, January 1, 1848.
4. Polk diary, December 31, 1847.
5. Polk diary, January 1, 1848.
6. Polk diary, January 4, 1848.
7. Ohrt, 137.
8. Ohrt, 138.
9. Ohrt, 139.
10. Ohrt, 139.
11. Ohrt, 140.
12. Ohrt, 140.
13. Ohrt, 140.
14. Polk diary, January 15, 1848.
15. Ohrt, 1414.
16. Polk diary, January 14, 1848.
17. Polk diary, January 25, 1848.
18. Polk diary, February 7, 1848.
19. Polk diary, January 23, 1848.
20. Polk diary, January 15, 1848.
21. Polk diary, January 6, 1848.
22. Polk diary, February 10, 1848.
23. CW 1, 422–23.
24. Outlaw to his wife, February 14, 1848.
25. *Intelligencer*, February 26, 1848.
26. *Intelligencer*, February 26, 1848.
27. Stephens, 22.
28. *Union*, December 6, 1847.
29. *Intelligencer*, December 13, 1847.
30. Outlaw to his wife, February 28, 1848.

31. Outlaw to his wife, December 7 1847.
32. John Strohm correspondence dated February 7, 1848.
33. Outlaw to his wife, December 14 1847.
34. Outlaw to his wife, December 14, 1847.
35. Caleb Smith Papers, Library of Congress (microfilm). From Thomas Dowling, January 19, 1848.
36. Smith papers, Greeley to Smith, February 18, 1848.
37. Armistead Burt papers, Duke University. Letter from constituent in Charleston, January 26, 1848.
38. George Houston papers, Duke University. January 7, 1848, to George Houston from Thomas Lockhart, Harysburg, N.C.
39. Peters to GH, March 1, 1848.
40. Winthrop to his son, Bob Winthrop, a student at Andover, January 6, 1848.
41 Winthrop, correspondence dated April 3, 1848.
42. Winthrop, correspondence dated April 3, 1848.
43. Outlaw to his wife, January 28, 1848.
44. Outlaw to his wife, January 30, 1848.
45. Outlaw to his wife, January 23, 1848.
46. Outlaw to his wife, March 3, 1848.
47. Papers of Joshua Giddings, Ohio Historical Society, Columbus, Ohio. Charles Francis Adams to JG, May 19, 1847.
48. Caleb Smith to JG, May 21, 1847.
49. Columbus Delano to JG, May 25, 1847.
50. Columbus Delano to JG, May 25, 1847.
51. Columbus Delano to JG, August 22, 1847.
52. Thomas Corwin to JG, August 18, 1847.
53. Horace Greeley to James Wilson, December 17, 1847, in the Papers of James Wilson, New Hampshire Historical Society.
54. Charles Francis Adams to JG, February 8, 1848.
55. Charles Sumner to JG, May 6, 1848.
56. Polk diary, December 27, 1847.
57. *Globe*, January 3, 1848.
58. *Globe*, January 3, 1848. The Globe reports 85 votes in favor, but lists only 82 names. The House Journal, which is authoritative, reports the vote as 82–81.
59. *House Journal*, February 14, 1848.
60. Outlaw to his wife, January 7, 1848.
61. Wheeler 1, 177.
62. Hale diary, December 31, 1847.
63. Outlaw to his wife, February 13, 1848.
64. Outlaw to his wife, February 13, 1848.
65. *Globe*, 107, January 5, 1848.
66. *Globe*, January 5, 1848.
67. CW 1, 430–31.
68. CW 1, 430–31.

69. Outlaw to his wife, December 9, 1847.
70. Papers of John Lumpkin Taylor, Ohio Historical Society, Columbus, Ohio. Correspondence dated December 20, 1848.
71. Outlaw to his wife, February 18, 1848.
72. Outlaw to his wife, February 18, 1848.
73. Riddle 2, 150.
74. Outlaw to his wife, February 22, 1848.
75. Watterston, 87.
76. Watterston, 145.
77. *Intelligencer*, December 6, 1847.
78. Emerson, 9.
79. Emerson, 9.
80. *House Journal*, March 1, 1848.
81. Dyer, 175.
82. Dyer, 176.
83. Dyer, 176.
84. Dyer, 176.
85. Dyer, 176.

CHAPTER NINE: THE QUESTIONS OF WAR

1. *Globe*, December 22, 1848.
2. Riddle, 36.
3. Riddle, 37.
4. Riddle, 36.
5. Burlingame, 778.
6. *Globe*, January 11, 1848.
7. Outlaw to his wife, January 12, 1848.
8. Notes for the Spot Resolutions speech, Papers of Abraham Lincoln.
9. Busey, *Reminscences*.
10. CW 1, 446–48.
11. CW 1, 449–50.
12. CW, AL to Usher Linder, March 22, 1848, PAL.
13. Outlaw, February 19, 1848.
14. *Globe*, January 18, 1848.
15. *Globe*, Appendix, February 2, 1848.
16. Boykin, Samuel. *A Memorial Volume of the Hon. Howell Cobb of Georgia*, 30.
17. Boykin, Samuel. *A Memorial Volume of the Hon. Howell Cobb of Georgia*, 30.
18. CW 1, 455–56.
19. Riddle 38
20. *Journal*, February 10, 1848.
21. Reprinted in the *Journal*, February 3, 1848.
22. *Journal*, February 10, 1848.
23. *Journal*, February 24, 1848.

CHAPTER TEN: WAR AND PEACE

1. Watterston, 21.
2. Outlaw to his wife, February 3, 1848.
3. *Journal*, February 3, 1848.
4. *Globe*, January 13, 1848.
5. Outlaw to his wife, February 1, 1848.
6. *Journal*, February 10, 1848.
7. Polk diary, January 13, 1848.
8. Polk diary, January 13, 1848.
9. *Globe*, December 15, 1847.
10. *Intelligencer*, December 16, 1847.
11. Solomon Cramer to Charles J. Ingersoll, January 22, 1848, Ingersoll papers.
12. Merry, 414.
13. W. Milton to George Marsh, January 29, 1848.
14. For unknown reasons, all of Stephens's February 2 speech appears in the Appendix to the *Globe*, beginning on page 159.
15. Schott, Thomas. *Alexander H. Stephens of Georgia: A Biography* (Baton Rouge: Louisiana State University, 1988), 9.
16. Outlaw to his wife, February 12, 1848.
17. Greeley, 227.
18. Paullin, Charles O. "Abraham Lincoln in Congress, 1847–1849," *Journal of the Illinois State Historical Society*, Vol. 14, No. 1/2 (April 1921), 85–89.
19. Outlaw to his wife, February 12, 1848.
20. *Journal*, February 3, 1848.
21. *Journal*, February 17, 1848.
22. *House Journal*, February 7, 1848.
23. *House Journal*, April 17, 1848.
24. Winthrop, 81.
25. Winthrop, 81.
26. Winthrop diary, February 2, 1848.
27. AH to his wife, February 3, 1848.
28. Winthrop letter, January 12, 1848.
29. Watterston, 140.
30. Outlaw to his wife, January 22, 1848.
31. AH to his wife, February 6, 1848.
32. Outlaw to his wife, February 3, 1848.
33. Polk diary, February 1, 1848.
34. Illegible constituent writing to John Strohm, January 18, 1848.
35. Albert Gallatin to George Marsh, January 3, 1848, Papers of George Marsh, University of Vermont.
36. *Globe*, February 8, 1848.
37. *Globe*, February 8, 1848.
38. *Globe*, February 8, 1848.
39. *Globe*, February 8, 1848.
40. John Strohm correspondence dated February 7, 1848.

41. *Globe*, February 16, 1848.
42. *Globe*, February 16, 1848.
43. *Globe*, February 17, 1848.
44. *Globe*, February 17, 1848.
45. *Globe*, February 17, 1848.

CHAPTER ELEVEN: NOT A SINECURE

1. I base these figures on a report found in the papers of the Committee on Post Offices and Post Roads, at the National Archives I legislative research center. It said that in one week in 1844, members of the House received 1,882 letters and sent out 1,505. This would be 8 and 6 letters per member per week, but adjusting upward for increases in population, literacy, and access to the post office, as well as Lincoln's status as the lone Whig of Illinois, this appears to be a very conservative estimate.
2. Findley, 171.
3. Donald, 103.
4. Marsh, 131.
5. Outlaw to his wife, March 13, 1848.
6. Outlaw to his wife, January 23, 1848.
7. Outlaw to his wife, February 17, 1848.
8. Outlaw to his wife, February 18, 1848.
9. Hale diary, January 8, 1848.
10. CW 1, 446.
11. *Globe*, January 17, 1848.
12. *House Journal*, January 24, 1848.
13. BH Gatton to JJH, January 13, 1844.
14. Constituent to AH, June 16, 1848.
15. Treasury Department to AS, July 17, 1848.
16. Embree papers.
17. Constituent to John Strohm, April 8, 1848.
18. John Chandler to EE, July 12, 1848.
19. Richard W. Thompson to constituent, June 8, 1847.
20. John J. Brown to JJH, November 8, 1843.
21. January 5, 1844.
22. CW 1, 453.
23. Graebner, Norma A. "James K. Polk: A Study in Federal Patronage," *Mississippi Valley Historical Review*, Vol., 38, No. 4 (March., 1952), 613–32.
24. Graebner, 615.
25. Papers of Caleb Smith, Indiana Historical Society, letter from CS to the Secretary of the Navy.
26. Winthrop papers. Letter dated December 14, 1847.
27. Winthrop papers. Letter dated December 14, 1847.
28. Outlaw to his wife, December 6, 1847.
29. Outlaw to his wife, December 16, 1847.
30. Polk diary, March 18, 1848.
31. Polk diary, April 6, 1848.

32. Polk diary, April 10, 1848.

33. Polk diary, December 16, 1847.

34. Polk diary, December 16, 1847.

35. Polk diary, December 16, 1847.

36. Polk diary, December 17, 1847.

37. Polk diary, January 14, 1848.

38. Outlaw to his wife, January 16, 1847.

39. Wentworth 10.

40. CW 1, 444–45.

41. Polk diary, December 29, 1847.

42. Polk diary, February 8, 1848.

43. Polk diary, August 15, 1848.

44. Polk diary, September 12, 1848.

45. Polk diary, February 8, 1848.

46. Watterston, 139.

47. Boas, Norman F. "Lincoln and John Quincy Adams," *The Railsplitter*, Vol. 8, No. 4, 10. Accessed online at http://www.railsplitter.com/wordpress/PDF/Vol8No4 .pdf, April 6, 2012.

48. Perley, *Reminiscences of sixty years in the national metropolis*, 338.

49. Poore, 339.

50. Outlaw to his wife, February 18, 1848.

51. Outlaw to his wife, February 18, 1848.

52. Outlaw to his wife, February 18, 1848.

53. Polk diary, February 19, 1848.

54. Polk diary, February 20, 1848.

55. *Intelligencer*, February 22, 1848.

56. *Intelligencer*, February 22, 1848.

57. Polk diary, February 21, 1848.

58. Polk diary, February 21, 1848.

59. President's message to Congress, as printed in the *House Journal* of December 7, 1848.

60. Polk diary, February 22, 1848.

61. *House Journal*, February 22 and 23, 1848.

62. Sargent 2, 332.

63. JG to his daughter, February 22, 1848.

64. Outlaw to his wife, February 23, 1848.

65. *House Journal*, February 24, 1848.

66. Outlaw to his wife, February 24, 1848.

67. *Intelligencer*, February 28, 1848.

68. *The Impending Crisis*, 15.

69. *The Impending Crisis*, 15.

70. Outlaw to his wife, February 26, 1848.

71. Outlaw to his wife, February 26, 1848.

72. Polk 4, 362.

73. Sargent 2, 333.

74. Polk 4, 363.
75. Watterston, 72.
76. Watterston, 72.
77. Watterston, 74.
78. *House Journal*, March 2, 1848.
79. Barringer to his wife, February 22, 1847.
80. Journal of George Grundy Dunn, Indiana State Historical Society, Indianapolis, Ind.
81. Ingersoll to his daughter, March 20, 1848.
82. Sargent 2, 333.
83. Sargent 2, 333.
84. *House Journal*, February 26, 1848.
85. Hunt, Gaillard. *Israel, Elihu, and Cadwallader Washburn*, 142. Thanks to Rhoda Sneller of *Abraham Lincoln Online*, for preserving the story of Lincoln's pilgrimage to Mt. Vernon. Her site can be found at http://showcase.netins.net/web/creative/lincoln.html.
86. Force, William Quereau. *Picture of Washington and its vicinity for 1848*, 140.
87. Force, 140–41.
88. Polk diary, February 25, 1848.
89. Polk diary, February 28, 1848.
90. Polk diary, February 28, 1848.
91. Polk diary, February 29, 1848.
92. Polk diary, February 28, 1848.
93. Polk diary, March 4, 1848.
94. Julian, George Washington. *The Life of Joshua R. Giddings*, 241.
95. Smith papers. E.W. McGaughry, Rockville, Ind., March 15, 1848.
96. Truman Smith to James Wilson, July 24, 1848, Wilson Papers.
97. Barringer letter of February 11, 1848.
98. CW 1, 452.
99. CW 1, 452.
100. CW 1, 453.
101. JG to wife, March 11, 1848.
102. JG correspondence dated April 21, 1848.
103. Outlaw to his wife, February 11, 1848.
104. Statutes at Large.
105. *Intelligencer*, February 28, 1848.
106. William Mitchell to AH, March 2, 1848.
107. Polk diary, April 27, 1848.
108. *Intelligencer*, February 28–March 4.
109. *Intelligencer*, March 3, 1848.
110. Polk diary, March 18, 1848.
111. Hale diary, March 10, 1848.
112. Outlaw to his wife, March 10, 1848.
113. *House Journal*, March 10, 1848.
114. CW 1, 454.
115. CW 1, 463–64.

116. CW 1, 463–64.
117. Dyer, 179.
118. Hale to Barringer, April 7, 1848.
119. Smith papers. Constituent letter to Smith, postmarked Indianapolis, April 4, 1848.
120. *Globe*, March 29, 1848.
121. Grant, 175.
122. Grant, 180.
123. Grant, 184.
124. Grant, 187.
125. Grant, 192.
126. Lee, 63.
127. Polk diary, April 27, 1848.
128. CW 1, 456–66.
129. CW 1, 456–66.
130. Papers of Robert Schenk, microfilm located at the Ohio Historical Society, Columbus, Ohio. Letter to his daughters, December 29, 1847.
131. Robert Schenk to his daughters, February 22.
132. AH to wife, February 6, 1848.
133. Outlaw to his wife, February 3, 1848.
134. Outlaw to his wife, December 5, 1847.
135. Outlaw to his wife, December 7 1847.
136. Outlaw to his wife, December 5, 1847.
137. Outlaw to his wife, February 1, 1848.
138. Outlaw to his wife, February 20, 1848.
139. Outlaw to his wife, February 3, 1848.
140. Barringer papers, University of North Carolina Chapel Hill, Southern Historical Collection. Barringer to his wife, January 28, 1848.
141. Polk diary, April 20, 1848.
142. *House Journal*, April 20, 1848.
143. *The Lincoln Reader*, 134.
144. Polk diary, April 29, 1848.

CHAPTER TWELVE: THE GALLOWS OF HAMAN

1. CW 1, 466–67.
2. CW 1, 474.
3. May 18, 1848.
4. *Intelligencer*, May 24, 1848.
5. *Intelligencer*, May 24, 1848.
6. National Party Conventions, 1831–1988, *Congressional Quarterly* (Washington, D.C.: 1991), 35 ("Conventions").
7. Polk diary, May 25, 1848.
8. Polk diary, May 25, 1848.
9. H. Battelle(?) to AH, April 12, 1848.
10. Webster, 288.
11. Weed 1, 575.

12. Dyer, Brainerd. "Zachary Taylor and the Election of 1848," *Pacific Historical Review*, Vol. 9, No. 2 (June 1940), 173–82.

13. *Intelligencer*, June 6, 1848.

14. *Intelligencer*, June 7, 1848.

15. Holt, 320.

16. *Intelligencer*, June 9, 1848.

17. Conn, Steven. "Where is the East? Asian Objects in American Museums, from Nathan Dunn to Charles Freer," *Winterthur Portfolio*, Vol. 35, No. 2/3 (Summer–Autumn 2000), 157–73, photo on page 158.

18. Zboray, Ronald, and Mary Saracino Zboray. "Between Crockery-dom and Barnum: Boston's Chinese Museum, 1845–47," *American Quarterly*, Vol. 56, No. 2 (June 2004), 271–307.

19. Conn, Steven. "Where is the East?," 157–73, photo on page 158.

20. *Intelligencer*, June 9, 1848.

21. *Intelligencer*, June 8, 1848.

22. *Intelligencer*, June 12, 1848.

23. *Intelligencer*, June 12, 1848.

24. *Intelligencer*, June 12, 1848.

25. *Intelligencer*, June 12, 1848.

26. *Intelligencer*, June 12, 1848.

27. *Intelligencer*, June 12, 1848.

28. *Intelligencer*, June 12, 1848.

29. Dyer, 283.

30. English papers, *Indiana State Sentinel*, July 26, 1848.

31. *Intelligencer*, June 12, 1848.

32. *Intelligencer*, June 12, 1848.

33. *Intelligencer*, June 12, 1848.

34. *House Journal*, June 15, 1848.

35. Illegible correspondent to JG, June 12, 1848.

36. Webster, 296.

37. Wentworth 30

38. Wentworth, 31.

39. Dyer, 288.

40. Mann, Horace. *Life of Horace Mann*, 264.

41. George G. Fogge to James Wilson, July 1848, Wilson Papers.

42. Letter to the Whigs of the Sixth Congressional District from George Ashmun, document located at the Boston Public Library.

43. Letter to the Whigs of the Sixth Congressional District from George Ashmun, document located at the Boston Public Library.

44. French, 204.

45. Isaac Strohm to John Strohm, June 29, 1848.

46. Amos Here(?) to John Strohm, March 7, 1848.

47. Correspondent to James Wilson, July 17, 1848, Wilson Papers.

48. John Miller to John Strohm, July 25, 1848.

49. Polk diary, June 22, 1848.

50. CW 1, 476–77.
51. Smith papers. Thomas B. Stevenson to Caleb Smith, June 12, 1848.
52. Mary Lincoln to AL, unknown date in May, 1848, PAL.
53. CW 1, 477–78.

CHAPTER THIRTEEN: INTERNAL IMPROVEMENTS

1. CW 1, 480–90.
2. *House Journal*, July 5, 1848.
3. *Globe*, July 24, 1848.
4. James L. D. Morrison to AL, June 25, 1848, PAL.
5. CW 1, 498.
6. Pratt, 101.
7. Pratt, 101.
8. Pratt, 101.
9. Winthrop, 84.
10. Hale diary, July 4, 1848.
11. Beveridge 2, 157.
12. Hale diary, July 4, 1848.
13. Beveridge 2, 157.
14. *Intelligencer*, July 6, 1848.

CHAPTER FOURTEEN: THE TROUBLE WITH OREGON

1. *The Impending Crisis*, 55–59.
2. *Impending Crisis*, 74.
3. *Impending Crisis*, 74.
4. Outlaw to his wife, July 20, 1848.
5. Polk diary, July 27, 1848.
6. *Life of Horace Mann*, 268.
7. Polk diary, July 28, 1848.
8. Outlaw to his wife (date illegible, probably July 24, 1848).
9. Outlaw to his wife, July 28, 1848.
10. *Globe*, July 27, 1848.
11. *Globe*, July 31, 1848.
12. *Globe*, August 1, 1848.
13. *Globe*, August 1, 1848.
14. *Globe*, August 2, 1848.
15. Outlaw to his wife, July 28, 1848.
16. *Intelligencer*, July 19, 1848.
17. *Intelligencer*, July 19, 1848.
18. *Reminiscences*, 330.
19. *Reminiscences*, 330.
20. *Reminiscences*, 330.
21. *House Journal*, August 14, 1848.
22. *Remembrances*, 221.
23. Tuck, 84.

24. Tuck, 84.
25. Tuck, 84.
26. Polk diary, August 7, 1848.
27. Herndon, 273.
28. CW 1, 517–18.
29. CW 1, 517, 18.
30. *Journal*, June 15, 1848.
31. *Journal*, June 15, 1848.
32. CW 1, 518–19.
33. *Journal*, May 4, 1848.
34. Findley, 218–19.
35. *Journal*, May 18, 1848.
36. Riddle 2, 120.
37. Riddle 2, 118.
38. Riddle 2, 121.
39. Polk diary, August 5, 1848.
40. Outlaw to his wife, August 7, 1848.
41. Outlaw to his wife, August 10, 1848.
42. *Globe*, August 5, 1848.
43. Polk diary, August 11, 1848.
44. *Globe*, August 12, 1848.
45. *Globe*, August 12, 1848.
46. *House Journal*, August 14, 1848.
47. *Globe*, August 14, 1848.
48. *Globe*, August 14, 1848.
49. Polk diary, August 23, 1848.

CHAPTER FIFTEEN: LINCOLN THE YOUNG INDIAN

1. Dyer, 286.
2. *Selected Works of Thaddeus Stevens*, 102–3. My thanks go out to Ross Hetrick, President of the Thaddeus Stevens Society, for his assistance in finding Stevens's reply to Lincoln.
3. Truman Smith to James Wilson, August 23, 1848, Wilson Papers.
4. Truman Smith to James Wilson, August 23, 1848, Wilson Papers.
5. Truman Smith to James Wilson, September 7, 1848, Wilson Papers.
6. Central Rough and Ready Club to EE, September 21, 1848.
7. Richard Wallach to EE, September 21, 1848.
8. Dyer 296–97.
9. Dyer 296–97.
10. Whig Central Committee to EE, September 27, 1848.
11. *General Taylor and His Staff*, 15.
12. Truman Smith to AH, September 9, 1848.
13. AH correspondence dated October 9, 1848.
14. http://www.archive.org/stream/proceedingsofmas24massuoft/proceedingsofmas 24massuoft_djvu.txt.

15. Dyer, 177.
16. Dyer, 177.
17. Dyer, 178.
18. Dyer, 177.
19. Dyer, 178.
20. Richard Wallach to EE, September 21, 1848.
21. Charles Sumner to JG, June 17, 1848.
22. JG to son, June 28, 1848.
23. JG to son, June 23, 1848.
24. JG to son, June 23, 1848.
25. Charles Sumner to JG, July 2, 1848.
26. JG to son, July 9, 1848.
27. Charles Sumner to JG, July 2, 1848.
28. Charles Sumner to JG, July 2, 1848.
29. JG to son, July 22, 1848.
30. Charles Sumner to JG, September 3, 1848.
31. Riddle 2, 134.
32. Burlingame (published edition), 1, 306.
33. Mann, 265.
34. Luthin, Reinhard H. "Abraham Lincoln and the Massachusetts Whigs in 1848," *New England Quarterly*, Vol. 14, No. 4 (December 1941) 619–32, 621.
35. Luthin, 622.
36. Schouler, 78, footnote 2.
37. Herndon, 1, 95.
38. Herndo 1, 95.
39. Donald, 131.
40. Beveridge, 2, 177.
41. *Memoir of Rufus Choate*, 112.
42. A description of Washingtonian Hall can be found in Charles Jewett's *Speeches, Poems, and Miscellaneous Writings on Subjects Connected With Temperance and Liquor Traffic* (Boston: self-published, 1849).
43. CW, 5.
44. Schouler, 77.
45. CW 2, 6.
46. Goodwin, Doris Kearns. *Team of Rivals* (New York: Simon & Schuster, 2005), 127.
47. Lincoln Log September 22, 1848, quoting the *Boston Atlas* of September 23, 1848.
48. Lincoln Log September 22, 1848, quoting the *Boston Atlas* of September 23, 1848.
49. Goodwin, 127.
50. Goodwin, 127.
51. Luthin, 631.
52. Riddle 2, 137.
53. CW 2, 10–11.
54. Emerson, Jason. *Lincoln the Inventor*, 5.
55. Emerson, 5.
56. Emerson, 5.

57. Emerson, 5.
58. Emerson, 6.
59. Papers of George Perkins Marsh, 124.
60. CW 2, 11–13.
61. Emerson, 6.
62. *Intelligencer*, November 11, 1848.
63. Dyer, 299.
64. Dyer, 299.
65. Polk diary, November 8, 1848.
66. Winthrop correspondence dated November 14, 1848.
67. W. W. Roman to AL, December 17, 1848, PAL.

CHAPTER SIXTEEN: MILES GONE BY
1. *Globe*, December 4, 1849.
2. Mann, 273.
3. *Globe*, December 5, 1848.
4. *Globe*, December 7, 1849.
5. *Globe*, December 11, 1849.
6. AL to C. U. Schlater, January 5, 1849, PAL.
7. Emerson, 18.
8. Emerson, 18.
9. Outlaw to his wife, December 15, 1849.
10. Smith papers. Letter to Caleb Smith from New York, December 6, 1848.
11. S. M. Gates to JG, December 5, 1848.
12. Greeley, Horace. *Horace Greeley: Recollections of a Busy Life*, 226.
13. Greeley, *Recollections*, 227.
14. Greeley, *Recollections*, 227.
15. Greeley, *Recollections*, 228.
16. Ingersoll, Lorton Dunham. *The Life of Horace Greeley: Founder of the New York Tribune*, 210.
17. Ingersoll, 210.
18. Ingersoll, 210.
19. Pratt, 118.
20. http://www.senate.gov/reference/resources/pdf/97-1011.pdf. Accessed March 25, 2012.
21. White, 145.
22. *Globe*, January 7 1848.
23. Force, 35.
24. Pratt, Harry E. *The Personal Finances of Abraham Lincoln*, 34–35.
25. Pratt, 84.
26. Pratt, 85.
27. Pratt, 85.
28. Papers of John Pollard Gaines, New York State Library, Albany, New York. January 3, 1849, letter to Gaines from constituent.

29. Ingersoll, 212.
30. Ingersoll, 212.
31. Ingersoll, 213.
32. Ingersoll, 216.
33. EE to the editor of the *Clarion*, March 20, 1849.
34. Ingersoll, 216.
35. Ingersoll, 219.
36. Outlaw to his wife, January 25, 1849.
37. Ingersoll, 219.
38. Ingersoll, 220.
39. Ingersoll, 221.

CHAPTER SEVENTEEN: THE VALIANT DEMOLISHER OF WINDMILLS

1. Wentworth, 15.
2. JG to Wendell Phillips, a public letter appearing in the *Ohio Statesman*, June 14, 1860. Papers of Johua Giddings, Ohio Historical Society, Columbus, Ohio.
3. Hudson, Charles. *The Character of Abraham Lincoln, 1863*, 5.
4. Hudson, 5.
5. Hudson, 6.
6. Wheeler 1, 374.
7. Tuck, 89.
8. Tuck, 89.
9. Tuck, 89.
10. Richard W. Thompson to constituent, June 8, 1847.
11. Thompson, June 5, 1847.
12. Winthrop to Gardner, December 29, 1848.
13. Outlaw to his wife, January 25, 1849.
14. Resolution of the North Carolina State Assembly, January 27, 1849, in the Barringer papers.
15. Papers of John McDowell, University of North Carolina, Chapel Hill, Southern Historical Society. John Harris to McDowell, January 14, 1848.
16. Foner, 4.
17. Foner, 28.
18. *Inner World*, 21.
19. *Inner World*, 22.
20. *Inner World*, 22.
21. Foner, 29.
22. Foner, 29.
23. Foner, 30.
24. Simon, 123.
25. Foner, 34–35.
26. Foner, 31.
27. Foner, 31.
28. *Impending Crisis*, 99.

29. *Impending Crisis*, 99.
30. Foner, 46.
31. Foner, 47.
32. Foner, 46–47.
33. Foner, 30.
34. Foner, 48.
35. Foner, 48.
36. Foner, 48.
37. Foner, 48.
38. Foner, 48.
39. Foner, 48.
40. Foner, 48.
41. *Inner World*, 26.
42. Simon, 124.
43. Riddle 2, 162.
44. Riddle 2, 163.
45. Polk diary, December 12, 1848.
46. *Globe*, December 13, 1848.
47. *Globe*, December 13, 1848.
48. *Globe*, December 13, 1848.
49. This story is found in correspondence of Joshua Giddings dated December 16, 1848.
50. This story is found in correspondence of Joshua Giddings dated December 16, 1848.
51. This story is found in correspondence of Joshua Giddings dated December 16, 1848.
52. *Globe*, December 18, 1848.
53. *Globe*, December 18, 1848.
54. *Globe*, December 18, 1848.
55. *Globe*, December 18, 1848.
56. *Globe*, December 18, 1848.
57. Anonymous to JG, May 4, 1848.
58. Anonymous to JG, May 26, 1848.
59. Winthrop correspondence, January 14, 1849.
60. Porter, Kenneth Wiggins. "Three Fighters for Freedom," *Journal of Negro History*, Vol. 28, No. 1 (January 1943), 51–72.
61. Porter, 66.
62. Porter, 66.
63. Porter, 67.
64. Porter, 67.
65. Porter, 67.
66. Porter, 68.
67. Porter, 68.
68. *Globe*, December 29, 1848.
69. *Globe*, December 29, 1848.
70. *Globe*, December 29, 1848.
71. *Globe*, December 29, 1848.
72. *Globe*, December 29, 1848.

73. Diary of Joshua Giddings, January 5, 1849.

74. Diary of Joshua Giddings, January 6, 1849.

75. *Globe*, January 6, 1849.

76. *Globe*, January 12, 1849.

77. *Globe*, January 8, 1849.

78. Diary of Joshua Giddings, January 6, 1849.

79. *House Journal*, January 19, 1849.

80. *House Journal*, January 19, 1849.

81. Winthrop correspondence dated January 14, 1849.

82. Winthrop correspondence dated January 20, 1849.

83. Winthrop correspondence dated January 14, 1849.

84. Winthrop correspondence dated January 14, 1849.

85. Diary of Joshua Giddings, January 8, 1849.

86. Diary of Joshua Giddings, January 11, 1849.

87. Diary of Joshua Giddings, January 11, 1849.

88. Johnson, Andrew. *The Papers of Andrew Johnson*, Vol. 1 (Knoxville: University of Tennessee Press, 1967).

89. Beveridge 2, 187.

90. Diary of Joshua Giddings, January 15, 1849.

91. Polk diary, December 22, 1848.

92. Polk diary, December 23, 1848.

93. Diary of Joshua Giddings, January 18, 1849.

94. Diary of Joshua Giddings, January 23, 1849.

95. Diary of Joshua Giddings, January 26, 1849.

96. Diary of Joshua Giddings, February 2, 1849.

97. Diary of Joshua Giddings, January 15, 1849.

98. Mann, 273.

99. Polk diary, January 16, 1849.

100. Polk diary, December 26, 1848.

101. Polk diary, January 20, 1849.

102. Polk diary, January 20, 1849.

103. Polk diary, January 26, 1849.

104. *Inner World*, 21.

105. *Inner World*, 21.

106. *Inner World*, 29.

CHAPTER EIGHTEEN: WITH MALICE TOWARD SOME

1. *House Journal*, January 6, 1849.

2. *Globe*, January 16, 1849.

3. *Globe*, January 18, 1849.

4. *Globe*, March 3, 1849.

5. *House Journal*, January 23, 1849.

6. *Globe*, January 22, 1849.

7. Outlaw to his wife, February 7, 1849.

8. Polk diary, February 13, 1849.

9. Polk diary, February 22, 1849.
10. Diary of Joshua Giddings, February 27, 1849.
11. Diary of Joshua Giddings, February 27, 1849.
12. Diary of Joshua Giddings, February 27, 1849.
13. Outlaw to his wife, February 2, 1849.
14. *Globe*, February 28, 1849.
15. CW 10, 14.
16. *Globe*, February 28, 1849.
17. *Senate Journal*, March 1, 1849.
18. *Globe*, March 2, 1849.
19. *Globe*, March 2, 1849.
20. *Globe*, March 2, 1849.
21. *Globe*, March 2, 1849.
22. *Globe*, March 2, 1849.
23. *Globe*, March 2, 1849.
24. *Globe*, March 2, 1849.
25. *Globe*, March 2, 1849.
26. *Globe*, March 2, 1849.
27. *Globe*, March 2, 1849.
28. *Globe*, March 2, 1849.
29. *Globe*, March 2, 1849.

CHAPTER NINETEEN: THE LAST FULL MEASURE

1. *Globe*, March 3, 1849.
2. *Globe*, March 3, 1849.
3. Greeley, 229.
4. Greeley, 229.
5. Greeley, 230.
6. Greeley, 233.
7. Greeley, 233.
8. Greeley, 233.
9. Greeley, 233.
10. Mann, 277.
11. Diary of Joshua Giddings, March 4, 1849.
12. Polk diary, March 3, 1849.
13. *Globe*, March 3, 1849.
14. *Globe*, March 3, 1849.
15. Greeley, 231.
16. *Globe*, March 3, 1849.
17. *Globe*, March 3, 1849.
18. Greeley, 232.
19. Greeley, 232.
20. *Globe*, March 3, 1849.
21. *Globe*, March 3, 1849.
22. Polk diary, March 3, 1849.

23. Polk diary, March 3, 1849.
24. Polk diary, March 3, 1849.
25. Polk diary, March 3, 1849.
26. *Globe*, March 3, 1849.
27. *Globe*, March 3, 1849.
28. *Globe*, March 3, 1849.
29. *Globe*, March 3, 1849.
30. *Globe*, March 3, 1849.
31. *Globe*, March 3, 1849.
32. *Globe*, March 3, 1849.
33. *Globe*, March 3, 1849.
34. Polk diary, March 3, 1849.
35. *Globe*, March 3, 1849.
36. *Globe*, March 3, 1849.
37. Mann, 276.
38. Polk diary, March 4, 1849.
39. Globe, 4/6/1849.

CHAPTER TWENTY: GENERAL TAYLOR'S GRAND TRIUMPHAL MARCH

1. French, 209.
2. French, 209.
3. *Intelligencer*, March 6, 1849.
4. Clark, 8.
5. *Intelligencer*, March 6, 1849.
6. *Intelligencer*, March 6, 1849.
7. *Intelligencer*, March 6, 1849.
8. *Intelligencer*, March 6, 1849.
9. Winthrop to Clifford, December 11, 1849.
10. Polk diary, March 5, 1849.
11. *Intelligencer*, March 6, 1849.
12. Polk diary, March 5, 1849.
13. Polk diary, March 5, 1849.
14. *Intelligencer*, March 6, 1849.
15. *Intelligencer*, March 8, 1849.
16. *Intelligencer*, March 8, 1849.
17. *Intelligencer*, March 8, 1849.
18. *Remembrances*, 19–20.
19. Donald, 100.
20. Watterston, 33.
21. Watterston, 33.
22. Watterston, 33.
23. Watterston, 33.
24. Emerson, 19.

CHAPTER TWENTY-ONE: THE COMET AT THE END OF THE WORLD

1. Stowell, 4.
2. Stowell, 4.
3. Riddle 2, 198.
4. Stowell, 6.
5. Anson G. Henry to AL, April 6, 1849, PAL.
6. CW 11, 1–2.
7. Nicolay and Hay 1, 294, footnote.
8. Riddle 2, 216.
9. Justin Butterfield to AL, April 10, 1848, PAL.
10. Nicolay and Hay 1, 294, footnote.
11. CW 2, 52.
12. Josiah M. Lucas to AL, April 12, 1849, PAL.
13. Josiah M. Lucas to AL, May 7, 1849, PAL.
14. *Intelligencer*, March 10, 1849.
15. Wentworth, 10.
16. Josiah M. Lucas to AL, May 9, 1849, PAL.
17. William H. Henderson to AL, May 19, 1849, PAL.
18. William H. Henderson to AL, June 11, 1849, PAL.
19. CW 2, 48–49.
20. "Presidential Patronage," accessed online at www.lincolnandfriends.org, November 1, 2012.
21. Josiah M. Lucas to Anson G. Henry, May 22, 1849, PAL.
22. Coleman, Charles Hubert. *Abraham Lincoln and Coles County, Illinois* (New Brunswick, NJ: Scarecrow Press, 1955), 128–29.
23. Justin Butterfield to AL, June 9, 1849, PAL.
24. Ewing, Thomas. "Lincoln and the General Land Office." *Journal of the Illinois State Historical Society*, October 1932, Vol. XXV, No. 3, 143.
25. William N. Bishop and Alexander P. Dunbar to AL, June 6, 1849, PAL.
26. The stories of Lincoln's travels back to D.C. are from Herndon, 303–6.
27. Richard W. Thompson to Abraham Lincoln, June 14, 1849, PAL.
28. Stowell, 10.
29. Stowell, 11.
30. Stowell, 12.
31. Stowell, 11, 13.
32. *Journal of the Illinois State Historical Society*, October 1932, Vol. XXV, No. 3, 153.
33. Journal ISHS, 153.
34. Journal ISHS, 153.
35. Stowell, 20.
36. Nicolay and Hay 1, 294.
37. CW 2, 55.
38. CW 10, 15–16.
39. CW 11, 3–4.
40. Thomas Ewing to Abraham Lincoln, July 18, 1849, PAL.
41. Riddle 2, 225.

EPILOGUE: THE EMANCIPATION OF ABRAHAM LINCOLN

1. *Impending Crisis*, 87.
2. *Impending Crisis*, 87.
3. *Impending Crisis*, 99.
4. *Impending Crisis*, 99.
5. *Impending Crisis*, 99.
6. *Impending Crisis*, 99.
7. Greeley, Horace. *Proceedings of the First Three Republican Conventions*, 71.
8. Burlingame, 1665.
9. Burlingame, 1670.
10. CW 4, 55.
11. Burlingame, 1678.
12. Ashmun, 194.
13. Burlingame, 1717.
14. Amos Tuck to Joshua Giddings, November 26, 1860.
15. CW 4, 160.
16. CW 4, 160.
17. Van Dyke, 15.
18. *Recollections of Alexander H. Stephens*, Introduction, vii.
19. Stephens, 82.
20. Van Dyke, 32.
21. Winthrop correspondence dated April 21, 1865.
22. Stephens, 141.
23. *The Works of James Abram Garfield*, Vol. 2, 534–42.

BIBLIOGRAPHY

—◆—

BOOKS

Angle, Paul (Editor). *The Lincoln Reader* (New Brunswick: Rutgers University Press, 1947).

Angle, Paul. *Here I Have Lived: A History of Lincoln's Springfield* (New Brunswick: Rutgers University Press, 1950).

Basler, Roy. *The Collected Works of Abraham Lincoln* (Springfield: The Abraham Lincoln Association, 1953).

Beveridge, Albert. *Abraham Lincoln: 1809–1858* (Boston and New York: Houghton Mifflin Co., 1928).

Bonham, Jeriah. *Fifty Years' Recollections* (Peoria, Ill: J.W. Franks and Sons Printers, 1883).

Booth, Asia. *The Unlocked Book* (New York: G.P. Putnam's Sons, 1938).

Booth, John Wilkes. *Right or Wrong, God Judge Me: The Writings of John Wilkes Booth* (Urbana: University of Illinois Press, 2000).

Boykin, Samuel. *A Memorial Volume of the Hon. Howell Cobb of Georgia* (Philadelphia: J.B. Lippincott and Co., 1870).

Burlingame, Michael. *Abraham Lincoln: A Life* (Baltimore: Johns Hopkins, 2008). Unless otherwise noted, this refers to the unedited manuscript hosted online by Knox College.

Burlingame, Michael. *The Inner World of Abraham Lincoln* (Urbana: University of Illinois Press, 1997).

Busey, Samuel Clagett. *Personal reminiscences and recollections of forty-six years' membership in the medical society of the District of Columbia, and residence in this city with biographical sketches of many of the deceased members* (Philadelphia: Dornan, 1895).

Cogswell, John. *Memoir of Rufus Choate* (Cambridge: John Wilson and Son, 1884).

Coleman, Charles Hubert. *Abraham Lincoln and Coles County, Illinois* (New Brunswick, NJ: Scarecrow Press, 1955).

Congressional Quarterly, National Party Conventions, 1831–1988 (Washington, D.C.: CQ Press, 1991).

Donald, David Herbert. *Lincoln* (New York: Simon and Schuster, 1995).

Eicher, John, et al, "Civil War High Commands" (Stanford, California: Stanford, 2001)

Emerson, Jason. *Lincoln the Inventor* (Carbondale: Southern Illinois University Press, 2009).

Evelyn, Douglas, et al. *On This Spot: Pinpointing the Past in Washington, DC* (Washington, D.C.: Capital Books, 1992).

Findley, Paul. *A. Lincoln and the Crucible of Congress* (New York: Crown Publishers, 1979).

Foner, Eric. *The Fiery Trial: Abraham Lincoln and American Slavery* (New York: W.W. Norton, 2010).

Force, William Quereau. *Picture of Washington and its vicinity for 1848* (Washington, D.C.: William Q. Force, 1850).

Garfield, James. *The Works of James Abram Garfield* (Boston: J.R. Osgood and Company, 1882–83).

Gary, Ralph. *Following in Lincoln's Footsteps* (New York: Basic, 2002).

Goodwin, Doris Kearns. *Team of Rivals* (New York: Simon & Schuster, 2005).

Grant, Ulysses Simpson. *Personal Memoirs of U.S. Grant* (New York: Charles Webster and Co., 1886).

Greeley, Horace, et al. *Horace Greeley: Recollections of a Busy Life* (New York: J.B. Ford and Company, 1868).

Greeley, Horace. *Proceedings of the First Three Republican Conventions* (Minneapolis: Charles W. Johnson, 1893).

Hawthorn, Julian, et al. *United States from the discovery of the North American Continent up to the present time* (New York and London: The Co-Operative Publication Society, 1904).

Herndon, William. *Abraham Lincoln: The True Story of a Great Life* (Chicago, New York, and San Francisco: Belford, Clark, and Company, 1889).

Hershman, Robert R. *Records of the Columbia Historical Society, Washington D.C., Vol. 50* (The fortieth separately bound book).

Holland, Josiah Gilbert. *Life of Abraham Lincoln* (Springfield, Mass.: Gurdon Bill, 1865).

Holt, Michael F. *The Rise and Fall of the American Whig Party* (New York: Oxford University Press, 2003).

Hunt, Gaillard. *Israel, Elihu, and Cadwallader Washburn: A Chapter of American History* (New York: Macmillan, 1925).

Ingersoll, Lorton Dunham. *The Life of Horace Greeley: Founder of the New York Tribune* (Chicago: Union Publishing Company, 1873).

Jewett, Charles. *Speeches, Poems, and Miscellaneous Writings on Subjects Connected With Temperance and Liquor Traffic* (Boston: self-published, 1849).

Johannsen, Robert W. *To the Halls of the Montezumas: The Mexican War in the American Imagination* (New York: Oxford University Press, 1988).

Johnson, Allen. *Douglas: A Study in American Politics* (New York: Macmillan, 1908).

Johnson, Andrew. *The Papers of Andrew Johnson* (Knoxville: University of Tennessee Press, 1967).

Julian, George Washington. *The Life of Joshua R. Giddings* (Chicago: A.C. McClurg and Co., 1892).

LaGumina, Salvatore John. *The Italian American Experience: An Encyclopedia* (New York: Garland, 2000).

Long, Armistead Lindsey, et al. *Memoirs of Robert E. Lee* (London: Sampson, et al, 1886).

Ludy, Robert B. *Historic Hotels of the World: Past and Present* (New York: David McKay and Company, 1927).

Mann, Mary Tyler Peabody. *The Life of Horace Mann* (Boston: Lee and Shepard, 1904).

Meigs, William Montgomery. *The Life of Thomas Hart Benton* (Philadelphia: Lippincott, 1904).

Merry, Robert. *A Country of Vast Designs* (New York: Simon & Schuster, 2009).

Mills, Robert. *Guide to the Capitol and National Executive Offices* (Washington City: W. Greer: 1847–48).

Nicolay, John, and Hay, John. *Abraham Lincoln, A History* (New York: The Century Co., 1890).

Northup, Solomon. *Twelve Years a Slave* (New York: Miller, Orton, & Mulligan, 1855).

Oates, Stephen B. *With Malice Toward None* (New York: HarperCollins, 1994).

Ohrt, Wallace. *Nicholas Trist: Defiant Peacemaker* (College Station: Texas A&M University Press, 1998).

Peck, William Farley. *History of Rochester and Monroe County* (New York and Chicago: Pioneer, 1908).

Polk, James K. *The Diaries of James K. Polk, During his Presidency* (Chicago: A.C. McClurg and Co., 1910).

Poore, Benjamin Perley. *Reminiscences of Sixty Years in the National Metropolis* (Philadelphia: Hubbard Bros., 1886).

Potter, David Morris. *The Impending Crisis* (New York: Harper and Rowe, 1976).

Pratt, Harry E. *The Personal Finances of Abraham Lincoln* (Springfield, Ill.: Abraham Lincoln Association, 1943).

Remlin, Robert. *Henry Clay: Statesman for the Union* (New York: Norton, 1991).

Rice, Alan Thorndike (Editor). *Reminiscences of Abraham Lincoln by Distinguished Men of His Time* (New York and London: Harper Brothers, 1909).

Riddle, Donald. *Congressman Abraham Lincoln* (Urbana: University of Illinois Press, 1957).

———. *Lincoln Runs for Congress* (New Brunswick: Rutgers University Press, 1948).

Sargent, Nathan. *Public men and events in the United States from the commencement of Mr. Monroe's administration in 1817 to the close of Mr. Fillmore's administration in 1853* (New York: DaCapo, 1970).

Sarmiento, Domingo. *Sarmiento's Travels in the United States* second edition (Princeton: Princeton University Press, 1971).

Schouler, James. *Abraham Lincoln at Tremont Temple* (Boston: Massachusetts Historical Society, 1909).

Simon, Paul. *Lincoln's Preparation for Greatness: The Illinois Legislative Years* (Norman: University of Oklahoma Press, 1965).

Smith, Jean Edward. *John Marshall: Definer of a Nation* (New York: Henry Holt and Company, 1996).

Smith, Justin Harvey. *The War With Mexico* (New York: Macmillan, 1919).

Stephens, Alexander. *Recollections of Alexander H. Stephens* (New York: Doubleday and Page, 1910).

Stevens, Thaddeus. *Selected Papers of Thaddeus Stevens* (Pittsburgh: University of Pittsburgh Press, 1998).

Taylor, Zachary, et al. *General Taylor and His Staff* (Philadelphia: Lippincott, Grambo and Co., 1851).

Thomas, Benjamin P. *Abraham Lincoln: A Biography* (Carbondale: Southern Illinois University Press, 1952).

Thompson, Charles Manfred. "Attitudes of the Western Whigs Toward the Convention System," found in *Proceedings of the Mississippi Valley Historical Association* (Cedar Rapids: Torch Press, 1912).

Tuck, Amos. *The Autobiographical Memoir of Amos Tuck* (Paris: N.P., 1902).

Van Dyke, John. *The autobiography of John C. Van Dyke, a personal narrative of American life 1861–1931* (Salt Lake: University of Utah Press, 1993).

Wallis, Michael. *Davy Crockett: Lion of the West* (New York: W.W. Norton, 2011).

Watterston, George. *New Guide to Washington* (Washington, D.C.: Robert Farnham, 1847–48).

Webster, Daniel. *The Papers of Daniel Webster* (Hanover: Dartmouth College Press, 1982).

Weed, Thurlow, et al. *Life of Thurlow Weed including his autobiography and a memoir* (Boston: Houghton, Mifflin and Company, 1884).

Weld, Theodore. *Letters of Theodore Dwight Weld, Angelina Grime Weld and Sarah Grimke, 1822–1844* (Gloucester: P. Smith, 1965).

Wentworth, John. *Congressional Reminiscences* (Chicago: Fergus, 1882).

Wheeler, Henry G. *The History of Congress* (New York: Harper & Brothers, 1848).

White, Ronald C. *A. Lincoln* (New York: Random House, 2009).

Williams, Harry T. *Lincoln and His Generals* (New York: Random House, 1952).

Wilson, Douglas (Editor), et al. *Herndon's Informants: letters, interviews, and statements about Abraham Lincoln* (Urbana: University of Illinois Press, 1998).

Wilson, Rufus Rockwell. *What Lincoln Read* (Washington, D.C.: National Capital Press, 1932).

Winthrop, Robert C. *A Memoir of Robert C. Winthrop* (Boston: Little, Brown, and Company, 1897).

MANUSCRIPT COLLECTIONS

Ashmun, George, Boston Public Library, Boston, Mass.

Barringer, Daniel, University of North Carolina, Chapel Hill, Southern Historical Collection, Chapel Hill, N.C.

Beale, Richard Lee Turberville, University of North Carolina, Chapel Hill, Southern Historical Collection, Chapel Hill, N.C.

Burt, Armistead, Duke University, Durham, N.C.

Cocke, William, University of North Carolina, Chapel Hill, Southern Historical Collection, Chapel Hill, N.C.

Donnell, Richard Spaight, University of North Carolina, Chapel Hill, Southern Historical Collection, Chapel Hill, N.C.

Dromgoole, George, Duke University, Durham, N.C.

Dunn, George Grundy, Indiana State Historical Society, Indianapolis, Ind.

Embree, Elisha, in the Lucius Embree papers, Indiana State Library, Indianapolis, Ind., and in the Elisha Embree Papers, Indiana State Library, Indianapolis, Ind.

Fries, George, Ohio Historical Society, Columbus, Ohio.

Gaines, John Pollard (microfilm), New York State Library, Albany, N.Y.

Giddings, Joshua, Ohio Historical Society, Columbus, Ohio, and at the Indiana State Library, Indianapolis, Ind.

Hale, Artemas, University of Michigan, Ann Arbor, and at the Library of Congress, Washington, D.C.

Hardin, John J., Chicago Historical Society, Chicago, Ill.

Houston, George, Duke University, Durham, N.C.

Ingersoll, Charles J., Pennsylvania Historical Society, Philadelphia, Pa.

Jones, George William, University of North Carolina, Chapel Hill, Southern Historical Collection, N.C.

Lincoln, Abraham, The Papers of Abraham Lincoln at the Abraham Lincoln Presidential Library and Museum, Springfield, Ill.

Marsh, George, University of Vermont, Burlington, Vt.

McDowell, John, University of North Carolina, Chapel Hill, Southern Historical Society, Chapel Hill, N.C.

Outlaw, David, University of North Carolina, Chapel Hill, Southern Historical Collection, Chapel Hill, N.C.

Palfrey, John, Boston Public Library, Boston, Mass.

Peaslee, Charles Hazen, New Hampshire Historical Society, Concord, N.H.

Schenk, Robert (microfilm), Ohio Historical Society, Columbus, Ohio.

Smith, Caleb (microfilm), Library of Congress, Washington, D.C.

Smith, Caleb, Indiana Historical Society, Indianapolis, Ind.

Strohm, John, Pennsylvania Historical and Museum Commission, Harrisburg, Pa.

Taylor, John Lumpkin, Ohio Historical Society, Columbus, Ohio.

Thompson, Richard W., Indiana State Library, Indianapolis, Ind.

Wick, William, in the English Papers, Indiana State Historical Society, Indianapolis, Ind.

Wilson, James, New Hampshire Historical Society, Concord, N.H.

Winthrop, Robert C. (microfilm), Library of Congress, Washington, D.C.

ARTICLES

Adams, William. "Louisiana and the Presidential Election of 1848." *Louisiana History: The Journal of the Louisiana Historical Association*, Vol. 4, No. 2.

Boas, Norman F. "Lincoln and John Quincy Adams." *The Railsplitter*, Vol. 8 No. 4.

Bray, Robert. "Abraham Lincoln and the Two Peters." *Journal of the Illinois Historical Association*, Vol. 22, No. 2 (Summer 2001).

Chroust, Anton-Hermann. "Abraham Lincoln Argues A Pro-Slavery Case." *The American Journal of Legal History*, Vol. 5, No. 4.

Clark, Allen C. "Abraham Lincoln in the National Capital." *Records of the Columbia Historical Society, Washington D.C.*, Vol. 27 (1925).

Conn, Steven. "Where Is the East? Asian Objects in American Museums, from Nathan Dunn to Charles Freer." *Winterthur Portfolio*, Vol. 35, No. 2/3 (Summer–Autumn 2000).

Dyer, Brainerd. "Zachary Taylor and the Election of 1848." *Pacific Historical Review*, Vol. 9, No. 2 (June 1940).

Ewing, Thomas. "Abraham Lincoln and the General Law Office." *Journal of the Illinois State Historical Society*, Vol. XXV, No. 3, (Springfield, Ill, October 1932).

Graebner, Norma A. "James K. Polk: A Study in Federal Patronage." *Mississippi Valley Historical Review*, Vol. 38, No. 4 (March 1952).

Kernell, Samuel. "Toward Understanding 19th Century Congressional Careers: Ambition, Competition, and Rotation." *American Journal of Political Science*, Vol. 24, No. 4 (November 1977).

Luthin, Reinhard H. "Abraham Lincoln and the Massachusetts Whigs in 1848." *New England Quarterly*, Vol. 14, No. 4 (December 1941).

Neely, Mark. "War and Partisanship: What Lincoln Learned from James K. Polk." *Journal of the Illinois Historical Society*, Vol. 74, No. 3 (1981).

Paullin, Charles O. "Abraham Lincoln in Congress, 1847–1849." *Journal of the Illinois State Historical Society*, Vol. 14, No. 1/2 (April 1921).

Porter, Kenneth Wiggins, "Three Fighters for Freedom." *Journal of Negro History*, Vol. 28, No. 1 (January 1943).

Sibley, Joel H. " 'Always a Whig in Politics': The Partisan Life of Abraham Lincoln." *Journal of the Abraham Lincoln Historical Association*, Volume 8, Issue 1, 1986.

Stowell, Daniel. "Abraham Lincoln and the Contest for the General Land Office in 1849." (Publication pending.)

Strubell, Robert. "House Turnover and the Principle of Rotation." *Political Science Quarterly* 94 (Winter 1979–80).

Sweet, William W. "Churches as Moral Courts of the Frontier." *Church History*, Vol. 2, No. 1 (March 1933).

Tarbell, Ida "Life of Abraham Lincoln." *McClure's Magazine*, May 1896. Vol. VI. No. 6.

Walton, Brian G. "The Elections for the Thirtieth Congress and the Presidential Candidacy of Zachary Taylor." *Journal of Southern History*, Vol. 35, No. 2 (March 1969).

Washburne, Elihu. "Abraham Lincoln in Illinois." *North American Review*, Vol. 141, No. 347 (October 1885).

Zboray, Ronald, and Zboray, Mary Saracino. "Between Crockery-dom and Barnum: Boston's Chinese Museum, 1845–47." *American Quarterly*, Vol. 56, No. 2 (June 2004).

DIGITAL

"American Memory," memory.loc.gov.

"Biographical Directory of the United States Congress," bioguide.congress.gov.

"The Law Practice of Abraham Lincoln," lawpracticeofabrahamlincoln.org/.

"Mr. Lincoln and Friends," lincolnandfriends.org.

"The Lincoln Log," thelincolnlog.org.

"Streets of Washington," streetsofwashington.com.

"United States Senate," senate.gov.

NEWSPAPERS

The Congressional Globe, Washington, D.C.

The Illinois Register, Springfield, Ill.

The Illinois State Gazette, Shawneetown, Ill.

The Liberator, Boston, Mass.

The Louisville Times, Louisville, Ky.

The Missouri Daily Republican, St. Louis, Mo.

The National Intelligencer, Washington, D.C.

The Sangamo Journal (later known as *The Illinois Journal*), Springfield, Ill.

The Springfield Republican, Springfield, Mass.

The Washington Daily Union, Washington, D.C.

OFFICIAL PUBLICATIONS

The Journal of the United States House of Representatives, accessed at the Library of Congress and the National Archives I, Washington, D.C.

The Journal of the United States Senate, accessed at the Library of Congress and the National Archives I, Washington, D.C.

The Records of the Thirtieth Congress, National Archives I, Center for Legislative Research.

Statutes at Large of the United States Congress.

ACKNOWLEDGMENTS

My name appears alone on the cover of this book, but it is through the efforts and energy of many that it has come to be.

I am grateful to God for providing me everything necessary to write this story and share it with the world. "A man can receive only what is given him from heaven" (John 3:27 NIV).

I am thankful for the constant love and support of my family, especially my mother, Anna, and my sister, Cathy, to whom this book is dedicated.

Abraham Lincoln was right when he said, "The better part of one's life consists of his friendships." The better part of mine has included Nolan Davis, who helped me plan it out and set it in motion, James Slattery, my best friend and who also loves history, as well as Nahiyan Ahmed, Chris Ashby, Paul Baben, Elliot Berke, Ed Brookover, Josh Daniels, Jeremy Duda, Ashley Fickel, Megan Flickinger-Wojtulewicz, Ruben Galego, Justin Herman, Eric Johnson, Gabby and Tom Kearney, Michael LaPidus, Cecilia Martinez, Danny and Bonnie Mazza, Pete and Theresa Nguyen, Mike Nimtz, Jim Ogsbury, Steve Orlando, Larry Pike, Katrina Shackelford, Jonathan Shuffield, Todd Sommers, Trey Terry, David and Caroline Van Slyke and our entire small group, Vinnie Vernuccio, and Jim and Kitty Waring,

For Ashley Baker, who made the writing of this book easier and better in so many ways, and for a thousand more reasons.

I want to thank especially those friends who served as sounding boards for this book. Heather Macre, who reads everything first and who, along with her husband, Steven Kruczek, have been tremendous supporters of my writing; Alan Gable, a fan who became a friend; and Rob Peck, whose vast historical knowledge has made this work better.

Behind every author and every book is a long list of great teachers. Karen Koenig encouraged my lifelong addiction to reading, Karen Miller indulged my love for storytelling, and of course history teachers like Sarah Seifert, Dawn Endler Strand, and Bill Jirkovsky, who first told me the story of Congressman Lincoln, Ed Mokrzycki, who always believed in me, and English teachers like Tom Fuller, as well as government teachers John Beasley, Michael Wyckoff, and Kyle Saunders. From Pepperdine Law there are Dean Jim Gash, Ambassador Doug Kmiec, Colleen Graffy, Tim Perrin, and Mark Scarberry, who have gone from valued instructors to friends, and I was honored to be welcomed back to campus to discuss my first book.

I have been especially mindful of my teachers this year while serving as a law professor for the first time, and thank the students and faculty of the Phoenix School of Law for that wonderful opportunity.

My search for Lincoln took me to many places, and I was often the beneficiary of gracious hosts. There were Dan Huber and Kate DeCleene in Indianapolis, Lauren Harmon in Columbus, Eli Fox-Epstein in Boston, Stephanie Dail in Raleigh, and Meaghan Cassidy in Manchester.

The assistance of Farar Elliot, Curator of the House of Representatives, was critical in helping me re-create the Capitol of the Thirtieth Congress.

This project was embraced and assisted from the beginning by the community of Lincoln scholars who have made it their life's work to bring the story of our sixteenth president to the world.

Many thanks to Daniel Stowell, Director and Editor of the Papers of Abraham Lincoln, and to his dedicated team, who have undertaken the monumental task of collecting everything Abraham Lincoln ever wrote or read, especially David Gerleman and Ed Bradley. I know of no more important historical research being done, or by a better group of people, and encourage everyone interested in Lincoln's legacy to support them (www.papersofabrahamlincoln.org).

Michael Burlingame, author of the definitive *Abraham Lincoln: A Life*, was generous with his time and insight, and his authoritative work has set a high bar for any who would follow him. Thanks especially to him and his publisher, Johns Hopkins Press, for posting an unedited copy of his manuscript online. His research has been especially valuable to this project.

Thanks also to Thomas Schwartz, the former Illinois state historian, for his enthusiasm and many great leads at the outset of this project.

I am indebted to every author cited in this book, and for all of the many librarians throughout the country who have assisted me in my research.

For as long as I can remember, I have been fascinated by the great events and figures of the past. In one of life's unexpected surprises, I have the privilege to research and write about history for a living. No acknowledgments could possibly be complete without thanking those who have made possible this exciting new chapter of my life.

For everyone who has ever read one of my books or recommended them to others, especially Congressman David Schweikert and his wife, Joyce, who have bought more than anyone, and for those who have taken the time to contact me personally to let me know that my writing meant something special to them, especially James O'Donohoe, the first person to think my signature on a book might be something worth having, for everyone who has come to one of my public appearances, and everyone who has helped publicize my work, especially James Hohmann of *Politico*, Patrick Mellody, who accosted George Will at a Nationals game in the hopes that he would write about it, and Chris Cillizza of the *Washington Post*, who named *Founding Rivals* among "the best political books of 2011."

Thanks to Jason Ashlock for his extraordinary representation, and the entire team at Movable Type Management in New York City. Two books in two years, Jason, and many more to come as time goes by.

Thanks also to all the professionals at Simon & Schuster—Threshold Editions, especially Anthony Ziccardi, who instantly saw the promise of this story and trusted me to tell it, as well as Mitchell Ivers, my editor.

INDEX